Lake St. John

Roberval

Shipshaw

Saguenay

Jonquiere   Chicoutimi

River

Laurentides

Park

Baie St. Paul

St. Lawrence River

La Tuque

Beauport

Quebec   Orleans Id

Levis

Three Rivers

L. St. Peter

Joliette

Sorel

Thetford Mines

Arthabaska

St. Jerome

River

Drummond-ville

Montreal

Que.

Granby

Sherbrooke

Maine

Valleyfield

Richelieu River

N. H.

Lake Champlain

Vermont

w YORK

QUEBEC
PORTRAIT OF A PROVINCE

BY THE SAME AUTHOR
    Storied Streets of Quebec
    Ruffles and Rapiers
    Storied York
    Saguenay
    Tom Thomson
    Planetary Democracy
        (with Oliver L. Reiser)
    Youth Speaks Its Mind
    Gaspe: Land of History and Romance

IN PREPARATION
    Ottawa: Portrait of a Capital

Jackson's ability to convey intimately to the observer the spirit of life in rural Quebec is exemplified in this At St. Hilarion, Quebec, in which he immortalized one of the old travelways of the Habitants. They followed the contours of the country in the unhurried days before tourism sacrificed the old twisting roads to the convenience of the hurried visitors to Quebec.

QUEBEC
PORTRAIT OF A PROVINCE

by

BLODWEN DAVIES

NEW YORK
GREENBERG :: PUBLISHER

First Published, 1951

Printed and Bound in Canada

by

T. H. Best Printing Co., Limited, Toronto

*To all my neighbours at Cedar Grove whose
kindness, generosity and helpfulness have been unfailing
and from whom I have learned so much*

Contents

Illustrations

Foreword

ALTHOUGH this is the fifth book I have written about my native province of Quebec I lay no claim to being an historian of Quebec or of any other part of Canada. This is is a portrait, not a photographic representation of the old province, for it is Quebec as I see it, at least, as much of it as can be contained within the covers of this book, — about half of the manuscript originally prepared. There are many more books to be written about the province of Quebec, just as there are about other parts of Canada. The cultural resources of our history have only been lightly turned over by our regional writers so far. The wealth of unused material available, not only in our archives and libraries, but in the lives of men and women still living, is the equivalent of the wealth of our natural resources. Unlike our physical resources there is too little interest in the exploration and use of this cultural wealth and far too little encouragement in the research and creative effort required to transform factual data into books that can be read for pleasure. The development of a regional literature of this kind depends not only on the writers but on some enlightened interest on the part of some of our eleven governments and upon publishers in Canada who have initiative and the long view. I have no doubt whatever that given this interest on the part of our administration, and practical encouragement by creative publishers, there would be no dearth of writers willing to put the time and effort into the research and travel required for regional writing. We might in time have a group of regional writers who by conference and exchange of outlook could provide the nation with the kind of books that

would give us a comprehensive view of our amazingly diversi-
fied history of settlement and development.

We still have many frontiersmen and frontierswomen with
us and many pioneers in countless projects, cultural, social,
political and economic. We should be at work learning their
histories at first hand. More than I could ever learn from
print I learned in my conversations with a magnificent ninety-
year-old farm woman who had lived for seventy-five years
on the land to which she had gone as a bride in a cabin in a
clearing in the forest, in Grey county, Ontario.

What I have tried to do in this and in all my writing on the
early days of this country is what the artist does when he
paints a sketch of a Canadian scene or a Canadian person. I
have tried to select something that is beautiful or significant
or interesting or essential to an understanding of ourselves.
I have tried to tell the stories of personalities, men and women
who have by their human qualities, aspirations and activities,
given substance to our history, whose loves and hates and
fears and achievements have been woven into the very fabric
of our Canadian consciousness. I have tried to say, as the
painter says, "here is something I think you would like to
know", "here is something that has significance", or "here is
something that may evoke your love or pride or indignation"
as the case may be.

My affection for the Canadiens is rooted in a childhood
lived in the old seigneurial town of Longueuil, among Canadien neighbours, and years of schooling in the old convent
that was built on land that was part of the site of the Chateau
de Longueuil. In my father's yacht I sailed up and down the
St. Lawrence just as the pioneers of New France must have
sailed, and we put into many of the little ports that had been
in use since seigneurial days. Knowing the Canadiens as I
do, I am more interested in their future than in their past,
anticipating what will happen to them as they seize the
instruments of the social and technical sciences of our day

for the expansion and development of their society. In some North American communities an over-eagerness for technical society has all but displaced an interest in the humanities and the art of living together. The Canadiens have never let go their hold upon the fundamentals of family and community life. Their apparent tardiness in moving abreast of the scientific age may in the long run prove to be an advantage for them, for now they will not sacrifice the art of living for the science of livelihood, but will find a way to integrate them. The Canadien in endowed with natural intelligence and manual dexterity and when to these he adds skills in the use of science and technology as a means of controlling the physical aspects of his society, he will have full play for his inate gaiety and the traditional use of the arts and crafts in his daily life. The song, the dance, the story-telling, the colour and design so natural to the Canadiens will, let us hope survive and flourish in their new scientific society which the wealth of the province makes inevitable. The Canadien has already made his province the magnet that draws a great many visitors to Canada because of his traditions and characteristics.

I am not providing a bibliography, partly because this is a book to be read for relaxation and partly because so many of my sources are not easily available to the reader. The standard books of reference are in every library but much of the material is taken, a line here or there, from documents in the archives and reports of historical societies; some from current government and industrial reports. Many good books on Quebec are out of print. Professor Wrong's books are invaluable, including *A Canadian Manor and Its Seigneurs*, *The Rise and Fall of New France* and *The Canadiens*. Parkman, of course, is indespensible. Stephen Leacock's *Montreal* is comprehensive and delightful. Marius Barbeau's books, including *Where Ancient France Lingers* and *Kingdom of the Saguenay* are important and good reading. *Old Quebec* by Alexander D. Angus leads into may byways. *Essai sur l'Industrie au Canada* in two volumes by Joseph-Noel Fateux provides much fascinating data. *Ile d'Orleans* and *Old Manors, Old Houses*, translations from the French, were publications of the Historical Monuments Commission of Quebec and are important sources.

A special word is due to *A History of Canada* by M. Jean Bruchesi. Canadians have long been in need of such a piece of work from the point of view of a Canadien. This book began as a series of lectures at the Sorbonne in Paris. It tells not only the story of French Canada's part in the creation of the nation, but clarifies the aspirations and cultural values in Canadien society.

W. H. Blake's writings, "*In A Fishing Country* and *Brown Waters* are Canadian classics and such books as *Chez Nous* by Adjutor Rivard and *Other Days Other Ways* by Georges Bouchard can be read with pleasure. *Thomas*, in the French by Damase Potvin, is the story of Thomas Fortin and the early history of the Laurentides Park.

For those who want to see more of Quebec without making the journey to the province there are many excellent and beautiful films available. Below are a few but more information is available from the film boards concerned.

From the National Film Board of Canada:
In sound and colour—
Historic Highway, Lower Canada
Montreal
Habitant Arts and Crafts
Painters of Quebec
Primitive Painters of Charlevoix
In sound only—
North Shore
Summer on a Quebec Farm
Saguenay
These run from eighteen to thirty minutes.

Other films are also available, with French or English titles from the Cine-Photography Branch of the Provincial Publicity Bureau, Quebec City.

I am once again indebted to many for help in writing *Quebec: Portrait of a Province*. First of all to M. Georges Léveillé, Director of the Provincial Publicity Bureau of Quebec for renewed help and interest. M. Gustave Bédard of the Department of Game and Fisheries introduced me to the Laurentides Park and infected me with his enthusiasm for that protected wilderness. Col. G. E. Marquis of the Legislative Library. M. Antoine Roy, Chief Archivist and M. Jean Bruchési, Under Secretary of State, of Quebec, have all been helpful. To all I offer my warmest thanks.

I am also happy to acknowledge my debt to Dr. A. Y. Jackson for permission to use prints of several of his canvases in this book. The jacket is from a canvas owned by Jane and Walter Stewart and used with their very kind permission. "April, Petite Rivière" is used with the permission of William Watson of Montreal and the print of "The Edge of the Maple Wood" is used with the consent of the National Gallery of Canada. "At St. Hilarion" is owned by William Phillips, former United States Ambassador to Ottawa.

My thanks are also due to the National Film Board, The Canadian National Railways, and the Aluminum Company of Canada for the use of photographs.

BLODWEN DAVIES

The Clearing,
Cedar Grove, Ontario,
May 15, 1951.

1

Introduction

THE destiny of Quebec was written in silver, by her rivers, against the green tapestry of her forests. The exits and entrances of her early history were made on her waterways. From the first bales of reeking beaver skins floated down to trading fishermen at Tadoussac in canoes, until today, when the energy of her rivers is forced through the turbines of great hydro-electric plants, the rivers of Quebec have shaped her economic and cultural patterns. Just as her first clearings and trading posts were on the riversides, so today her latest industrial towns, modern as newly minted coins, come to birth around the power plants where her portages once began.

Long before any white man crossed the Atlantic, the native people of this country had spelled out the charter of Quebec's story. Tadoussac, Quebec, Three Rivers, Montreal were trading places from time immemorial and the travelways of the Indians were the routes the white men used to "discover" the country and claim it for their king.

The Europeans who first came to the St. Lawrence were so ignorant of the geography of the planet that they did not know they had found a new world. They commemorated their ignorance by calling the inhabitants "Indians" because they believed these wild and beautiful coasts were the outskirts of ancient India.

The chief reason, apparently, why the St. Lawrence country was not known and claimed hundreds of years before its written history began, was that its waters produced no

1

cod. The western boundaries of the known world, until the days of Jacques Cartier, were fixed by the fins of the cod-fish. Wherever there were good spawning conditions for cod, and good gravelled beaches upon which fishermen could dry and salt their catch, there Europeans travelled with all their gear and equipment to harvest cod.

The rebirth of intellectual curiosity that characterized the Renaissance displayed itself in many ways. Curiosity about the geography of the planet was one of them. Exploration upset the old order of that day, as atomic energy is upsetting the old order of today. Jacques Cartier was one of the "moderns" of the sixteenth century, a man of scientific mind and well disciplined curiosity.

It is believed Cartier made voyages to the Grand Banks and Gaspé with French fishermen long before he served officially as discoverer and mapmaker. Doubtless he knew about the trade in furs and native curiosities carried on by the fishermen in the western Atlantic and it set him think-ing. Beyond the Grand Banks and the cold, cod infested waters of the Atlantic lay what? India? China? Cartier secured the king's commission to explore, to break through the barrier of silver cod, to chart and name the land marks of the unclaimed continental lands on the western shores of the Atlantic.

We have seldom given the natives of this country the credit they deserve for the opening up of the land to Europ-eans. Without them the charting of North America would have been a vastly more difficult task. It was two Indian lads who had gone home with him to France, who told Cartier that the Great Bay of Canada led into a great river, and that into this river flowed many other rivers, pathways to the wilderness beyond, the home of the Indian tribes.

Cartier returned to the St. Lawrence with the two lads. He had been kind to them and now his goodness was rewarded by a friendly attitude on the part of the Indians he encountered at Quebec. Perhaps it was from these boys that Cartier learned the word "Canada". For it is to Cartier that we owe the name of this country.

The British, grown to maritime power, loved the seas but they had little interest in the freshwater highways of the new continent. While the British colonists quietly built up numerous and prosperous settlements along the Atlantic coast, Frenchmen paddled and portaged their way as far as the Rockies and the Gulf of Mexico. The settlements of the French, however, were small and insecure.

Today Quebec is in a state of transition. Its enormous natural wealth is making industrialization inevitable. Its vast power resources are being turned into magnificent hydro-electric projects. And where there is power there will be factories. The Canadien is a naturally ingenious fellow, and as he gains technical training and scientific education he will astonish his neighbours with his ingenuity and inventiveness. Yet Quebec is a province of traditions. Men and women in the medieval garb of the monasteries are numerous upon its streets. Hundreds of parishes, some of them with histories centuries long, are purely French and Catholic, without a single stranger.

Industrialism and tourism will change the whole face of Quebec. It will bring higher standards of living and of education, and the scientific society of the new Quebec will be built upon the foundation of a cultural heritage that goes back to the troubadours. Young Canadians will honour the traditions of Quebec but will realize that tradition is established by those who break with outworn conventions. Those who go to Quebec to enjoy the antiquity of its relics, the romance of its history and the charm of its kindly culture, will also see a new world people stirring into a new awareness.

The fabled richness of the Kingdom of the Saguenay, the dreams of gold and diamonds on the banks of the St. Lawrence, the hope of trade in silks and spices, all these were little indeed compared with the actual wealth developed in the

3

Province of Quebec by the ingenuity, initiative and technical skills of the people who inherit the dreams of Cartier and Champlain, of Frontenac and Talon, of Carleton and Haldimand, of Simpson and Molson. The history of the past three and a half centuries is a prelude to new adventures.

Throughout this book, in order to avoid the cumbersome hyphenation of French-Canadian and English-speaking-Canadian, I have referred to the French speaking people by the name they use for themselves, *Canadiens,* and to the people of non-French origin as *Canadians.* Where there is no differentiation I speak of Canadians.

2

Quebec's Royal Mile

AMONG all the cities of North America, none has achieved a more distinctive character than the old fortress city of Quebec. Even the high tides of tourists cannot entirely erase its natural serenity. All too many go to Quebec only in July and August; the wise will plan their visits to the old city at other times,—when spring, delicate and yet exuberant, lies like a lustre over the city and its environment, or when autumn flows like molten gold over the countryside. Or even when snow adds the final touch of enchantment to the St. Lawrence Valley.

It is in these quiet seasons that the real Quebec reveals itself, as the people of the city go about their accustomed ways of life, unconscious of the visitor. If we go in search of old Quebec, the city of saint and savage, of seigneur and censitaire, we want to see the city in its unspoiled moods. We want to stroll quietly through streets familiar to coureurs de bois and rapiered adventurers; we want to explore what remains of the haunts of pioneer nuns and King's Girls. The romantic city of the past is still there,—half stone, half shadow,—and those who will may still sense the presence of friendly spirits who walk abroad in the legend-haunted streets. Another life still moves on in old Quebec, half-remembered,—a generation that goes about its ghostly business in cuirass and gauntlet, in powdered wigs and high red heels.

Perhaps it is because Quebec is so many-faceted that it preserves its charm. It is at once feudal and modern; it is

5

a fortress bristling with obsolete guns and it is a little Rome, the daughter of an ancient faith. It is a dreamy city of the past, living on memories and legends, and it is a modern capital, involved in the problems of its own restless age. It is a port where ships from the seven seas cast out their mooring ropes and yet, unlike so many ports, it is a lovely city, superbly set in a magnificent landscape.

Nor is Quebec all French and Catholic. The Anglican Cathedral is of the very essence of Protestant England, and there is no spot more staunchly Scottish and Presbyterian in all Canada than the little area that encloses Morin College and St. Andrew's Church.

The city of Quebec has adapted itself to the natural demarcations of the rocky plateau from which it has so long dominated the river. The old city of the French regime was almost entirely within walls. The walls are still there, not the French fortifications, but those that were built to replace them in the early part of the nineteenth century by the Royal Engineers.

These walls, roughly speaking, are in the form of a huge triangle, its base along the St. Charles River, its apex atop Cape Diamond. The citadel, crouching on the highest point of the Quebec promontory, occupies that point. Old Laval University lies in one of the angles, overlooking the St. Lawrence, and the Dominion Arsenal lies in the other angle, overlooking the St. Charles.

The chief gates out of the city were, first, St. Louis Gate which led to the Plains of Abraham and the Sillery Road; second, St. John's Gate which opened onto a forked road, the upper branch running to St. Foy, (where the new Laval University has established itself) and the lower branch of the road went by way of Côte d'Abraham to the lowlands along the St. Charles and to the ferry to the Beauport shore; third, Palace Gate, giving way down a steep decline past the Hotel Dieu to the Palace of the Intendant at the mouth of the St. Charles.

6

Again, to characterize roughly the origins of Quebec, it might be said that church and state occupied Upper Town and commerce the Lower Town. High above the river rose the fort and chateau of the governors, Chateau St. Louis, the monastic institutions, schools and churches; while down by the river were the markets, quays, storehouses, the residences of the rich merchants, the inns for sailors and traders, and the Palace of the Intendant, into whose care the mercantile welfare of the colony was entrusted. The Upper Town is still largely devoted to education and administration and Lower Town to commerce. Modern Quebec has spread far beyond the old walls and has overrun what were once fields and meadows, as far as Sillery on the one hand and along the St. Charles on the other. The Second Great War brought phenomenal expansion to Quebec, so that it hums with new enterprises and branch factories of many well known American and British firms.

There was one other outlet from the walled city and perhaps the most picturesque of them all. It was a road, the oldest in Quebec, traced out by the feet of Champlain himself, that led from the King's Wharf to Place d'Armes. It was called Côte de la Montagne,—the Royal Mile of Quebec.

There is no more fitting introduction to Quebec than this ancient footpath, which was an Indian trail. Up and down this steep, entwining road went all the great, the dramatic, the romantic and the villainous of Quebec. The first we see upon it is the Indian sovereign, Donnacona, "King of Canada". His tribe encamped here when Cartier sailed up to Quebec more than four hundred years ago. He went to visit the Renaissance court of Francis the First, but strange to the ways of white men, Donnacona died in France.

It was three quarters of a century later before Champlain came to establish a Huguenot trading post at Quebec. At the foot of the trail he made a clearing in the woods and built L'Abitation, the dwelling place, the plantation. It was a cluster of log buildings within wooden walls and sur-

7

rounded by a moat, a log castle, with a courtyard within, little brass cannon on the walls, a dove cote and a sundial on the roof. There is an excellent model of it in the Quebec Museum.

Round about were the first streets of Quebec, Sault au Matelot, named for Champlain's dog, Sailor; Sous le Cap, Notre Dame and Champlain streets. Here beside the river in the shadow of the Rock, the little town was born.

Champlain later moved up the trail and built Fort St. Louis on the plateau above, where he spent the rest of his life. He died on Christmas day in 1635.

Côte de la Montagne is still the only road from Lower Town to Upper Town on the St. Lawrence front of the city, as it was in the earliest days of the colony. Here came the nuns, gentle and unshakeable heroines of the seventeenth century, to nurse and teach and serve, and to temper the rude manners of the outpost with their graciousness. Here came the King's Girls out of the bride ships, dowerless daughters of families on the fringes of the court to be wives for the officers, and buxom maids from the countryside as brides for the discharged servicemen at the close of the campaign against the Iroquois, all to be mothers of young Canadians. Here, too, came the Marquis de Tracy with a staff of officers in gorgeous uniforms, pages in livery, and fighting men fresh from the campaigns against the Turks.

It was up this road that the seigneurs came from their outlying seigneuries to pay homage to the king's deputy, in the ancient rituals of feudalism. Missionaries with rosaries swinging as they trod the road from river to cliff, painted savages to treat with viceroys, spies and explorers, soldiers and sailors, traders and prisoners of war, all these and many more mounted this steep, rough path.

3

The Terrace

THE people of Quebec love the scenery of the St. Lawrence and the Laurentian foothills laid out before them in such splendour from The Terrace and ramparts of the city. There is some magic here that even a hurried tourist cannot escape.

When we try to understand why the men and women who first settled this country (a wilderness, inhabited by strange, and for the most part unfriendly tribes of natives) endured so much suffering and loneliness and uncertainty, we may be puzzled, until we have time to wander at our ease by these famous paths of Quebec. The early settlers came here to isolation, privations, dangers, to live under the unpredictability and indifference of absolute kings and their courtiers, divided by the months of sea travel from kindred and friends. Grant that Europe of the seventeenth and eighteenth centuries was such a sad and bad place for the great mass of people, that even the limitations of colonial life might seem good in contrast to the famines and plagues of the homeland. Yet over and above that there were those who had less reason to dread life in Europe, men and women of the aristocracy, the military and administrative classes, who came and saw and were conquered. These men and women gave years of devotion to New France, many of them bearing great names, great by inheritance or by achievement. Some of them stayed until all they could claim of New France was a grave. Some of these graves we know. Some, like that of Champlain, were forgotten. Yet all down the corridors of

9

our past we can see the niches these people made for themselves in our history, niches before which we may well pause to lay tribute of understanding and appreciation.

The scene from the top of the Rock of Quebec has been loved by many long generations of red men and white. All across the wilderness the wandering hunters talked of Quebec, "The Place Where the River Narrows", when they turned their thoughts toward home. When the white men came to Quebec they often walked and talked along the rim, feasting their eyes upon the views which nursed their dreams of empire.

Champlain was the first white man who seriously undertook the creation of a European colony on this site. L'Abitation, at the foot of Côte de la Montagne, was put there for convenience in living and trading and administering the affairs of the infant colony, close by where the little ships could anchor and discharge their cargoes, and where the Indian flotillas could glide in to ground their fur-laden canoes on the shore. But in his leisure hours it was to the heights above that Champlain turned to plan for the future.

Nearly a decade after Champlain had settled in Quebec, the first European family settled there. It was the family of his good friend, Louis Hébert, a Paris apothecary, who could act as physician and surgeon to the colony while he farmed the homestead Champlain granted him, part way up the slope towards Cape Diamond. You may see this family today, in bronze, before the City Hall, the apothecary holding aloft his first sheaf of wheat, Madame Hébert teaching her children from an open book, and Guillaume Couillard, who married one of the daughters of the Héberts,—the first bride in New France. Couillard is shown standing by his plough, for he was the first Canadian to have a plough drawn by oxen. On the back of the monument is a list of the names of the first colonists in Quebec. There are few Canadiens today who cannot boast that in their veins flows the blood of the Héberts. To many he is "the first ancestor", the very Adam of New France.

Champlain was a Huguenot in childhood and youth, and he fought for the Huguenot, Henry of Navarre, until he became King of France as Henry the Fourth. But having arrived at the throne, for the sake of French unity, Henry became a Catholic, although maintaining as long as he lived, his interest in the welfare of the Huguenots. Champlain apparently followed his royal leader into the church of Rome, although he too maintained his association with the Huguenots, founding the colony at Quebec for the French Protestant traders who were so much in need of Canadian beavers for their beaver hat trade. It was two years after the founding of Quebec, in the last days of 1610, that Champlain married a Huguenot bride, but their marriage was within the historic walls of the old Roman Catholic church of St. Germain l'Auxerrois, in Paris.

This marriage of Champlain's is one of the romances of New France, a strangely curious and tender story. Champlain was forty, Hélène Boule was twelve years of age. After the wedding Hélène went back to her home and resumed her studies. Champlain went back to New France to begin his explorations of the interior. It was eight years later, when she was twenty, that Hélène de Champlain came to Quebec, the first French gentlewoman to set foot ashore at the King's Wharf.

Champlain may have hoped that the example of his young wife would encourage other women like her to venture to live in the new world. But Hélène came to a sagging and leaking log home; one wing had fallen into decay during Champlain's absence, the winds howled through the cracks and rain dripped in through the broken roofs. Moreover there had been an Indian plot to drive the white men away. Prisoners and hostages were held for Champlain's arrival.

Hélène settled down to make the best of the place for the time being, setting up her pewter plates upon their shelves and hanging her copper kettles in the kitchen while her maids scrubbed the old bachelor quarters into shining comfort.

When they were settled and the lovely autumn days had come, Champlain and his young wife would walk up the road to the top of the cliff in the sunset hours and sit with all the splendour of the valley at their feet. In the very year of her coming Champlain began the building of Fort St. Louis, where the Chateau Frontenac stands today.

So lovely was this Hélène de Champlain that the Indians thought she was one of the angels of which the Recollets had told them, and they were more willing to worship at her feet than at the shrines of the Unknown Manitous of which the Frenchmen showed them images. At her waist there hung a little mirror, a novelty from Paris. In it the Indians saw their own faces reflected and they believed that she carried their images close to her heart.

The chateau that Champlain built was renovated, and rebuilt, and extended by a whole line of Governors until it was burned in 1834 while Lord Aylmer was in residence. The cellars of the old chateau are still below the wide wooden walks of The Terrace, and The Terrace itself is still technically a part of the defences of Canada.

On the face of Chateau St. Louis was the first Terrace of Quebec. Champlain built a gallery that looked out over this very scene as it was when Quebec was merely a clearing in the woods, when no one lived on the south shore or on the Island of Orleans, or on the Beauport Shore. For four years Hélène lived in Quebec. Then as no other gentlewomen came to join her, and as Champlain had to be away from Quebec so much it was decided that life in New France was still too difficult and dangerous and she returned to Paris.

For a hundred and fifty years the lilies of France floated above the cliffs of Quebec. There is an undeniable magic about the place, and many great souls willingly exchanged the vassalage of Versailles for imperial dreams fostered by New France.

In the days of Louis the Fourteenth the Chateau took on something of the reflected glory of the Sun King. Frontenac was his deputy and Frontenac had a sense of the spectacular. He rebuilt the chateau, and the gallery he built had a stone paving and an iron rail. Many a petitioner came here in the mellow after-dinner hour to broach some project or to seek some favour from the great old Governor. There is an old inventory in the Provincial Archives which describes the furnishings of the Chateau St. Louis in the early days of the 18th century. It had its great beds with tapestry hangings and curtains of white damask embroidered in flowers of gold and silver, mirrors in gilded frames and paintings of the Kings of France. It had little carved cherrywood chairs and cushions of *petit point* and fine old silver and china to lend beauty and dignity to the lives of men and women in the little court of Quebec.

4

Lower Town

WHAT ghostly crews must sometimes sail the river before Quebec! Cartier in his medieval vessel of four hundred years ago, sailing westward in search of China,—Champlain on his way to Georgian Bay,—Frontenac on his way to found a fort at Kingston,—La Salle on his way to build a ship at Niagara,—how many there are of them who sometimes come back in the quiet of a summer evening!

We may see them, as we lean over the railings on the ramparts above, among the river ships from ports across the world. Every line in this landscape is imbued with historical memories. Across the river is Levis and the south shore where Wolfe's batteries were planted for the bombardment of Quebec; to the left is the Island of Orleans; farther along on the lovely north shore, at the foot of the purple Laurentians, is Beauport with its ancient villages now woven into one long community.

Two hundred feet below, between the rocky cliff and the river's edge, is Lower Town, now as always the busy quayside area. The street under the cliff is Little Champlain Street running eastward, and Champlain Street running westward to the Sillery. Little Champlain Street arrives at Cul de Sac, and continues to Notre Dame Street. Along this ancient roadway is the oldest church in Canada, Notre Dame des Victoires.

This quaint church was built in 1688. The little town was very proud of it. It stood on the town square close to the water's edge. Farm produce, catalogne carpet, homespun cloth and maple sugar all came to market in the square under the benign walls of the Little Church of the Christ Child as it was first called.

The church was only two years old when ships from New England arrived in the basin before Quebec with the ambitious plan of taking Quebec. There was no love lost between the French and British colonists and when the overland raids of the French became intolerable, the New Englanders got together to plan a private conquest of the northern neighbour.

The man in charge of the attack was a picturesque American. When Sir William Phipps came to Quebec he was not quite forty but he had packed a great deal of experience and adventure into his life. He was one of a family of twenty-six children, twenty-one of them boys. He became a shepherd and later a ship's carpenter. When his apprenticeship was over he was a skilled craftsman, but still unable to read or write. He had the courage to begin then to acquire an education. The history he must have read inspired him to go treasure hunting in the Spanish Main, and he found it in a Spanish galleon wrecked off the Bahama Islands. He became rich and famous, and seemed to be just the right person to take charge of the expedition against Quebec; he set off with thirty-two ships and twenty-five hundred men.

The Gulf of St. Lawrence gave him no welcome but kept his square-rigged ships at bay for days on end. The fleet had to run before the wind and take shelter in Gaspé Basin. Phipps did not reach Quebec until the sixteenth of October, more than two months from the time he sailed out of Boston harbour. He sent a letter to old Count Frontenac ordering him to surrender. Frontenac told the messenger that Phipps would have his reply by the mouths of the French cannon. Phipps landed an army on the Beauport shore and then began a bombardment of the town. His cannon balls fell harmlessly against the cliffs and did almost no damage.

Parkman says: "Phipps lay quiet till daybreak, when Frontenac sent a shot to waken him." Another shot from the heights cut Phipps' flagstaff right off and the flag of St. George fell into the river, much to the delight of the Canadiens. It drifted with the tide over to the north shore and several Canadiens jumped into canoes and paddled out to pick it up. They carried it ashore in triumph. "On the spire of the cathedral in Upper Town," writes Parkman, "had been hung a picture of the Holy Family as an invocation of Divine aid. The Puritan gunners wasted their ammunition in vain attempts to knock it down. That it escaped their malice was ascribed to a miracle, but the miracle would have been greater if they had hit it."

The New England ships were so badly battered that one by one they cut their moorings and drifted down stream to safety. Presently they repaired what damage they could, and sailed back home.

The people of Quebec were delirious with joy over their victory and so they changed the name of the little church by the quayside. They called it Our Lady of Victory (Notre Dame de Victoire).

Twenty years later Sir Hoveden Walker sailed out of Boston on the same errand, but he did not even reach Quebec. Storms in the gulf beset him and he lost ten ships and more than nine hundred men. The New Englanders sailed home empty-handed, and again Quebec re-named their little church of the Lower Town. This time they called it Our Lady of Victories. For nearly three centuries Canadiens have taken their griefs and their joys to this sanctuary so closely interwoven with their history.

Along the Sault au Matelot are old stone houses that were once fashionable homes of successful merchants, where elegant parties were given to display the accumulations of wealth. Now the old mansions are converted into warehouses and shops and tenements. Where princely fortunes once were made and spent, the less successful today eke out a livelihood in drab surroundings.

Sault au Matelot leads into Sous le Cap Street, the narrowest street in America. In the seventeenth century the builders of Quebec had no ideas about city planning; the river drove them to building nose to nose. They made the best of what little toehold there was under the cliff. The old-fashioned windows and low doorways cut into stone walls, give us glimpses of the crowded life within. The neighbours of Sous le Cap have learned a careless tolerance of each other in the intimacies of their life, for not only must they live at such close quarters with each other, but in the holiday seasons they have to tolerate also the stream of visitors who wander through.

Until Nature and the engineers gave Lower Town room to grow, this was the only outlet from Lower Town to the lands along the St. Charles. The junction of Sous le Cap with St. Paul Street, that leads into the thickly populated St. Roch district, is still called La Canoterie,—the Canoe Landing, for here was a beach where travellers, Indians and Frenchmen alike, drew up their canoes when they landed in Quebec. Probably it was at this very spot that hundreds of young French settlers landed when they were on their way,—eager or bashful or determined,—to find brides among the King's Girls waiting on the heights above in the convent of the Ursulines. St. Paul Street led around the foot of the cliff to the Palace of the Intendant, one of the most celebrated,—and at one time the most notorious,—buildings in New France.

This side of the city lies in the valley of the St. Charles river. The slope from the heights of Quebec down to the meadows along the St. Charles was called Côte Ste. Géne- vieve. The heights were granted in the earliest days of the colony to three men. Louis Hébert and his son-in-law, Guillaume Couillard, who occupied the lands near the fort, and to Abraham Martin whose lands lay to the west.

Abraham Martin was one of those exiled Scottish royalists who found haven with the French people, some in France, a very few in New France. Martin was the King's Pilot, and down in the harbour there is a memorial to this man who was the first of his calling and who guided the ships from France up the treacherous waters below Quebec and into safe channels. It was on Martin's farmlands that the Battle of the Plains was fought,—the Plains of Abraham.

But as a farmer, Martin had the same problem as Hébert and Couillard had faced, the problem of watering cattle. The road that was cut down the slopes overlooking the St. Charles was the path of the cattle who were driven down to the lush meadows by the waterside for both food and drink. So all the territory between the hill and the river became known as La Vacherie, the place of the cows, and the roadway was known as Côte d'Abraham, and so we still call it.

There is another twisting road which runs from Palace Hill to the foot of Côte d'Abraham, called St. Vallier Street. This is a part of a trail beloved by Bishop St. Vallier, who often walked from the Bishop's Palace, down Palace Hill and so through the riverside meadows to the General Hospital, near the St. Charles. It must have been a lovely walk in the early years of the eighteenth century, as the sunset light flowed into the purple bowls of the Laurentian hills. We can imagine St. Vallier resting his tired spirit on this quiet stroll, feasting his heart on the loveliness of the valley and its guardian hills beyond, and coming at last to the picturesque buildings that had once been a Recollet monastery, surrounded by gardens and well tilled fields, and now a place of refuge for the aged, the crippled, the homeless and the chronically ill. Perhaps in the hospital he would spend an hour talking with the old men who had fought the Iroquois in their youth, or had paddled away as coureurs de bois into the unexplored west; or perhaps he listened as some lonely widow told him of the unfulfilled hopes and dreams of some young couple, soldier and King's Girl, settling in a clearing and looking towards the peace and security of a little farm, dreams shattered by a tragic death, raiding some frontier English town. As he walked back again, perhaps by moonlight, the Bishop must have had a great many strange things to think about. Not

18

least the sadness of so many warped and unhappy lives in so young a colony.

When Intendant Talon decided that Canadiens should drink beer of their own brewing rather than the wines brought at such expense from France, he built them a brewery at the foot of the hill, in 1688, the very year that Notre Dame des Victoires was built, and not very far from it. The colony grew by leaps and bounds and Talon's successors found their work growing so fast that they needed a Palace of the Intendant in which to transact it. So they made the brewery into the Palace that gave its name to Palace Hill. The rivalry between the Governor in Chateau St. Louis on the top of the hill, and the Intendant in the Palace at the foot of it, was not diminished by this display of importance.

A fortune was lavished on the Palace of the Intendant, on its furnishings and its gardens. It was a little Versailles in Canada, but by the time of the Cession it had become the equivalent of the Bastille, as a symbol of tyranny and exploitation. Intendant Bigot, the last of the Intendants, was a ruthless, greedy, villainous man. To him France owed in large degree the loss of the colony to the British. Because of the regime of Bigot, the British military regime was almost welcomed by the hungry and destitute Canadiens. During the siege of Quebec the Palace was partly destroyed. It returns to history in the winter of 1775 when Arnold and his American rebels tried to take shelter there from the blustery winter weather while they waited for Montgomery and the time for the attack on Quebec. Then Carleton turned his guns upon it and brought the old building to its final dissolution. Now it is again part of a brewery, for the ancient vaults are still good and useful.

Even in the French regime there were a few houses beyond the Palace, and Quebec hoped that some day there would be a suburb of the city on the St. Charles. Today the meadows of La Vacherie are completely swallowed up in the busy industrial district that grew out of the tanneries and shipyards of the nineteenth century.

5

A Bishop's Grave

THE time came when that old aristocrat, Bishop Laval, felt his strength failing him. After years of strenuous service to New France, he made the journey to Paris to beg the king to allow him to retire from his episcopal honours and to serve Quebec as a humble priest.

Neither church nor state could refuse his reasonable request. When it was granted he was also given the privilege of choosing his own successor.

Laval looked about the court, for he wanted a man who had powerful associations. He discovered in one of the royal chaplains a young man, as nobly born as himself, whom he believed to be well fitted for the post at Quebec. He was Jean Baptiste de la Croix Chevrièrs de St. Vallier. Fortunately he became known by the simple title of St. Vallier.

St. Vallier was the same age, when he was created Bishop of Quebec, as Laval had been when he had been elevated to that post,—thirty-five. Laval served as Bishop for thirty years, but lived on in Quebec for another twenty. St. Vallier served in his turn for forty years and died in office.

The new bishop was an earnest and painstaking young man, and so he was well equipped for the arduous tasks and numerous responsibilties of his colonial office. These responsibilities he multiplied and magnified. He assumed control of the whole moral life of the colony and did not hesitate to interfere with anyone, governor, intendant, or commander-in-chief, if he suspected that anything was amiss in any of these administrative departments. He worked hard and he

20

travelled much, visiting the parishes of his huge bishopric as far away as Acadia and Newfoundland. He even went from house to house to see for himself how his people lived.

The weight of his austere authority was unbearable to the lighter-minded elements in society, so frequently the bishop's windows were broken and he was sometimes jeered at by the rebellious. There were, too, some amazing quarrels over precedence; once he put the Recollet church in Montreal under an interdict after a quarrel over the placing of the prie-dieu of the Governor of Montreal.

The bishop was once recalled to France where King Louis the Fourteenth tried to induce him to resign. He refused to accede even to the wishes of the king and so succeeded in keeping his bishopric and his power for many years thereafter.

When St. Vallier first reached Quebec in 1685 he found that the little town already had a pressing problem of dependent poor and chronically disabled. The life in the colony was hard and dangerous. Voyageurs and coureurs de bois were all too likely to end their lives crippled or in ill-health and poverty. So many were killed in the Indian wars that many a widow was left dependent on public charity. Quebec had to raise money for its charitable needs by taxation. One of St. Vallier's first responsibilities was to organize the charities of Quebec and plan for their extension.

The Recollet priests, who so often found more favour with the leaders of the colony than did the powerful and ambitious Jesuits, came to New France with Champlain. As early as 1620 they began the building of a monastery at Quebec. They did not choose to build on the Rock at Quebec where the traders and administrators were crowded together, but selected a spot on the meadows by the St. Charles. The church and monastery they erected while Champlain was Governor of New France, were fine bits of seventeenth century architecture. They named their institution Notre Dame des Anges, a name which the Jesuits later on transferred to their own seigneury east of the St. Charles.

The Recollet monastery with its chapel, dormitory, court and cloisters, was a fine specimen of the religious institutions of that day. It was beautifully situated, surrounded by lush meadows with the river meandering in picturesque curves nearby and charming landscapes in every direction, backed, of course, by the Laurentian hills to the north and east. Fish and game were plentiful in the neighbourhood, and the place was assured safety because of its protection from the fort. The land itself gave them peace and quiet and abundance in its fields and gardens.

St. Vallier looked upon the monastery with an approving eye and a good deal of envy in his heart. He wanted to control it and perhaps also he wanted to have the Recollet priests under closer observation. He induced them, by a combination of guile and authority, to exchange their monastery, now seventy years old, already a venerable institution in the young colony, for a site in the heart of the city. They must have had a great deal of regret in moving out of their lovely old monastery, and no doubt surrendered it with sorrow in their gentle hearts. The land which they were granted in its stead faced on Place d'Armes and included that on which the Anglican Cathedral stands to-day, and also that where the Court House was built, right in the heart of the town.

It was in 1691 that St. Vallier began additions to the Recollet monastery as a means of converting it into a General Hospital. He spent some hundred thousand crowns on building and furnishing. When the place was ready for use he borrowed from the Hôtel Dieu a superior and a few sisters, whom he set to work organizing a refuge for the poor, the helpless and the insane of New France. To support the General Hospital he succeeded in diverting the poor taxes of the city and in return he undertook that the sisters would supervise the problem of relief. The new institution was one of Bishop St. Vallier's dearest cares and interests. Event-

ually he made his home at the General Hospital and took over
the duties of chaplain to the convent.

Presently the sisters of the Hôtel Dieu who had gone up
the St. Charles to organize the refuge for the distressed were
encouraged to found a new order which was made independent of the other conventual orders in the colony. The work
that fell to their hands increased with every year, but the
interest and sympathy of the bishop compensated for their
unremitting work and the sisters were both elated and content with the project they had established. To this day the
sisters carry on their work of caring for the helpless and distressed.

This is the only pioneer institution in Quebec that has
never been burned. It was far enough away to escape the
shells of the British bombardment in 1759 and so it escaped
the perils of war to which the rest of the city was exposed.

During the siege of Quebec in 1759 wounded British
soldiers were carried to the General Hospital from Beauport Flats after the unsuccessful British attack on the French
lines there. The sisters were so kind to their enemies that
General Wolfe promised that when Quebec was taken the
sisters would have special attention and protection. True
to the promise of their dead commander, the staff officers, as
soon as the Battle of the Plains had ended, sent a guard to
the hospital to protect the convent from molestation by the
victorious troops. So here French and British wounded lay
side by side. A special plot was set aside in the convent
cemetery for the graves of Protestants who died in the hospital.

After the American rebels had been defeated in their
attempt to take Quebec in 1775, wounded soldiers were
again carried to the General Hospital to be cared for by
the sisters. Among them was Benedict Arnold.

In the year of the siege the convent was the scene of one
of the most exciting escapes in the history of New France.
Frequently British officers and men, and even civilians, were

taken prisoners by the French in border forays or expeditions into the western frontier country. Five years before the fall of Quebec, three young officers, all Scots, were among the prisoners in Quebec. One was a very charming Captain Robert Stobo. He was a favourite with all the hostesses in Quebec and a welcome guest everywhere, for his French captors were very kind to him. But in spite of all the kindness and attention paid to him, he was neither happy nor content and spent a good part of his time planning with his brother officers an escape from the fortress city. The rendezvous was a windmill on the grounds of the General Hospital beside the St. Charles. On a dark night in May they stole a birch bark canoe and slipped silently down river to the St. Lawrence. They paddled all the way to Kamouraska and there they lay concealed by the river until they discovered Chevalier de la Durantaye, seigneur of the Islands of Kamouraska, rowing a boat loaded with grain. They fell upon him and laid claim not merely to his boat but to his services as well. The Chevalier protested that he was a Canadien aristocrat and kin to the Duc de Mirapoix. Captain Stobo assured him that if he was King Louis himself he would still be under the necessity of helping them to row the craft down towards the gulf.

So willy-nilly the seigneur was put to work. Some days later they captured a small French ship and turned the seigneur loose again in his rowboat to make his way home as best he could. Progressing in the importance of their enterprises they at last ventured upon the capture of a French sloop. In this the three young daredevils made their way to Louisbourg.

The fleet had already sailed for Quebec. However, another ship was about to follow the fleet up the river and Captain Stobo took passage in it. So it was that in the harbour of Quebec he finally overtook General Wolfe and offered him his services as one familiar with every inch of the city.

In July Captain Stobo was sent up the river to Descham-

bault to round up all the ladies of Quebec who had fled
from the British and taken refuge there from the bombardment. Wolfe did not want all these Quebec ladies up-stream
from the operations of his siege where their curious and
observant eyes might see too much. It is not hard to imagine
the astonishment of all his hostesses when they saw the rogue
Robert Stobo, come to fetch them back to Quebec. With the
gallantry and charm for which he was already famous among
them, he conducted them down the river to the city. As the
boat filled with the great ladies of the town came near the
city the British guns were silenced. In peace and quietness
they were conducted to the quay. The truce continued until
the ladies had plenty of time to get beyond danger.

But all this lay far in the future. When Bishop St. Vallier
cherished the General Hospital and planned for its growth
and security, he had not thought of the perils that lay ahead
for New France. As the years passed he grew more and
more fond of the monastery by the St. Charles and in his old
age he prepared a grave in the Church of Notre Dame des
Anges so that he might rest there forever. Then, at last,
death came to the arrogant and devoted priest on the twenty-
first of December, 1727.

Now in his forty years in Quebec, St. Vallier had achieved
a reputation for extreme saintliness, so that the ecclesiastics,
looking hopefully into the future, believed that some day
miracles might occur at his grave and perhaps,—who could
tell?—the old bishop might be canonized.

The canons of the Quebec cathedral, jealous for the honour
of the bishop's seat, planned an elaborate ceremonial for his
funeral. The body of the prelate was to be carried through
the snowy December streets, from church to church, to
rest before all the altars of Quebec. The procession was to
end at the high altar of the Cathedral, with all the pomp and
ritual that chapter could command.

But suspicions fell upon the over-eager canons and it was
whispered about that once the body of the bishop got into

the cathedral it would never come out again. The grave he had prepared for himself, and which the nuns regarded as such an honour to their order, would probably yawn for its bishop. The Archdeacon Lotbinière, who was anxious to bury the old bishop as he had desired, spoke out for simple and immediate burial in the crypt of Notre Dame des Anges. The canons of the Cathedral were stubborn. The intendant intervened and called for the help of the Sovereign Council of New France. The whole of Quebec was in an uproar. Ten days went by and the bishop was still unburied while the wordy war was waged.

When the canons of the Cathedral refused to appear before the Sovereign Council to thrash the matter out, the Intendant took speedy action. He sent an armed guard to the General Hospital with an order to the Sisters to bury their friend and protector.

Hastily the clergy were summoned that winter evening and the nuns were gathered from their daily tasks, rustling along the dim corridors, carrying candles that threw mournful and wavering shadows on the white walls. Their eyes were downcast under their white coifs and their serene faces barely concealed their emotions on this most dramatic moment in their order's history. The wooden rosaries clattered gently as the nuns fell at last into a solemn procession, the weary feet falling softly on the polished floors. As they gathered in the dim chapel the haunting perfume of incense suffused the darkness. The voices of men and women, chanting and responding in service for the dead, filled the century-old vault of Notre Dame des Anges. There was need for haste and caution, so the body was hurriedly lowered into its resting place and the great stone was pulled over the grave.

No sooner was the ceremony ended and the sadly excited nuns back at their tasks than the news spread like a grass-fire throughout the city. The canons from the Cathedral, their cassocks flapping angrily in the winter winds, hurried one and all to the distant hospital. There the serene-faced nuns met them only when they had forced their way past the military guard at the door. They were told that the bishop was buried. The canons stormed and even threatened to have the bishop exhumed. Finally, however, quieter councils prevailed and the bishop was left to the care of the sisters.

Visitors can see the grave at Notre Dame des Anges, for to this day it is a venerated spot in the old General Hospital.

6

Quebec's Last Siege

BETWEEN the Conquest of New France and the American Revolution, — that is, between 1760 and 1775, — Canada was one of fourteen American colonies under British rule. During that time Benjamin Franklin was Postmaster General of Canada as well as of the thirteen other American colonies. For fifteen years our history was a common one.

But when the people of the Atlantic Colonies, as they were called, went into open rebellion against the king, they were determined that the Canadians would join them. It was part of Washington's strategy to command Quebec. Indeed it seemed quite logical to the Americans that the conquered people of New France would be among the first to welcome a chance at rebellion.

What a difference a few years can make! The Conquest of New France was undertaken for the benefit of the Atlantic Colonies which had suffered so long at the hands of the French and Indian raiders from the north. But once New France had been overcome and Canada had become a British colony, the Americans were no longer in need of the protection the British army and navy gave them. The way was open for revolution. And at the end of those fifteen years of common history, the revolt of the American colonies was in effect.

As part of the primary plan of revolution, two armies were sent into Canada to "free" the Canadians from the British. The first army went by way of Lake Champlain. It was under the command of General Richard Montgomery, a brilliant young Irishman, something of a military genius, endowed with fine powers of leadership and plenty of courage. Nevertheless, he would have preferred to stay at home with his adored young wife and his books; instead he found himself at the head of a republican army invading the St. Lawrence country. St. John, and eventually, Montreal, fell before the invaders, and the Americans appropriated Chateau de Ramezay in Montreal as their military headquarters. Almost all of Canada came under rebel control, except the grim old fortress at Quebec.

The second army came by way of the Kennebec and Chaudière valleys. It was under the command of the dashing and ambitious Benedict Arnold, a horse-trader, who had often been in Quebec on business, and who dreamed of repeating the achievements of General Wolfe and winning a like fame in this new siege of Quebec.

Guy Carleton, the commander-in-chief in Canada, was having a bad time of it. London sent him equipment for six thousand men, whom he was to enlist. But the Canadiens were not enlisting in an army which might be sent to fight at Boston or New York. By September of 1775 Carleton discovered the first Canadien trooper on duty and gave him a guinea, so pleased was he to find one enlisted in the army. The bishops and the seigneurs, pleased with their relationships to the British administrators, urged enlistment, but the common people of Canada had had enough of war. Besides, most of the British merchants were openly on the side of the rebels.

Montreal was defended by only two hundred men and surrendered without a shot, but under cover of the excitement Carleton, disguised as a habitant, slipped away down the river to Quebec. He tried to get his little garrison away in boats, but at a point where the Americans held both sides of the river, they were seen and forced to surrender. Meantime, the destiny of Canada hung in the balance there upon the river where Carleton and his two canoemen floated. The three men lay motionless in the bottom of the canoe so that it looked like a drifting log. There they lay until they were far enough away into the dusk to elude the eyes of the invaders.

It was the nineteenth of November when Carleton reached Quebec, already under siege. Arnold's ragged army was on the Plains, so when the disguised commander got inside the city walls he was welcomed with genuine joy.

Washington sent Benedict Arnold to Quebec warning him that he must appear as a liberator of oppressed Canadiens and a friend of their religion. It took grim purpose to attempt the journey through the wilderness. Arnold gathered twelve hundred men and set off up the Kennebec river valley at the coast of Maine to follow the old route of French and Indian raiders up the Kennebec, across portages to the source of another river, the Chaudière, which flowed into the St. Lawrence opposite Quebec. It was a journey of two hundred miles.

The Americans set out in a sunny September, full of hope and ambition, but it was not long before the travel, dragging heavy bateaux over portages and through swampy lands, took all the glamour out of the project. They found the Chaudière in flood. Food gave out, the weather was bitterly cold, illness devastated them, and so at least half the force turned back. Arnold pressed on. For thirty-one days the Americans met not one human being. On the frontiers of the French settlement, habitants and Indians began picking up and caring for the sick and weak that Arnold was forced to abandon as he went on.

Finally in November, the remnants of the gay revolutionary army reached the south shore of the St. Lawrence. Staggering on foot through a blinding snowstorm they peered across the river at Quebec. Only five hundred men of the twelve hundred had arrived, without artillery and without boats. Yet Arnold, the liberator, with a ragged, hungry horde at his heels, demanded the surrender of the fortress!

All that Arnold could do was to settle down to await Montgomery. He was on his way down the river with his army of republicans endeavouring to join Arnold for the assault on Quebec. While Arnold set up his headquarters in the old Intendant's Palace outside the walls of the city, Montgomery chose Holland House, one of the celebrated homes on the St. Foy Road, as the perch from which to swoop down upon the city. The hungry and ill-provided men looted the country homes roundabout in search of food and trophies.

Carleton, behind the walls of Quebec, was making the best of what little he had to command. Time was his most powerful ally and so he refused to be drawn out to fight the invaders beyond the walls. He knew they were suffering badly in their winter encampments, and the besieged were at least snug within the city. For six weeks the two American armies shivered in their encampments unable to accomplish anything.

Finally the two leaders decided to make a frontal attack on the city under cover of a snowstorm. But the winter weather was clear, bright, and bitterly cold. It was the last day of the year that the blizzard, which was to be the signal for their combined attack, began to brew. Grey clouds, heavy with snow, gathered over the valley. Cold east winds roared and grew hourly more menacing and icy. Finally as snow fell over the whole countryside, the Americans began to move. Montgomery and his men began the descent from the Plains and took the River Road towards the city, carrying their red and black rebel banners through the storm, with heads bent and the locks of their guns hidden under the lappets of their coats to keep the snow out of them. Arnold's men came up from the St. Charles shores through Lower Town to the posts long since allotted to them.

The two armies, converging on the fortress, between the cliffs and the icebound river, waited for the signal for the assault. When it came they were to dash up Mountain Hill, spring upon the ramparts, force the gates and hew their way into the stronghold while the city slept.

Then, suddenly, before the signal for the assault was given, out of the darkness and the storm, from the edge of the cliff above and from the barricades, thin red tongues of musket fire spat out. Black-mouthed cannons snarled an unholy welcome to the rebels. A chance wayfarer, who had seen the marching men, had given the alarm. The defenders, huddled at their posts behind the walls, electrified into action, had caught the attackers almost in the act of assault. Canadiens and Canadians, grimly keeping their monotonous watch on that night of storm, suddenly found themselves in battle.

It was not long before the good news spread that their defenders had not been caught unawares, that Carleton's men had won a quick and decisive victory. Before two o'clock in the morning, the last siege of Quebec was over.

Down in Champlain Street, in a shroud of fleecy snow, the brave young Montgomery lay dead, far from his wife and his books. Arnold, wounded in Lower Town, was carried off with many of his men to the General Hospital. Between four and five hundred men were prisoners.

When the remnants of the American force had withdrawn to their camps, Quebec gathered up the rebel dead and treated them with military honours. Montgomery was carried to a house on St. Louis Street and there he lay until the fourth of January. Then he was buried near Citadel Hill, along with two of his aides-de-camp and some of his soldiers. His body rested there for forty years before it was carried back to New York.

A memorial plaque marks the spot where Montgomery met his death. It reads: "Here stood the undaunted fifty, safeguarding Canada, defeating Montgomery, at Pres de Ville on the last day of 1775, Guy Carleton commanding at Quebec." Still another on the walls of Molson's Brewery reads: "Here stood her old and new defenders, uniting, guarding, saving Canada, defeating Arnold at the Sault au Matelot barricade, on the last day of 1775, Guy Carleton commanding at Quebec."

7

Along the Ramparts

WHEN Carleton shelled Arnold out of the old ruins of the Intendant's Palace, its history came to a full stop, except for the beer vaults below ground. There were still Canadiens in Quebec who remembered the Palace with bitterness. It is hard to imagine this part of Quebec as a place of luxury, with elegant and formal gardens surrounding the palace, and within all gay with the light of hundreds of candles and aglitter with silver and glass. But even this the poor colonial French would have overlooked but for the fact that the palace was a storehouse and into it flowed the grain that should have been feeding the people. Bigot forced the farmers to sell to him at low prices, and he paid them with worthless paper money. Then he either sold the produce again at high prices to those who could buy it, or fed grain to his chickens to fatten them for his banquets. The storehouse was called by the people "La Friponne",—The Cheat.

Bigot went home to France and was put on trial after the fall of New France, and in the articles of capitulation and of the peace treaty the British insisted that France redeem the worthless paper notes held by her ill-used subjects.

The echoes of the revelry in the palace below the hill rose to shock the ears of the nuns in the Hotel Dieu at the top of the hill. Palace Hill rises towards the hospital and there is a bronze plaque on the wall to point out where Palace Gate once stood.

The great hospital which stands today on the slopes of the

hill has a history that goes back to 1639, for it was then that three women in the white habits of nursing nuns came out to New France in a cockle-shell of a ship, to take up the task of nursing French and Indian alike. These carefully nurtured French gentlewomen came from the cloisters of a French convent to the wilderness to win souls by healing bodies.

They came under the patronage of the Duchesse d'Aiguillon, whose portrait still hangs in the hospital. She was a niece of Cardinal Richelieu, a woman he dreamed of placing on the throne of France, so say the gossips of that day, if the French queen could be dislodged. Though she was a pawn in the politics of her age, the Duchesse is well-remembered in Quebec as the foundress of this ancient institution.

The nursing sisters went first to the Sillery where there was an Indian mission village. One of the most touching stories of those days tells of the sisters, blinded by tears of mortification, dipping their white serge habits in pots of dye made from bark. They wore the drab garments with what grace they could muster, for it was impossible to keep them white while they worked among the greasy Indians.

When they began building their hospital in Quebec, they moved into the town, and part of that original building still stands, while the great modern hospital has grown up around it. In their library, the sisters have more than three thousand books of the seventeenth century and earlier. They have rich treasures in altar silver and mementoes of early Canada, but most important of all, they have their convent register complete since the first three sisters entered their names in it, and a register of patients that have passed through their hands since 1689.

Probably no register was kept before that date, but it marks the coming to Quebec of Bishop St. Vallier who was so conscious of the social needs of the colony, and who immediately began to put the social services into order in New France. He succeeded in securing special taxes for the care of the sick, the needy and the homeless, and these taxes were distributed among the institutions that undertook the work of mercy. Doubtless it was then that the sisters began to keep records of those whom they nursed, so that they might prove their right to a fair share of the tax funds set aside for the welfare of the colony.

The road along the ramparts begins in a rock cutting beside the hospital, and turning to the left comes to the city walls built by the British a century and a quarter ago. In that day there was still danger of attack and invasion.

The new American Republic had already twice attempted to pry Canada from its allegiance since the Conquest of Quebec, in 1775 and 1812. It was in Quebec that the defence of Canada was planned in the War of 1812, for the Americans were still trying to repay an old promise to France,—a promise to invade the old province and rouse the Canadiens to rebellion.

It was just a few years after the end of the War of 1812 that Great Britain began the expenditure of many millions of pounds upon these massive stone walls and fortifications. Never since has an enemy come within reach of the city's guns. The obsolete guns that line the ramparts add a sense of age to the walls of Quebec and the ramparts themselves have assured modern Quebec of very pleasant views of the river and countryside. Between the guns of the Grand Battery there lies, in the distance, Point Levy, to the south of the river and the Beauport shore to the north. For here we face down the river, over the St. Charles valley and away to the lovely Island of Orleans.

Along the Ramparts you will come to some very old houses and on one of them is a plaque to commemorate the fact that here for two years lived the unfortunate and unhappy Marquis de Montcalm.

Montcalm was in command over all the French troops in New France in the years before the conquest. But as usual, there was so much bickering and quarrelling between the factions in New France, that his life was made miserable much of the time. On the one hand were the merchants conspiring with the Intendant to enrich themselves at the expense of the people; on the other was the governor, the Canadien-born Marquis de Vaudreuil, well-meaing, honestly devoted to his country's welfare, and focusing in himself the growing awareness of the Canadiens of their infant nationalism. The Canadiens born in the valley of the St. Lawrence, fumbling their way towards some sort of civic integrity and knowing very little about how to go about it, began by resenting the royal officials named by the king to rule over them. Vaudreuil was in a curious position. He was appointed by the king, but he was also a colonial born, as was his mother. He was confused in his loyalties and lacking in personal power and wisdom. Montcalm was not only the military chief in New France, he was also an aristocrat of the same rank as Vaudreuil—but he was a "Frenchman from France", not a colonial, and on him Vaudreuil vented his resentment and his half-awakened nationalism. Montcalm wanted above all else to be back in his old home, Chateau Candiac, with the wife that he loved so dearly and the many children that he longed to see. "When shall I see my dear Candiac again?" he wrote home forlornly. He was never to see it again. One of the saddest memories in the story of Quebec is that of the wounded Montcalm, riding his white horse back from the Plains of Abraham on the morning of that brief and decisive battle of 1759, through the frightened and sorrowful people along Grande Allée, to the house of the surgeon, where he died.

The ramparts end in a little park filled with old trees. This is one of the most historic spots in all Quebec, the very tip of the Quebec promontory, and an angle in the great triangle of the walls of Quebec. On this spot was once the parliament of Canada and it was here that the celebrated Quebec Conference sat to debate the proposal for the confederation of the colonial peoples into the Dominion of Canada. This was the birthplace not only of the Canada of today, but also of the British Commonwealth of Nations, perhaps the most significant democratic development in world history.

Curiously enough this historic conference of Quebec took place just where New France and Canada were born, where Champlain once built a chapel, Our Lady of the Recovery, to celebrate the withdrawal of the English Kirkes from the Quebec they had seized in 1629. Here, too, lived the first family, the Héberts, hereabout was married the first bridal pair in Canada, and the first Canadian-born came into the world. Here was the first farm, and here the first plough was used.

In this angle of the walled city today stand a great accumulation of buildings that constitute the university and seminaries of Laval. This was part of the first seigneury granted in New France by Champlain to his friend, Louis Hébert. Hébert's son-in-law, Couillard, built a stone house close to the brim of the promontory, and it was in this house that Bishop Laval opened his first school and began the first of a long series of educational adventures. On entering the courtyard of Laval, we see on the other side of it, Le Petit Seminaire, built under the very eye of Laval himself in the seventeenth century. It is in Le Petit Seminaire that the most beautiful chapel in all Quebec is to be found, that of Bishop Briand. It is of unpainted wood, beautifully carved by artists trained at Cap Tourmente school of arts and crafts, founded by Laval as a part of his educational program.

Eight million acres of land were granted to the ecclesiastical bodies during the French regime and of this seven hundred thousand went to the seminary of Quebec. Only the Jesuits got a larger share of the land grants, for they acquired nine hundred thousand acres. The schools of Laval were supported by the incomes from some of these lands, including the Seigneury of Beauport.

Laval's monument stands before the Post Office beside the Côte de La Montagne, up and down which he travelled for fifty years. He was the third son of a very old and aristocratic French family, a branch of the Montmorency. He chose the church as his way of life, but while he was at his studies his two elder brothers died and he became heir to the title and estates. The young aristocrat was now facing a great dilemma. Would he renounce the church and become the head of the family and its affairs or would he renounce his inheritance in loyalty to the life he had elected to live? Laval decided for the church, and in spite of the pleading and upbraiding of his family, he renounced the title and estates and became a priest.

In time he came to Quebec and engraved his name deeply on the history of New France. He established the Quebec Seminary in order to educate native-born priests for the church. He discovered that many of the boys had more aptitude for the arts and crafts than for the academic and ecclestiastical life, so he opened a school for these boys on the Seminary Farm at Cap Tourmente. Some of the old school buildings still remain and are incorporated into the farm buildings of the modern farm. From these lads came the painters, sculptors, cabinet makers, ironworkers, and the craftsmen who did so much for the cultural life of New France. Their work is today prized by art galleries and collectors from coast to coast. The last of the men trained in the tradition of the Cap Tourmente school died not far from the school, in 1928,—Louis Jobin, the fine old wood sculptor who was so surprised to find himself famous when he was discovered by modern Canadian artists.

Laval arrived in Quebec in 1659, just exactly one hundred years before the fall of New France. He lived there for fifty-one years in the seminary he had founded. He tortured his body with a vermin-infested bed and he sometimes ate food that had become putrid, in his zeal for self-mortification. Even when he became a feeble old man he rose long before dawn and spent hours on his knees before the altar of the seminary chapel, in summer and winter. At last, in the fireless chapel, the feet of the old priest were badly frost-bitten one winter morning. As a result of shock and cold, he sickened and died.

The middle of the twentieth century saw Laval University, the child of the old seminary, "hurdling its cloistered walls" as one Quebec writer put it, to migrate outside the city walls to St. Foy to build a University City. The University was created in 1852. It continued the classical tradition of Canadian education with faculties in theology, medicine and the arts. Indeed it clung to the old outlook on life and education for more than fifty years, ignoring the fact that around Laval had grown up a scientific world. It declined to face the fact of the industrial revolution. The old classical school that did so much to produce cultured sons of Quebec, depended largely on the old seigneurial revenue which had come to the seminary. But with the twentieth century, the university roused itself. Young Canadiens became restless, they asked why they did not have a share in the prosperity of the managerial and technical executives in the province, nearly all of whom were English speaking. Some of the wiser among them, instead of reverting to resentment and jealousy realized that if they expected to become executives in the industrial life of their times, to become industrialists on their own account, they must have modern, scientific, utilitarian education. In 1920 with grants from the province, Laval began to expand. Since then it has outgrown its old quarters and its old limitations. As one of the chief officers of Laval University said of the new professions which young Canadiens wished to enter: "These professions . . . would soon change, without our co-operation, the economic structure of our province." So very reasonably the policy was developed to train Canadiens for the life that they naturally sought to share, "to assure our people the minimum of prestige necessary for their survival . . . and prepare competent men who will occupy executive posts in the nation's economy, that are unfortunately inaccessible to French Canadiens because of the insufficiency of their universities."

So today, with a great master plan for a University City, and many millions of contributions for their task, the men of Laval plan to celebrate their centenary by building such a school as even Laval could not have dreamed of, the greatest French University in America.

8

The River Road

FROM the clatter of rosaries and the clash of swords in the streets of Quebec, we turn along the river road to walk with rogues and bullies, hard fisted seamen and swaggering, singing lumberjacks. Below The Terrace lies this road, Champlain Street on the maps, the road that some day a novelist will make famous, for it is certainly a street in search of an author.

This long street, with its back against the cliff, has witnessed nearly everything that has taken place in Quebec since the days of Champlain. The beach under the cliff, in the early days, was very narrow and the docks were close to the cliff. The canoes of Indians and traders might be drawn up anywhere along the way, close to the homes of the merchants. The tall grey houses on Champlain Street had thick-walled vaults beneath them in which the goods for barter, and furs, could be safely stored. The French street was badly battered in the seige of Quebec, but after the cession it was quickly rebuilt and French and English merchants settled down side by side to carry on the traditional trade of the country.

However, as the fur trade declined and made way for other commercial enterprises, the fortunes of Champlain Street declined and in the early nineteenth century most of the houses had been converted into inns and taverns where immigrants sought shelter, ships' crews made merry and the lumberjacks came to squander all their earnings.

In 1832 one of these inns was run by a family named

Roche. On a warm June day a traveller from Dublin engaged a room there. He had come up the river in the vessel *Carrick* which was still in quarantine but in some way he had been granted permission to go into the city. A few days later a sinister rumour began to circulate in Quebec. The stranger at the Pension Roche, so it was said, was dead of cholera. The health department admitted that the *Carrick*, tied up at Grosse Isle, had cholera sufferers aboard when she docked, but they had been taken to hospital, the ship was disinfected and free from all danger of disease. The city officials made the greatest effort to reassure the citizens and subdue the excitement. Next day six people died of cholera. Fifty-six people died in Pension Roche that summer.

During that summer, thirty thousand immigrants landed in Quebec. The voyage across the Atlantic might take anywhere from four to six weeks and all the ships were plague-ridden. Hundreds of the wretched people died at sea and were buried hurriedly over the gunwales. Many hundreds more were buried in huge graves at Grosse Isle.

Quebec suffered with the exiles. Never since the days of the conquest had there been such scenes. Instead of the rack and crash of cannon, the bells tolled for the dead. None escaped the horrors of the plague. The death carts prowled through the streets at night and the drivers cried the terrible, old cry of "Bring out your dead."

From the eighth of June until the winter frosts put a stop to the ravaging plague, thirty-five hundred people died in the city of Quebec, as many as a hundred in a day.

The plagues raged again and again, in 1849, in 1851, in 1852 and in 1854. The immigrants, driven out of a depressed and hungry homeland, crowded into quarters aboardship unfit for occupation, living for weeks on a starvation diet, had no resistance to disease, and those who escaped death, began life in this country bereaved and weakened and bewildered.

From Quebec westward Champlain Street is a roadway

strung with quaint houses all the way to Sillery. Summer or winter, a walk along this way is an amusing and interesting jaunt, for it is a part of Quebec little known to most visitors. Above the road towers Cape Diamond, its rugged and familiar outlines queerly distorted and out of focus from this point of vantage. To the left the restless river moves downstream with the impetus behind it of all the freshwater lakes and rivers stretching as far away as the boundaries of Manitoba.

Away across the river on the southern shore the rippling ridges of hills and the sweep of meadows are broken by little villages of peaked roofs under the shadow of shapely spires. Rolling fields of green and gold, groves of maple trees, straggling fences, uniting, not dividing these neighbours of a dozen generations past, together spell out the story of the country's past.

But the habitations along this road have little in common with the serenity, the domestic traditions, of those villages yonder on the southern shore. Now, indeed they are reduced to twentieth century respectability so that it is difficult sometimes to imagine the riotous days of the nineteenth century. Here and there a house front bulges, ready to collapse. Here a curving eave has sagged wearily under the weight of neglected years, the door beneath hangs low, the windows are hitched up by the pull of the gables and the whole house-front leers at the passerby.

They press their faces against the road, some with neat white curtains behind their small-paned windows; some have little shelters to house a few chickens or a pile of yellow kindling. Here and there, utterly incongruous, a bright new brick house with straight new edges and shiny doors, makes its neighbours seem a little more decrepit, a little more interesting by comparison. Here and there en route we come upon some fine old dwelling, backed up against the rocks, at bay, defying its inevitable fate.

What means all this evidence of a once busy, prosperous exciting life along this long river front? We feel them striding

43

by, hear their boisterous greetings in ghostly voices, their riotous river songs and sea chanties. Even as ghosts they are vigorous and restless, these seamen and rivermen of long ago. The sea has always bred a race of devil-may-cares. Eighty, ninety, a hundred years ago from the forests of Canada came a new race of hard-living men, the lumber giants of all ranks, from the timber princes who lived in some of those gaunt, stone mansions, to the rank and file of lumberjacks who drank and fought and revelled in the inns and taverns along this way.

In those days this quiet road was one of the busiest highways on the continent, for ten miles up from Quebec lay the timber coves. There are remnants of them still to be seen in rotting cribwork and broken pilings along the water's edge. But in the middle of the last century the forests of the interior were laid low and their virgin timber, bound into rafts, swept down the river to Quebec. Muskoka, Algonquin, the Ottawa Valley, the Gatineau country, all these paid tribute to the trade. Pine and cedar, maple and oak, felled in winter and rolled into icy streams to be washed down in the spring floods from a thousand tributaries, travelled for months before they came to Quebec. Some timber took two years to reach tidewater, so great were the distances to be covered and so complicated the business of getting the logs through the rapids that had, in earlier times, made the fur trade and exploration so difficult. Indeed, the canals that were built a century and a quarter ago, were largely to encourage the timber trade, and the great long timber shoots to pass the logs over dangerous passages in the rivers were regarded as "rapids under control". There was an art and a science of keeping the great logs moving, some of them long enough for the tall masts of ocean-going ships and war ships. There was a skill in building cribs and especially in tying them together for the more peaceful journeys down broad deep river stretches, when they seemed like floating villages, with their tents and cook-houses.

The men who cut the trees and followed these mad
streams, who unlocked the log jams and sailed the rafts,
were Canadien lumberjacks for the most part, heirs of the
traditions of the coureurs de bois, though there were plenty
of brawny Scots and Irish among them. What men they were,
this race of lumberjacks, reckless, skilful, graceful with the
swift, strong beauty of hardy men; they worked, they fought,
they sang and drank with dynamic energy.

When at last they reached tidewater they turned over their
rafts to their owners and collected their year's wages. Then
foolish, childish creatures, with their pockets stuffed with
money and their minds with anticipation, they landed on the
river road. Along they came under the cliff, finding temp-
tation in many a guise. They made their way from inn to inn
until, penniless, but neither wiser nor sadder, they started
upstream again for another year in the woods and on the
rivers of the interior.

The lumberjacks loved big leaders and so giant bullies in
red shirts with checked trousers tucked into the tops of their
oiled leather shupacs, drew around them tribes of followers
and supporters. The rivalry between these groups was fierce
and bitter, whether in the woods, on the rivers or in Quebec;
and the men were always ready for a riot when the opportunity presented itself.

Prior to the nineteenth century Europe depended chiefly on
the Baltic countries for wood. Then came the Napoleonic
wars. The Little Corsican closed the Baltic ports to British
ships. Britain was forced to look elsewhere for timber. A
lanky New Englander, Philomen Wright, had dreamed for
years of cutting the pines of the Ottawa Valley and running
them down the river to Quebec. By one of those queer
quirks of fate he had the timber available just when Britain
needed it most. The first raft of Ottawa timber arrived at
Quebec in the summer of 1807. By 1809, thanks to the urgent
war needs of Britain, the balance of trade was in Canada's

favour for the first time in history and Canadian timber traders had captured the British naval market.

From then until 1864 the business in timber and shipping increased steadily. After that peak year it began to decline. During the square timber age Quebec became the greatest timber market in the world. Side by side lay the timber coves as far as the eye could see on each shore. As many as thirteen hundred and fifty great sailing ships came into port in a summer season. To stout sea chanties, their cargoes were discharged. Then huge square timbers were stowed away below decks and thousands of oak casks and barrels were hoisted aboard for the rum and molasses trade of the West Indies, the hard spirits of Britain and the wines of France.

It was Jean Talon who began rafting timber to Quebec as far back as the sixteen-sixties and it was the same wise Intendant who built the first ship here. From his day on ships were launched at irregular intervals from Quebec shipyards. Once a frigate of seventy-two guns was launched by Quebec shipbuilders. From the Cession to 1900 twenty-five hundred ships were built in and near Quebec, all square-rigged barques, brigs, brigantines and schooners, many of them as big as two thousand tons.

It was natural that Quebec businessmen should seize the opportunity at their doors. Timber was plentiful, Canadiens ingenious workmen and ships were in demand. So along the St. Charles and the St. Lawrence shores dozens of shipyards were established. All winter long thousands of Quebec workmen laboured at the fashioning of swift and beautiful sea-going ships, so that in the spring they could be launched and in summer sailed away to European markets. As boys today dream of becoming airmen, in those days they dreamed of becoming sailors and even sea captains. Captain Joseph Bernier, the old explorer of the Arctic, was a captain at seventeen and retired twenty-five years later with a tidy fortune. But there were not enough native lads to man the ships built in Quebec, and that was why there were so many terrible nights on Champlain Street.

The shipbuilding trade produced some curious characters. One of them was old John Munn who built ships for many years. He was a devoted Protestant so he named three of his ships *John Calvin, John Knox,* and *Martin Luther.* At one time he had a fleet of one hundred ships at sea.

Now while Canadiens were great lumbermen and ship-builders, they were not inclined to be sailors. They had learned to love the land so well that they were not anxious to sail away out of the Gulf. So when forty or fifty ships were launched in a year, their owners had to import crews to sail them away. To man a ship was therefore an expensive and ticklish business, for other shipowners and sea captains were always on the lookout for men. Lucky indeed was the man who could import a crew and keep it intact until the ship was ready to sail. Out of these conditions grew the notorious age of crimping. A crimp was a man who under-took to secure sailors by fair means or foul,—usually foul. Along this river road lived many of the crimps, who used their inns and taverns to lure unwary men into their clutches. They stopped at nothing and murder was all too common when anything interfered with their plans. Many of these notorious crimps were known as good citizens of Quebec, and the public could not be brought to believe that an apparently honest, tax-paying innkeeper was a villainous fellow. The shipowners and the sea captains knew them from another point of view but they could not induce the city police to interfere with the dark and deadly gang warfare that was waged along the river shores.

Bodies were frequently disposed of and men who had fallen foul of the crimps were quietly hurried down the gulf and out to sea to save their lives. The whole nefarious busi-ness is the blackest page in Quebec's story. Armed crimp gangs actually boarded ships at anchor to kidnap sailors and shot them dead if they resisted. Captains who fought the gangs were despatched out of the way. Sometimes it was a famous crimp who disappeared but no questions were asked. With as many as three or four hundred ships in port at a time, with scores of taverns doing a roaring business, the timber trade was a law unto itself. In spite of all efforts to cope with the lawlessness and the evil trade in men, crimping declined only when the trade declined. So little wonder if along this sunny river road there prowl strange, shadowy figures, murdered and murderer, captain and crimp, lumberjack and salt sea sailor.

The River Road was known in the French regime as Chemin des Foulons, and the name was used until fairly recent times. Long ago the Quebec Seminary built two mills in St. Michael's Cove for the manufacture of thread and linen cloth.. Flax was grown extensively by the farmers around Quebec and what they did not use at home in spinning and weaving they sold to the mills. The men engaged in the mills were called "foulons" or fullers, and as they built their homes within easy reach of the mills, the road soon came to be called the Road of the Fullers, or Chemin des Foulons. Wolfe's Cove, before it was renamed after his ascent to the heights, was Anse au Foulon, or Fuller's Cove.

Along the road, too, were woollen mills where the "etoffe du pays", the strong serviceable homespun, was made for the markets.

Under the old battleground where the fate of Quebec was decided, a railway tunnel has been cut from St. Malo on the St. Charles to Wolfe's Cove, and the Cove itself has been transformed into docks for the largest ships that sail into the St. Lawrence. There are two berths here seven hundred feet long, and six others as well.

The sides of the Plateau at Wolfe's Cove today do not suggest any insurmountable difficulties. It would seem that any able-bodied man or woman could scale the bluff if the necessity arose. But, because of landslides and other changes hereabouts Wolfe's Cove today is a much gentler declivity than

it was in 1759. Even then there was a path from the top
to the bottom of it, steep, but serviceable. This was one of
the points the French watched with anxiety and the pathway
had been purposely broken up and a barricade built at the
top. There was also an outpost there with a hundred men on
guard. Wolfe's plan was to scale the rough sides of this
"wooded gulley", as he called it, a little to the east, surprise
the guard and make the pathway available for the regiments
and the artillery that were to follow his landing party.

Every Canadian schoolchild knows the story of the boats
drifting downwards in the misty dawn, with Wolfe in his new
uniform wistfully quoting that "the paths of glory lead but
to the grave". This was the zero hour and Wolfe, relaxed and
a little nostalgic, let his mind wander in the quietness to
meditative thought. But once his vessel scraped its keel on
the shore, Wolfe was the first to land. The success or failure
of the whole campaign hung in the balance in the dawn of
that September day. There was the tall, lean, red-headed
Wolfe in his scarlet coat and cocked hat, with his sweet-
heart's handkerchief tucked away in his pocket. Young
Wolfe, so certain that he would not return from this splendid
venture. The time for poetry was past. Wolfe planned to
have his army up on the heights and in battle array before
the morning light warned the French of the impending
attack.

Poor, stricken Quebec! All her gallantry and courage could
not avail against the weakness, the stupidity, the greed and
folly of some of her leaders.

Wolfe found only a handful of sleeping Frenchmen to
impede his way. By six o'clock in the morning of September
thirteenth Wolfe had nearly six thousand men on the field.

He had excellent information concerning this and other
parts of Quebec long before he landed there. Down into this
cove one night in the previous May there came a certain
Major Patrick MacKellar, who had been known in Quebec
as a French trader from the west. The visitor, handsome,

amusing, entertaining, had been a welcome guest in the bored society of Quebec. During the late winter he had been a visitor in every fashionable home in the city. But this so-called coureur de bois was an English spy who had made his way to Niagara by way of Downing Street. The orders he acted under were those of William Pitt. This night in May he had completed his task. He carried with him a detailed map of the city and he believed that this cove, through which he now descended to the river, was the way the British could hope to make their way into the fortress.

In the darkness, after his escape from Chateau St. Louis, where he had left an effigy to avert suspicion for an hour or two, MacKellar made mental notes of the cove and its steep bluffs. He paused as he reached the road by the river. Everything was silent. He plunged into the river and in due time he dragged himself out on the southern shore. He had left nothing to chance. At a rendezvous he met a party of Indians who had been sent to help him. With their guidance he travelled up the Chaudière and down the Kennebec and came at last to Boston. He sailed to London and then followed Wolfe to Quebec with his map and his journal.

So when Wolfe reached the Plains of Abraham he had a mental picture of Quebec and its environs. In the pale golden light of a September morning he crossed the Plains and looked down into the Valley of the St. Charles. There lay the French camp, but all was silent and undisturbed. Montcalm, the military genius who commanded the French army, was already astir, it was true, but no instinct warned him of what was afoot.

Meantime a sick French officer at the General Hospital, astir early in the morning, saw the moving mass of scarlet on the St. Foy Road. He seized a horse, and pounding off along the road, over the bridge of boats and down the Beauport Road, found Montcalm himself and told the dumbfounded commander that the British were on the Plains of Abraham.

Montcalm feared that Wolfe would descend into the Valley of the St. Charles, cut the bridge and prevent his army from

Indian Statuary at Legislative Buildings, Quebec Cit

going to the help of the garrison in Quebec. Hasty alarms were sounded and presently Quebec's defenders, breakfastless, were running up Côte d'Abraham to face the enemy at the city's gates.

By eleven o'clock that morning Wolfe, in his great cloak, was carried down the steep slope, now beaten flat by thousands of heavy feet and the weight of great guns. He was carried aboard one of the boats that had brought the British so quietly to the landing place and the dead general was rowed to the *Lowestoft* by sad but victorious men. The young soldier was never to see within the walls of the city he besieged and conquered.

Towards the end of the Chemin des Foulons stands the oldest building in Quebec, the old Jesuit House. Since the people of Quebec were not subject to the Iroquois raids that made life in Three Rivers and Montreal such a perpetual terror, it was possible to build outside of Quebec in comparative safety. In such a way the Recollets went to the shores of the St. Charles to build their monastery and settlers made their homes along the north shore as far as Cap Tourmente. The Jesuits built their house at the Sillery as headquarters for the first Jesuit missionaries to the Indians. The founders of the Mission were Father Paul Le Jeune, Superior of the Jesuits in New France, Noel Brulart de Sillery, commander of the Order of the Knights of Malta, for whom the place was called Point Sillery, and Francois Derre de Gand, the Canadien representative of the Company of One Hundred Associates. The object in founding this mission station outside of Quebec was to attract to the area a settlement of Algonquins. The missionaries had set their hearts not merely on converting the nomadic Indians to Christianity but on making them civilized Frenchmen as well. All through the history of New France runs the dual thread of rival interests, missions and fur trading. The church wanted to win the natives to a settled, civilizing society which would be a reflection of Catholic France, while the traders and monopolistic trading companies wanted the Indians to stick to

e Ottawa River, Showing the Interprovincial Bridge

their pagan and nomadic ways, hunting and trapping, in order to bring to the trading posts the rich furs on which the companies depended. On this conflict of interests was based the constant feuding between the church and the governor in New France, for the governor had to represent the king who was quite as interested in his subjects who were business men, or patrons of business men, as he was in priests. The struggle for balance of power kept New France simmering in difficulties throughout its history as a French colony.

In the struggle the colonists were the sufferers no matter which side won, and the whole system prevented demo-cratic enterprise on the part of the hardworking habitant.

The Jesuit House represents one of the efforts to civilize the Indians. De Gand, the trader, as a gesture of acquies-cence, gave the land on which the mission was to be founded, and de Sillery provided the funds from France. It was in July 1637 that six workmen began the stone-work for the foundations and walls of this house. Nine months later, in April of 1638, Father Le Jeune and his co-worker, Father de Quen, took possession and two Algonquin families joined them. This is the first we hear of Indians trying to live within the walls of a French house.

The house is today a museum and a very interesting one. The Mission church is gone. The first of its kind in Canada, it was built near the Mission house and was called the Church of St. Michel de Sillery. Its location was realized when the body of Father Massé, one of the first Canadian missionaries, was discovered, in 1868. He had died in 1646 when the church was in the course of construction, and before it was dedicated. The church was paid for out of the estate left to the missionaries by Michel de Marillac, who died in 1644 and bequeathed everything he owned to them. Massé's body was discovered more than two centuries after his death, and it was then that the people of Sillery erected a memorial to him.

The house is interesting for its construction and for its

memories. Here are the bevelled roof-boards and the hand-forged nails of the French regime; and old iron candle holders, by the light of which the missionaries may have written their "Relations" home to France. Here are the fireplaces around which they taught their curious but reluctant Algonquins and around which they must have exchanged many strange reminiscences.

They were ingenious men, as many things about the house will testify. Not long ago while making repairs around the house, workmen discovered outside the walls the remains of wooden water pipes by which water was piped into the house from a spring on a hillside nearby. Some of the pipes are still exposed to view.

It was not far from this house that Monsieur de Puiseaux built his home, the finest in New France in those early days of the colony, and here it was he welcomed Maisonneuve and Jeanne Mance in the winter of 1641.

What tales may have been told around these fireplaces! The men who lived here had lived colourful lives of much adventure. Father Massé was a missionary at Port Royal in Acadia as early as 1611. In 1613 Captain Argall from New England carried Massé off prisoner to New England and so he came to Boston. A year later he was sent home to France and then in 1625 he returned again to Quebec and spent his life there. Father Le Jeune, who was his superior at the Mission House, was a younger man and a professor of philosophy at three French universities before he went to the Sillery. In Canada he spent his time establishing missions, schools and hospitals, and after his return to France he was proposed as Bishop of Quebec before Laval was chosen. The rules of his order prevented him from taking the office. Here, too, came other Jesuits from time to time, to rest, to renew their contacts with their order, and to enjoy for brief interludes the comparative luxury of monastic life after their experiences in the filthy wigwams of the red men.

9

Ile d'Orleans

ISLAND communities, whether the islands be large or small, have a way of maintaining distinctive characteristics. The water separates and protects, it builds an invisible wall around the traditions, manners and customs of the island. This applies particularly to Ile d'Orleans. In spite of a bridge and the ease in getting to the island in recent years, and in spite of a few commercial buildings and some spots where inappropriate summer resort life has cropped up, for the most part Ile d'Orleans is untouched by its proximity to the commercial and industrial life of the mainland.

It was relatively late in colonization and the Beauport shore and Côte de Beaupre were well established communities before anyone ventured to live on the island. The reason, of course, was that it was too exposed to raids by the Iroquois and settlers preferred the mainland.

The island had no natural defences. It was an ideal area for settlement because its land rose in gentle slopes from the river towards a low ridge midway across the island. It was forty miles long. At its western end, just below Quebec, the water was sweet, but at its eastern end it was brackish for the sea water reached so far up the St. Lawrence. There is a rise and fall of six or seven feet of tide around the island.

In the old days, before the bridge, it was reached by an old-fashioned ferry boat from Quebec that landed at the quay at Anse du Fort after a trip downstream of twenty minutes. This was the old route of the dug-out canoes, used as ferries on the St. Lawrence in the early days.

On the plaque on the Hébert memorial before the Hôtel
de Ville in Quebec, bearing the names of the first colonists,
there is the name of Eleanor de Grandmaison. By that name
she was known throughout the fifty-odd years she lived in
New France, although she had no less than four husbands.

Eleanor de Grandmaison was a widow when she came to
Canada, but after coming here she married Francois de
Chavigny de Berchereau. She went to live the life of a
pioneer woman on lands up the St. Lawrence, but in 1648
they decided, probably for the sake of safety, to move to
the tip of the Island of Orleans where settlement was just
beginning. She seems to have been one of the first women to
live on the island. In the following year a seigneury covering
the end of the island nearest to Quebec was granted to her
husband.

They built a manor house, which is still standing, on a bit
of rising ground overlooking the Beauport shore and set
about colonizing and cultivating their lands. Shortly afterwards Chavigny made a trip home to France and died at sea.

Eleanor was a very enterprising woman as well as a brave
one. She had a family of young children, so she stayed on in
the manor house and struggled with seigneurial affairs.
Within a few months her house was burned, but she immediately rebuilt it. And since she was an attractive woman and
a rich widow to boot, she married for the third time, Jacques
Gourdeau de Beaulieu. She was married in a little chapel
on the island, apparently the first bride to make her wedding
vows on the Island of Orleans.

It is as Madame Gourdeau de Beaulieu that Eleanor is
chiefly celebrated and a long line of Gourdeaus commemorate her third matrimonial venture. There has always since
been a Madame Gourdeau de Beaulieu in the old stone
house. The house has been too big for one family for a long
time, so it has been divided, making two homes. Years ago
when I first visited the old house there was a very aged
Madame Gourdeau sitting in a rocker by a fire, a tiny, bright-

eyed woman, incredibly old, but witty and alert, her wrink-
led face peering out of a little white starched bonnet. The
daughters of the *grandmere* took a lantern to light our way,
and led me down into the cavernous cellars of the manor
house to point out the very fireplace where Jacques Gourdeau
de Beaulieu met his untimely end and the wall where the
Gourdeau treasure may, for all we know, still lie hidden.

For Jacques Gourdeau de Beaulieu was murdered by a
valet, who threw his body into the fireplace and set the house
afire. The valet was convicted and executed for his crime.
According to tradition the gold he was seeking was hidden
somewhere in the thick dividing wall of the cellar. The Gourdeaus have lived for three hundred years in the house without pulling the wall down to look for the treasure!

Five months later Eleanor married again, for the fourth
time. But to her contemporaries she went on being Eleanor
de Grandmaison. Perhaps it was a little confusing trying to
keep up with her change of names. Eleanor of the Big
House,—what was her story before she ventured, a young
and ambitious and charming widow, away from Clamecy
de Niverais to the colony of New France?

Her fourth husband was Jacques Gailhaut de la Tesserie.
She led a happy life with him for ten years. She was a woman
of fifty when she was widowed for the fourth time and
apparently had had husbands enough, for she devoted the
rest of her life, another score of years, to the affairs of her
large and increasingly important family, and her considerable fortune.

Lands to the east of the estate of Beaulieu fell into the
hands of Charles de Lauzon Charny. He was one of the
family of Governor de Lauzon who brought three sons to
New France. They belonged to a famous family of the
French aristocracy and it was quite a romance when young
and wealthy Charles married young Marie Louise Giffard,
the daughter of the seigneur of Beauport, just across the
river. The story had a tragic outcome, for although her father

was a physician, Marie Louise died four years later in child-
birth and left young Lauzon with an infant daughter. He
was overwhelmed with grief, put the child into the hands of
the sisters at the Hotel Dieu and next summer crossed the
Atlantic and sought solace in a cloister. He was ordained a
priest and two years later returned to Quebec in the train
of Bishop Laval. He was a useful man to the bishop and
among the duties he assumed was that of vicar to the Hotel
Dieu. There he watched his little flower of a daughter blos-
soming from babyhood into girlhood and from girlhood into
womanhood. No one knew better than Charles de Lauzon
how hard and self-sacrificing was the life the white sisters
lived. He tried to shield his daughter from the rigours of
convent life, yet when she was sixteen she told him that
she wanted to be a nursing nun and to share the life of the
nursing sisters. Lauzon was alarmed. In desperation he
offered the nuns a dowry of twelve thousand pounds for his
daughter if they would serve her an extra course at every
meal when she became a nun. The austere Laval remon-
strated. The bishop and the priest quarrelled bitterly and as
a result, Lauzon took his daughter back to France. But she
was still insistent about her calling and entered a convent at
La Rochelle. Longing to be near her, all that remained to
him of Marie Louise, Lauzon entered a Jesuit monastery at
La Rochelle, in order to see her sometimes, and there he lived
until his death.

Another of the Lauzon brothers,—Louis,—settled on the
Island and he too made a romantic marriage. For some unre-
corded reason a young girl by the name of Catherine Nau de
Fossambault had been sent out, against her will, by the
Duchesse D'Aiguillon, to take the veil at the Hôtel Dieu.
Catherine was a high-spirited girl and would not submit to
the will of a duchess, nor to the discipline of a mother superior, even in exile in New France. The nuns ruefully admitted that she had no vocation for the religious life. But she
had a dowry. Louis de Lauzon had lands but no money. So

somehow the two young people managed to find each other and decided to pool their resources. Probably the sisters were glad to have the wilful Catherine off their hands. The young couple retired to the island and built themselves a home. Their happiness was short-lived, because four years later, in 1659, when Louis was crossing from Quebec to the island in a canoe, he ran into trouble and was drowned.

The bridge that since 1935 has linked the island with the mainland, is a beautiful cable suspension bridge two and three-quarter miles long. It leads to the road that encircles the island through typical habitant country. Here are farms running from the water's edge, in long narrow fields, towards the interior of the island, for the means of communication was by water and each farm had its own landing place. Here are the low, white-washed stone houses, the big white barns, the wayside shrines, the weathered rail fences.

Thirty-one families on the island were awarded the Quebec tercentenary medal in 1908, to honour their allegiance to the soil since the seventeenth century. One family had lived on the same farmlands since 1658, and three families proved unbroken occupation since 1662. No less than thirteen families had been on the land since 1666.

The head of the family that had the longest record was Francois Gosselin of St. Laurent, a descendant of the first settler on the island. In the history of that family are one hundred and thirty sons who entered the priesthood.

The village of St. Pierre lies along the north shore, facing Montmorency Falls. It has a beautiful church in the centre of the village. It was built in 1718. In the summer of 1758 word ran round the island that British ships were nosing their way through La Traverse and were at their very doors. The Islanders fled their homes. When the soldiers landed they found the little white homes deserted and the church silent and lonely in the June sunshine. Many of the homes were destroyed in the war that followed but the church escaped and when the fighting was over, the villagers returned and went on with the enriching of their church. Much of the lovely woodcarving dates back to the first and second quarter of the eighteenth century, when fine craftsmen were at work in Quebec. The church has a single door and an oeil-de-boeuf window in the facade and two small projecting lateral chapels.

Little St. Pierre had two curés who became bishops. The first was Monseigneur Mariauchau d'Esgly. He was born in Quebec and at twenty-four became a priest and was sent to the Parish of St. Pierre. He did not leave his village for the fifty-four remaining years of his life. When he was sixty and quite content with his rural peace, his mother's family, the Lotbinières, determined to have him appointed to succeed Bishop Briand of Quebec. Curé d'Esgly held aloof from the intrigues of his family but they succeeded and had him consecrated as a bishop, the first Canadian-born to hold that high rank in the Roman church. But when it was all over, he returned to St. Pierre and to his duties as curé. He did not actually take possession of the see until he was seventy-four and then made trips to Quebec only when he had to administer the rites of ordination. When he was seventy-eight he died, and amid the most solemn ceremonies that the church of St. Pierre had ever seen, he was buried within the crypt, in his robes of office. No fewer than forty priests assisted in the five-hour ceremony one hot June day.

The other curé who became a bishop was a rollicking Irish priest, Father Burke, who came to Canada in 1787. In the estimation of the times, Father Burke was "a great genius". He had oddities enough to indicate that he was at least a most unusual man. When he was thirty-five he came from his native Kildare, via London, to act as professor of philosophy and mathematics at the Seminary of Laval. His Irish brogue sat so badly on his French conversation that his classes frequently became uproarious over his mispronunciations. At last, as a solution to the problem, he was appointed curé of St. Pierre. There he went in September of 1791 and in spite of the peculiarities of his speech he made himself beloved by his parishioners. A century later St. Pierre was still laughing over the tales of his lazy horse and his famous sermons. Proper names were beyond him altogether and one of his parishioners helped him out by interpreting for him. "You say that, Gosselin," the priest would shout down from the pulpit when he was reading banns, or making an announcement of some kind.

A few years later Father Burke moved on to other fields and ended a long and interesting life as Bishop of Halifax.

Between St. Pierre and St. Laurent, which is on the other side of the island, runs a beautiful road called La Route des Prêtes, which got its name from a ceremonial procession that ended a famous island quarrel. In the late eighteenth century the church at St. Laurent was called the church of St. Paul. Bishop St. Vallier asked the church of St. Pierre to divide its honours with the church when he renamed it St. Laurent. The curé at St. Pierre said that if the other church would give to St. Pierre a relic of St. Paul which was in its possession, then he would give the church of St. Paul three relics of St. Clement the Martyr. The bishop agreed and the exchange was made.

However, the parishioners of St. Laurent were very unhappy about losing their familiar relic. So one night an audacious habitant entered the church of St. Pierre and deposited there the bones of St. Clement and calmly appropriated the bone of St. Paul and walked back over the hill and returned it to the church of St. Laurent.

There was a furore when the exchange was discovered, the two parishes were up in arms and every household was agog over the affair. The bishop arrived and angrily ordered the return of the relics to their respective churches. Moreover, it had to be done with ceremony and ritual. A day was set aside and in each church the parishioners gathered and set out behind their priests, who carried the relics, for the rendezvous, midway between the villages. On the Route des

Prêtes they walked until they met and there the exchange was solemnly made. Where the exchange was made a cross was set up to mark the end of the quarrel.

One of the things for which St. Pierre is famous in the markets of the mainland is *fromage rafinné*. In spite of its pungent bouquet, this cheese is considered a great delicacy, and the queer, rough yellow cakes are bought eagerly in the markets of Quebec. It is from a recipe that has remained a secret in certain families of St. Pierre from the earliest days of the colony.

Beyond St. Pierre the highway runs between fields that have supported a dozen generations of Canadiens, and comes at last to Ste. Famille. The church which gives its name to this village and parish is one of the most celebrated in the province for its history, its architecture and its wood carvings. It it named for the holy family and in niches on the facade are the famous statues of St. Joachim, and Ste. Anne, St. Joseph and Mary with the Christ child. The first church on this site was built in 1669 and the more imposing stone building was begun in 1743.

In the seventeenth century the parish of Ste. Famille ranked next in importance to Quebec and Charlesbourg. When the church was rebuilt the parish wanted to depart from the simplicity of the small country church and so this was built in the form of a cross with three steeples. Again the wood-carvers and the ironworkers were commissioned to make the church as rich and ornate as possible. Unfortunately much of what they did then has been removed and replaced by later generations. The altars, however, are the original ones, the main altar the work of the brothers Levasseur in 1749. Some of the work is very fine, among the best surviving from the workshops of the famous craftsmen working in the tradition of the Cap Tourmente school.

Ste. Famille is now the only church standing which was consecrated during the French regime. Very few churches underwent this important ceremony, although all the churches are blessed. Only two others were consecrated and both have been destroyed.

Under the feudal regime in Quebec the seigneur was always a person of very great importance in the community. He had special rights, such as a grave within the church, the first communion bread after the clergy, the first candles blessed on Candlemas Day, the first ashes and the first palms. He also had the right to a specially placed pew. There is still a bitter memory in the parish over a famous lawsuit concerning the seigneurial pew of St. Famille. It came about in this way. In 1779 Malcolm Fraser, a captain in the Royal Emigrants, (loyalists from the American colonies) bought the parishes of Ste. Famille and St. Jean as a seigneurial estate. Fraser was a Protestant and he assigned his pew to his miller, Louis Poulin. In 1803, since the seigneurial rights had been allowed to lapse, a new pew was built in front of the original pew of honour at the right of the altar. Then trouble began. Which was pew number one and which was pew number two? Poulin continued to use the seigneurial pew and in 1805 he bought the seigneury from the Frasers and became in actual fact the feudal lord of the two parishes. The puzzle lay dormant untiil 1848 when Poulin's son attempted to assert his rights to the seigneurial honours. The matter had to be carried to the Superior Court and the Court of Appeal, before it was settled and it became a *cause célèbre* over which much good ink was spilled. The miller's son won the case.

The drive towards the end of the island, from Ste. Famille to St. Francois is one of continual interest, for all the homes are built along the highway in the tradition of Quebec. Below, at the foot of each long field, the river glistens on its restless way to the sea. Across the water the sister villages of the north shore spread themselves over the sloping land. And behind them in rolling masses, low against the sky, are the Laurentian hills.

At the eastern tip of the island is the parish of St. Francois de Sales. It is a sleepy village. Living and dead alike crowd around the walls of its old church facing the highway. While not one of the most important architecturally or historically, the church of St. Francois is one of the most charming in Quebec. There is a sense of grace and unity about it, within and without, that makes its simplicity very appealing. It was built in 1732 and still retains much of its original austerity and peace. When the British troops landed on the island in 1759 this church was converted into a hospital.

An old lament is still sung in the village to tell the story of a tragic wedding party. Louis Beaudoin crossed the river from St. Francois to St. Joachim to bring home his bride. A day and a night were spent in festivities and then, with thirteen of their relatives, the bridal pair set out on the return journey to St. Francois. As they approached the shore the boat capsized and all but two were drowned, including the bride and groom. Of the original twenty verses some thirteen survive in the capacious memories of the folk-singers.

St. Jean lies round the island on the way back to Bout de l'Ile. St. Jean is the largest village on the island and many from Quebec spend the summers here. St. Laurent is the next village, and it was here that Wolfe landed in June of 1759 in search of encampments for his men and strategic positions to command Quebec. About two thousand five hundred islanders were ordered off by the French command and took refuge in the woods around Charlesbourg. The farms had to be abandoned while the fields were green with the young crops and the apple trees still rosy with blossoms. They might have stayed quietly at home, but fear and divided councils in the French camp drove the habitants into exile and left the island deserted when the British landed. With not a living soul to oppose them, Wolfe's men landed and walked up the beach to the empty village. Wolfe was with them and as he walked, eager and curious, through the long sunny street, he came to the door of the Church of St. Laurent. There, nailed to the door was a paper addressed to

"The Worthy Officers of the British Army". It was the famous letter from Curé Martel which begged the invaders, in the name of humanity, to respect the little house of God. After an eloquent plea for consideration for the unfortunate parishioners he added, out of transparent guile, mingled with the pride of a host: "If you had arrived sooner you could have tasted the vegetables from my garden, such as asparagus, radishes, etc., but now they have all gone to seed."

Amused by the naiveté of the good curé, Wolfe spared the village church and the rectory and Curé Martel came back to it in due time, when New France had become a British colony.

10

"La Mauricie"

WHEN we drive out of Quebec on our way towards "La Mauricie" we begin to realize what the new highways, built for speed, have done to the old travelways and the historic spirit of the province. The old roads, on which history was made, followed the contours of the country side. Because the old seigneuries were laid out along the waterfronts and the fiefs were cut ribbonlike from shore to the interior boundaries, the pioneer travelways were along the river's edge where the homes were built. The road from Quebec to Montreal was like one long village street.

The Canadiens were rarely in a hurry. A journey was broken up by visits to friends along the way. In summer the travel was by water but the little vessels tied up at sunset at some friendly dock and the evenings were spent in visiting. If there were people of importance aboard the boat, the nearest seigneur would undoubtedly give a dinner party. Only in winter did the Canadiens use the road for long journeys. It was a beautiful route with pleasant and gracious homes, busy and cheerful farmhouses, churches and presbyteries, convents and seminaries along the way, all unfolding like pages of a story book.

Now the graceful curves of the old road have been sacrificed to speed and efficiency, slashed off by the surveyors' instruments. Here and there is a crescent of ancient highway lying north or south of the speedway and on these fragments there may stand some old house, an old mill, a quiet church, set aside from the rush of twentieth century life, shielded by venerable maples that recall a more leisurely generation.

Fifty-six miles out of Quebec at Ste. Anne de la Pérade there is a marker at the side of the road to indicate the location of the home of Madeleine de Verchères. We shall discover Mareleine as a girl when we get to Verchères, but here we are reminded that she was not only the heroine of Verchères but that she was afterwards a woman of character and perhaps one of the first Canadian women yearning for a career of her own. The Verchères story was forgotten for two hundred years. It was only revived when by chance a manuscript was discovered in the Archives of France which told Madeleine's story in her own words.

Madeleine admits, when she was only twenty-one, that she frankly "entertained sentiments which urge me to aspire to fame quite as eagerly as many men". In those days,—for she grew up in the seventeenth century,—a woman with this urge to express her own competence or ambitions had only two alternatives from which to choose: she might enter a convent or she might become a courtesan. There was no other life in which a woman could act freely as an individual in working out a career of her own. But in New France, with its strictly supervised society, there was no place but a convent for a woman who was not a wife and the mother of a family. Madeleine had no taste either for the monastic life which was open to her or the role of courtesan which would be too difficult in New France. Yet Madeleine was twenty-seven before she married. That was an unheard of thing in New France where parents were called to account when a daughter of sixteen was unmarried. Certainly, even when she came as a bride to this manor house of La Pérade, she was anything but a clinging vine. We read in her report of the attack on Fort Verchères of her contempt for Madame Fontaine who was in the fort with husband and children. Madame Fontaine wanted to leave and seek refuge elsewhere, but Madeleine said that was just the kind of timidity that stamped all Parisian women. Madeleine saved her husband's life from the Indians and fought a lively battle with them in her own kitchen, and from all accounts was a lusty, gusty woman who shocked the clergy and her more sedate neighbours in many ways.

The strange structure we see now is all that remains of a fine old manor house, on a hill-side looking down upon the St. Lawrence, with a seigneurial mill near by. The old house itself is in ruins and all that is habitable is a box-like structure that was built on its foundations and what Alexander Angus in "Old Quebec" calls "a little one-story excrescence on the west end (built) for the better reception of Governor General Lord Dalhousie" by its owner in 1825. What we see from the highway was originally the rear of the house, for the old road was re-routed.

It was in 1706 that Madeleine married a retired officer, Pierre-Thomas de Lanaudiere, whose father was the first seigneur of La Pérade. There is a novel yet to be written about this house and its mistress. It was in the kitchen of this house that a drunken Indian, said to be an Abenaki, attacked her husband. But Madeleine seized his hatchet from him and put him out of action.

The original house was built in 1673. Shortly after the marriage the house was enlarged. Only the walls remain, overgrown with trees and weeds. It was here that Madeleine lived until her death, at sixty-nine, in 1747. No one marked the place where she was buried. But of recent years the occupants have come upon a grave near the house which they believe to be Madeleine's. No one has done anything about it, and in her own home town of Verchères no one seemed to know or care anything about Madeleine's resting place. Yet here even in the ruins there lives the spirit of this rugged woman who grew out of the heroic child, a woman who was strong-minded, ambitious, perhaps a little frustrated, more than a little ribald and probably a bit of a vixen, ruling the great manor house of Ste. Anne de la Pérade, where the Marquis de Vaudreuil and the Marquis de Beauharnois and other of the great and near-great of her time, were frequent guests.

Madeleine is still awaiting recognition although the heroic child who defended the fort against the Iroquois is beloved by school children from coast to coast. How strange that the mature and heroic woman should be so neglected by Canadians. Is it because the memory of her "burlesque litanies", composed and sung when she was in her buxom 'forties, still echo down the ages?

Twenty-two miles beyond Ste. Anne de la Pérade we come to the outskirts of *La Mauricie*, the valley of the St. Maurice River, a region with a very distinctive character. It was into *La Mauricie* that the French went in search of Indians and furs, a great Laurentian wilderness teeming with game and broken by short and turbulent rivers. The valley, except for the area lying near the shores of the St. Lawrence, is still largely wilderness and is the source of great wealth, but not in furs alone. No river valley in any part of the North American continent, or perhaps anywhere in the world, is as completely and thoroughly organized as a producer of hydro-electric power as the St. Maurice Valley.

We don't know what the Indians called it, but perhaps they had a name for it as majestic as the name they bestowed upon the Saguenay. It lies wholly within Quebec province as it rises in several lakes just south of James Bay and on the St. Lawrence side of the watershed. It is not a long river, as rivers go in Canada, for it is only two hundred and forty miles, but for beauty, forest wealth, power and dramatic scientific interest, it is unexcelled.

It is a river with a history of five hundred million years, but it emerged from the mist of geological antiquity only three centuries ago when Frenchmen discovered how rich a fur trading centre there was at the triple mouth of the turbulent river.

In those days young boys,—so young that today they would scarcely be allowed to choose their own ties,—played quite important roles in the politics and administration of the colony. They were brought out from France in order that they might be placed with the hunting tribes of Indians to learn their language, customs and travelways. The Indians accepted the boys because of the adaptability of adventurous youth to the nomadic life of the tribes. The boys, as they grew up, became the guides and interpreters of the explorers and fur traders. So we find that in 1634, while Champlain was still Governor of New France, Pierre Boucher, at the age of twelve, came to Quebec with his father. He was sent off one summer with a party of Indian hunters. Four years later, when he was only sixteen, he was so well versed in Indian dialects and Indian ways that he was sent to the mouth of the St. Maurice to act as interpreter at the trading post. In the next thirty years his fortunes and those of Three Rivers were as one. Whatever he may have been by birth, he became a man of substance and importance in New France. He was the first Canadian ennobled by King Louis the Fourteenth and he had influence at court because of his services in New France. When he was raised to the nobility during a visit to Paris in 1661, he returned with a party of colonists who became censitaires on his seigneury up the river about what is now Boucherville.

It was Pierre Boucher who induced the King and Colbert to send help to the colonists in their struggle against the Iroquois and it was after a visit to court that the Carignan Regiment was sent to Canada.

For fifteen of his thirty years at Three Rivers, Pierre Boucher was governor of the district. At forty-five he retired to his seigneury. But for him life began at forty with his elevation to the nobility, for he lived on his seigneurial lands, in the manor house at Boucherville for fifty years. He died in 1717 at the age of ninety-five, leaving one hundred and fifty descendants. He was one of the first Canadian authors, for he wrote a book called *A True and Frank History of the Customs and Products of the Country of New France.* Too bad he did not spend his long retirement in writing more about New France in those crucial years of the half century from 1667 to 1717.

In the days of Pierre Boucher the wealth of *La Mauricie* was in furs, but later the French found iron near Three Rivers and later still the forests were turned into wealth. But all this was preliminary, just the little prelude played on the Pipes of Pan before the curtain went up on the great drama of *La Mauricie*.

The first act of this drama is around a bottle in a famous Montreal hotel where a few business men were talking over the new-fangled hydro-electric power just as men now wonder whether or not atomic power will ever come into general industrial use. There was not much hydro-electric power being generated anywhere in the world while these late Victorian Montrealers were letting their imaginations soar over Scotch and soda. Perhaps one of them had looked into the history of this strange new energy and recalled its story for his friends. He probably told them that six centuries before the time of Christ, Thales, one of the seven sages of Greece, absent-mindedly rubbing a piece of amber that traders had brought down from the Baltic, discovered that the friction had done something to it which made it attract other substances. That was the discovery of electricity. It was twenty-two centuries before a physician at the court of Queen Elizabeth recognized what had happened to the amber in the hands of Thales and knew that the magnetism it generated represented a new principle. He used the Greek word for amber and called the principle *electricity*.

It was to be another two centuries before men of science began exploring the idea in their laboratories. Nobody knew what the power could be used for; it was just another of those ivory tower ideas. Some thought perhaps it was related to lightning.

It is here that the story of electricity moves nearer home. When the American rebels tried to force the Canadians into the revolution, they sent up a committee of Americans to Montreal, to try to win over the fourteenth colony. One of the committee was Benjamin Franklin. In the years between the Cession of New France and the outbreak of the revolution, 1760 to 1775, Franklin was postmaster-general of all the British colonies, and therefore the first postmaster-general of Canada. It was Franklin who had experimented with a kite in a thunderstorm and brought electrical energy down into his laboratory, twenty-five years before he came to Montreal, where the bottle of Scotch was getting low as the excitement of the business men rose. These men had heard about a falls in the St. Maurice Valley on the Shawinigan River, a tributary, that was said to be an ideal site for an experiment in hydro-electric power. Some of them decided to go to Three Rivers to learn more about it.

From Three Rivers they rode off in a buckboard with a team over a rough lumbermen's road. They were so impressed with what they saw at Shawinigan Falls that they decided to buy the power rights. There was no settlement in the vicinity until the power project began at Shawinigan Falls.

It was an impressive venture. Two generators of five thousand horse power each were installed, the largest ever built up to that time. The transmission line to Montreal was eighty-five miles and it carried fifty thousand volts, the longest line and the highest voltage ever attempted. The generators that began work in 1903 are still in use, perhaps partly for sentiment's sake.

Before we turn off the highway onto the road that leads into *La Mauricie* there is one relic of the far off days of Indians and Pierre Boucher that we must see. It is the little mission church of Cap de la Madeleine. Pierre Boucher helped to found the Indian mission on the east side of the St. Maurice, just far enough away from Three Rivers to protect the Indians from the disadvantages of the white man's life. The little mission church is now part of a large modern church, which has been built on to one

71

side of the simple and lovely little chapel. From some points of vantage it is still possible to get a view of the little grey stone building which suggests what it must have been like when the power development of the St. Maurice began. It was about the time that the Shawinigan Power project brought many people into the district, that the little chapel first became a miracle-working shrine. Today more than a quarter of a million pilgrims visit each year the great institution that has grown up around the modest and beautiful mission church of the Indians. But in its original architecture, the mission is one of the purest examples of fine seventeenth century Quebec architecture. At the turn of the century the St. Maurice Valley was still a great wilderness and the church of Cap de la Madeleine a sleepy, almost unknown place. Today it rivals Ste. Anne de Beaupré, and the valley beyond is one of the most modern industrial areas on the continent.

The source of the St. Maurice is the lake-fretted Abitibi country, south east of James Bay. Much of this country is now the Gouin Reservoir, at an elevation of 1328 feet, where two hundred and eight billion cubic feet of water is controlled for the power plants below. There are two other great dams, one on the headwaters of the Manouan River, and third at the headwaters of the Mattawin, both tributaries of the St. Maurice.

Laurentian history begins with volcanoes pouring molten lava from the earth's boiling interior over the land. When wild seas roared over this part of the world, mountains were thrust up, only to be eroded by icefields and floods. Science says that the oldest rocks on our earth are two billion years old. Anything older than five hundred million years is called Pre-Cambrian. The Laurentian country is Pre-Cambrian. In *La Mauricie* water from ice sheets miles thick formed these power sites by flowing in around the roots of ancient mountains and making lakes in crevices.

The last of the glaciers retreated probably twenty-five

thousand years ago. The temperature rose, the glaciers melted
at their southern edges, rivers and streams were born, and at
the same time all the great rocks, gravel and sand that had
been held in the glaciers as they ground over the continent,
were released. Old river valleys were sometimes choked by
the debris and new courses had to be formed. The St. Maurice
from its source flows over these glacial deposits to the southern edge of the Laurentian Plateau at Grand' Mère, in a series
of rapids that lie between quiet stretches of the river, drop-
ping seven hundred and fifty feet in two hundred miles. The
river follows parts of several pre-glacial rivers but where the
glacial deposits blocked the old channels, the river was forced
to flow over divides between valleys in a series of rapids.
Two of these divides cause a drop over rapids of one hundred and forty feet in eleven miles. Behind Rapide Blanc the
river formed a great lake at one time. So all the way down the
river the geologists have discovered great depths of glacially
deposited rock above the original river beds and can trace
the changes that were made by the higher temperatures and
their effect. They have discovered by geophysical methods
that at La Tuque, for instance, the original rock bed was
about sea level, and that there is now more than five hundred feet of sand choking the original river bed. The town of
La Tuque is built on this sand terrace. Below La Tuque the
river is again in a pre-glacial channel to below Grandes Piles.
Where the pre-glacial channels are followed by the river, the
river is sluggish and the valleys are broad, but where the St.
Maurice jumps over the gaps and low ridges from one valley
to another there are rapids. The Shawinigan River is older
than the St. Maurice, and Cross Hill in the town of Shawinigan is one of the deposits formed by the loosening of the grip
of the glacier upon its accumulations of stone and gravel in
its long travels southward. But the dam builders of today
must seek the original rock of the Laurentians as foundation
for their great dams and power houses for the engineers say
that "a dam is only as effective as the material on which it

stands". These stand on Pre-Cambrian rock, the oldest in the world.

So when we start up the valley towards Shawinigan Falls we are entering an area which is a dramatic industrial theatre with a backdrop of a geographical divide in the far north, a setting of sixteen thousand lakes, the greatest of which is the five hundred square miles of Lake La Loutre, created by the government-owned Gouin Dam, and great forests which produce not only furs and famous sports fishing, but millions of logs of pulpwood for paper for the printing presses of the world.

One of the characteristic sights of this area is a great cone-shaped hill of pulp-wood at some paper mill. It may be a pale gold or a weathered grey, depending upon the season of the year and the age of the pile. For with the development of hydro-electric power came industry. With a storage capacity of three hundred and fifty billion cubic feet of water behind publicly owned dams to the northward, the power supply could be depended upon for industrial operations. There are ten great power sites on the St. Maurice, in its quarter of a mile drop from its source to the St. Lawrence, about three-fifths of which is already developed. The water out of the silent north will ultimately be put to work ten times before it escapes to the sea, for it will be forced through generators at each of the sites of the ancient fur traders' portages.

What stories there must be behind the names of the old portages, now the names of modern electric plants. For instance, the first plant from the St. Lawrence is La Gabelle, a reference to an old French salt-tax. Why did the voyageurs and coureurs de bois call this the portage of the salt-tax? Did some one from Three Rivers collect a little graft from the traders as they came here with their furs? Long afterwards in the British regime a law was instituted to prevent greedy traders from going up-stream to meet the hunters before they had a chance to get their furs to the market at Three Rivers.

The portage at Grand' Mère was named for a rock which looked like an old woman, the one at La Tuque for a rock that looked like the hunter's headdress. Then there is the Rapid Without a Name, with a potential of two hundred and fifty thousand horse-power, the Rapid of the Hearts, and the Rapid of the Hare. If the old hunters and traders who paddled and portaged their way up and down this river two and three centuries ago could return to their old haunts, what a satisfaction they would feel in seeing these white waters and terrible rapids put to work as the servants of man, and no longer his master.

At Shawinigan Falls, the heart of the power empire, the Shawinigan Water and Power Company, the parent of the modern chemical industry of the valley, has its headquarters. Here, the lovely falls that first inspired the hydro-electric development has practically disappeared. It is only in times of a surplus supply of water that it is again routed over the ancient one hundred and fifty foot ledge. All the rest of the time the water pours through stocks and turbines to become power.

The St. Maurice valley produces fifteen per cent of all the power generated in Canada. Half a million horse-power is generated at Shawinigan Falls alone. This is a spot to which engineers from all over the world are attracted because it demonstrates so vividly the history of electrical power. Here they can trace the evolution of hydraulic machinery and equipment for the generation of power over a period of more than half a century, in the three power houses built in that time.

Ninety per cent of the power produced in the valley is sold to large industries such as pulpwood and chemical plants. The first industrial use of power was in 1901 when aluminum was made at Shawinigan Falls. In 1903 the pulp and paper industry originated also at Shawinigan Falls. Today this industry uses about half the power generated by the St. Maurice, in plants at Three Rivers, Cap de la Madeleine,

Shawinigan, Grand' Mère, and La Tuque. But in addition today great textile and chemical plants are operated near the power sites. The power travels far afield, from La Tuque to the United States border, and from Oka in the west to Murray Bay in the east. It crosses the St. Lawrence on transmission lines at Three Rivers and at Sorel. These are fed by those very beautiful high-voltage transmission towers that straddle the wilderness, emerging so dramatically out of the forests when we travel the roads that cross the forest lands and fishing and game country to the north. Some one has called them "silver giants who cross the fields, leaping over hills and striding over streams."

When we approach the vicinity of St. Jean des Piles we begin to realize the immensity of the pulp-wood industry. Here from a quiet spot on a high bank we may sit and watch the motion of the great floes of pulp-wood. Twenty-four million of these logs are floated down the St. Maurice every year, through special channels incorporated into the power developments. The forests protect the water supplies of the Laurentian country, the river takes the logs to the mills and turns them into paper, in a great co-ordinated engineering and conservation plan. As a result, here in this valley is the greatest concentration of pulp and paper plants in the world.

11

Three Rivers

WEST of the St. Maurice is the city of Three Rivers, the second oldest city in Canada. Today it is an industrial city but there are parts of Three Rivers that bespeak its antiquity; some very old houses, the Ursuline convent, a daughter house of the old convent in Quebec city and an eighteenth century mill.

During the French regime there was a church and monastery of the Recollet Fathers in Three Rivers. After the fall of New France, the British who came to settle in the old trading town, took over the home of the Recollets and turned the property into an Anglican church and rectory. The old Recollet buildings, the Ursuline convent and some of the oldest houses in the city are grouped together on one street which has preserved its eighteenth century atmosphere.

The city of Three Rivers takes its name from the three-mouthed estuary of the St. Maurice. Its history goes back to a time only seven years after the founding of Quebec, for it was a trading post from 1615. In 1634 the first settlement was begun under Laviolette and it became a fortified town. The site of some of the early fortifications is today a public promenade. The greatest son of Three Rivers was La Vérendrye, the explorer.

Pierre de La Vérendrye was the son of a seigneur, born at Three Rivers, and her most illustrious citizen. La Vérendrye went to France as a young man to fight for Louis the Fourteenth in his last war against the English. In September of 1709 the French and English fought the famous battle of

Malplaquet. Among the many, many thousands of the dead who lay on the battlefield, young Pierre lay, left for dead, too. But presently, in spite of his almost fatal injuries, he came back to life and was a prisoner of the English for a year. When he was released he found that a defeated king had no rewards for a young colonial with his nine wounds. Pierre returned to New France. The only career open to him there was fur trading and exploration. To get a permit to trade with the Indians, the trader had to undertake exacting explorations for the government. In this way La Vérendrye began his travels westward through the Great Lakes and beyond. He cared little for the profits from the fur trade but he had to earn a living for his family. Three of his sons grew up to love the travels of exploration their father undertook and they shared his adventures and his fame as the discoverer of the West. One of his sons was murdered by Indians in the west, but the other two pressed on with him year after year. Finally one year, when La Vérendrye was too ill to go forward, from a trading post he had established where Portage La Prairie now stands, the two sons went on alone and were the first white men to see the Rocky Mountains from the plains. But France had no gratitude for his work. He was accused of making a fortune and neglecting the king's commands; he was spied upon and defamed and in 1743 he returned to the St. Lawrence for the last time, a broken man. It was half a century before his achievements were repeated or excelled. Only when Sir Alexander Mackenzie pressed on to the Rockies and beyond to the Pacific was La Vérendrye's dream of a route to the Pacific realized.

Three Rivers brings to life a notable and unpretentious little Swiss gentleman, Sir Frederick Haldimand, who is one of the most likeable characters in the history of the British regime in Quebec. There is something about this meticulous, honest and kindly man, with his love of good living, of the companionship of friends, of time for quiet thought and privacy in which to keep his voluminous journals, that attracts the curiosity of those who turn over the pages of Canadian history.

He was a well-educated young Swiss gentleman when he began his life as a mercenary soldier, for the Swiss encouraged their young men to join the armies of friendly powers. Haldimand began with the King of Sardinia and moved on later to Prussia where he served under Frederick the Great, whom he always called "my old master." Later he joined the Swiss Guards in Holland and found himself welcomed at the Dutch court. He always kept a diary, and today there are scores of his letters and journals in the Archives of Canada. They reveal the integrity of his life and his devotion to any duty he assumed.

It was while Britain was building up her armies for the Seven Years War that Haldimand first comes into our picture. There were many Swiss and German Protestants who had settled in Pennsylvania and Maryland. London decided to recruit a regiment among them and except for the commanding officer, the other officers might be non-British. Haldimand was invited to join this regiment. So in 1754, when he was thirty-six years of age, he left the Prince of Orange and entered the service of George the Second. The new regiment was the Royal Americans, and Haldimand had a command at Philadelphia. There he learned his first lesson in living with people who did not look upon soldiers as little tin gods, and there too, he learned to speak English, for his native tongue was French. He looked a good deal like George Washington, and he shared many of Washington's good qualities.

In 1758 he was offered a command in an expedition against the French in Canada. He was wounded in his first battle on Lake George. Later he trained men as rangers in native methods of warfare, and in the year that Wolfe besieged Quebec he was at Oswego, building a dozen galleys for the descent on Montreal in the following year. He was interested in the scientific horticulture for which the Dutch were already famous. Wherever he went he set out gardens and experimented with plants. He was one of the earliest experimental gardeners on the continent. At Oswego, and also at Niagara he planted large gardens which were tended by convalescent soldiers, partly to give them some interesting occupation and partly to provide them with fresh vegetables to aid their recovery.

Lord Amherst arrived at Oswego in June of 1760 with the army that was to go down Lake Ontario and through the St. Lawrence to take Montreal. By a curious chance it was Haldimand who was sent to the gates of Montreal with the party which was to accept the surrender of the French and take over the city when the capitulation became effective. Levis had twenty-two hundred French regulars, but the city was defenceless against Amherst's army of eighteen thousand. Levis asked that his men might leave the city with the honours of war, their flags flying, and with their arms. But Amherst was adamant. He believed that the French had been responsible for the "unheard-of-barbarities" of their Indian troops, and by refusing them the honours of war he was showing his "detestation of such practices." Every French officer bitterly resented the indignity but the capitulation was signed. Col. Haldimand, who spoke French, was chosen for the task that he might "prevent differences on both sides." So it was this Swiss gentleman who went to the gates of Montreal to accept the surrender of the city and aid in the evacuation of the French army. When General Gage became governor of Montreal, Haldimand served two years on his staff, before going to Three Rivers. He was made a British subject as one of the rewards of victory.

When Haldimand settled in Three Rivers, New France continued under military rule for the first two years of his office. The military governors found that a good deal of their time was spent in protecting the Canadiens from the greed of the American traders who flowed in behind the armies and who felt that the French should be treated as conquered people. By all accounts these British Americans, and the new-comers from the British Isles were for the most part an unprincipled lot, for both Murray at Quebec, and Haldimand at Three Rivers were constantly fighting on behalf of the inhabitants and against the encroachments of the new-comers. The French had been badly exploited by the same kind of people from France for years before the Cession and so we have the curious situation in which the men who conquered New France became the defenders of the Canadiens against the rapacious men of their own nation, and later on against the Canadiens who returned from France to claim their old places in the colony.

Haldimand was well liked by the Canadiens for the justice and mercy by which he ruled them. Government House in Three Rivers was a busy place. There were seven thousand inhabitants, including the Indians who lived in three settlements on the outskirts. He divided the district into four parts and in each established a "chamber of audience" with militia officers in charge, where most of the affairs of the country were settled according to old French laws. Only criminal offences were tried by court martial.

Haldimand, in his bachelor quarters, created a home and planted a garden and settled down to live quietly among his people. When there was a bad fire in the town he asked the citizens to make contributions for those who were burned out, as a thank-offering for having escaped a similar fate. He appointed priests to administer the fund, or goods in kind that were collected. He taught the citizens how to fight fires. There were no ladders in the town. He ordered every householder to provide one.

Then he looked at the highway which ran through Three Rivers connecting with Montreal and Quebec. He ordered that the roads in his district be made thirty feet wide and rounded in the centre with the earth dug from ditches which were to be made on each side.

All this time the clergy and the noblesse merely waited

the return of the Bourbons. The habitants and the bourgoise were better off than in the days of the nefarious Intendant Bigot who was now cooling his heels in the Bastille, but those who had the coveted Cross of St. Louis and who lived on glamorous memories of the past made a lot of trouble for men like Haldimand. Not more than a dozen holders of the Cross, a decoration from Louis the Fourteenth, remained in Canada, but they were the core of a movement of frustration and resentment. It was not that they wanted to return to France, because they could have done so if they chose, but because they wanted more attention, more honours, more concessions from the new government. They found it hard to realize that the feudalism of France had passed. Haldimand shrewdly wrote that the great body of Canadiens had settled down to appreciate their new liberties. "I am satisfied," he said, "that they would be in despair were they to see a French fleet and troops arrive in this country in any number whatsoever; they begin to taste too well the sweets of liberty to be dupes of the French; they are now engaged at their harvest peacefully and it is a good one this year." For the repose of the soul of Bigot, he said, there would be not a mass. He supervised the cutting of timber, tall pines for masts from the north shore, oak for the hulls of ships from the south shore.

In his day the great event of the month of May was the arrival of the Têtes de Boule, or the Roundheads, as these Indians were called, from the north, paddling down the St. Maurice with their winter's catch of furs. English traders had swarmed into Three Rivers and some of them travelled up the river to intercept the Indians and get the pick of their packs. Haldimand stopped that. The Têtes de Boules were to be allowed to bring their bales right into the public market at Three Rivers. When they arrived the town crier was to go about giving fair notice to everyone so that all should have a fair chance to buy and the Indians an equal chance to trade without unfair risks.

Fort Chamb

The governors of Montreal, Three Rivers and Quebec were asked to raise militia regiments among the Canadiens, to prove to the restless Indians that the French were satisfied with their new rulers and did not want to drive them out. Only Haldimand was able to complete his unit with Canadien volunteers, for they trusted him and realized that althought he was stern and often inflexible, he was just and he had their interests at heart. The corps of Canadiens never had to fight, but the very fact of their enlistment astonished the Indians and made them realize that the Canadiens would never join them in guerilla warfare against the British. Instead of war, Haldimand's thought was all for the ways of peace. He longed for the immigration of some well-trained agriculturists who would help the Canadiens to modernize their methods and to rise above the serfdom under which they had farmed their lands.

But Haldimand is chiefly remembered for his development of the iron mines near Three Rivers. They were the first thing to attract his attention on his arrival. Just west of Three Rivers there is a cairn by the roadside commemorating Des Forges and nearby a little path runs down to the ruins and to the stream that runs through them. An old chimney still stands, almost lost in the trees and there is a gentle muttering from the stream, like the garrulous chatter of an old-timer, anxious to tell the visitor the story of his life.

Des Forges is the birthplace of Canada's heavy industries, her iron and steel manufacturing. The place has a curious history and it is not easy to think of this quiet spot as one of the biggest enterprises in the history of New France, with smelters, foundries, offices, staff houses and an "industrial town" where some thousands of people lived.

Like so many of the enterprises of the French regime, it was top heavy with the expenses of supervisors and inspectors and royal guards, and, of course, Bigot had a finger in the financial pie. Here was a primary industry producing cannon,

tern Townships

shells and stoves for civilian use, as well as industrial iron for the use of smiths and bell-makers throughout the colony.

It was scouts of Intendant Talon who first discovered iron in this vicinity in 1666. It was 1730 before a serious attempt was made to mine the ore and smelt it as marketable iron. For in addition to the smelters built here, there were also, eventually, foundries for casting the iron into armaments and into articles for domestic use. Intendant Hocquart induced the king to grant to Francois Poulin, Sieur de Francheville, a rich Montreal merchant, a twenty-year monopoly of the iron mines and to confer on him two seigneuries, Yamachiche and Cap de la Madeleine, as sources of fuel, in return for working the mines and building the forges. But where were the men with the "know how", the technicians to direct the work?

The smelting of ore into iron was at that time a rare skill. Smelters and foundrymen were few and there was a great deal of rivalry between mine owners for their services. There was no one in New France who could attempt the work. Francheville, with his mines and forest lands already secure, appealed to the king for two foundrymen. They arrived with their tools in 1731.

The foundrymen agreed that the ore was excellent and then began devising ways and means for the most economical working of the mines and the forges. New England already had the reputation of working its mines competently so Francheville got permission from the Intendant to send a man named Labrèche, an intelligent native workman, to New England to learn their methods. On his return Labrèche began experiments and declared that it was possible to extract from the ore deposits at Cap de la Madeleine supplies of the first quality. He sent a specimen bar of the iron home to France. Then he set men to work on the basis of the methods used in New England. The ore had to be floated from Cap de la Madeleine up the the St. Lawrence to the site of the forges, a spot where Ruisseau St. Maurice, a steeply falling brook, emptied into the St. Maurice River. The Ruiseau was to supply the water needed in the processing.

Labrèche was now superintendant at Three Rivers. He decided to go again to New England and take with him two men to be instructed as he had been. On their return things really began to hum. But also misfortunes piled up. Francheville died in Montreal and although the company decided to carry on it was badly handicapped without his leadership. Moreover, in the two months the forges had been operating they had produced much less iron than was anticipated and no profits. The installation proved to be very defective.

At this point an expert arrived on the scene. He had been sent from France to look the whole situation over. His name was Olivier de Vezin and he quickly pointed out the faults. They were many. The whole plant had to be rebuilt. The amateur foundrymen had done their best but it was not good enough. They were faced with the extreme necessity of getting some really competent men.

By this time the government at Paris was thoroughly roused because of the growing need for iron in the new industrial development of the day, iron for ships and armaments and other new uses. So the king sent out two master ironworkers. Now these men were really expert technicians and there was a big row in France about taking them away from the French companies. Years before, in the days of Colbert, some Frenchmen had been sent to Sweden to study the iron processes in which the Swedes excelled, for they surpassed all other people in the working of iron in those days. On their return the Frenchmen had trained others, but good ironworkers were still few and every one of them was precious to the French economy. It was difficult to persuade any of these men to leave France because they could command high wages at home and were reluctant to exile themselves in a lonely colony. It was in 1735 that the Minister of Marine announced that he had put his hand on a certain number of workers who would undertake the journey in return for very high wages. Meantime a model of the forges at Three Rivers had been sent to Paris, and when the chief of the French ironworkers had examined it he was so impressed that he decided to follow his workers to New France. He was welcomed with great warmth and was turned loose to plan an enterprise that would produce both plenty of iron and plenty of profit.

In those days, as in these, Canada was bedevilled with problems of the balance of trade. The colony brought so much from France that it could never balance its export trade with its import trade. Now it was hoped that the export of iron and its products and the building of ships in which native timber and native iron could be used, would at long last bring about a favourable balance. Vezin decided to stay and become a partner in the new company which would operate the mines and the forges.

Then the government at Paris began to worry over the effect the colonial mining venture might have on the industry of France. There might be advantages for New France but old France would have to face competition. Business men in the provinces were howling blue ruin because the people of Quebec were being encouraged to develop their own resources. However, the king gave Quebec the signal to proceed and presently he even sent them a second expert, Sieur Jacques Simonet, who could work with Vezin, and if necessary, replace him. It was 1738 before the new plant was set in operation.

About this time Simonet returned to France to look for more foundrymen now that full production was near. He actually recruited fifty-five workers, attracted by high wages and the excitement the new enterprise was creating. But there were more howls of dismay from the French industrialists over taking away their best men. A Comtesse de Grancey was delegated to carry the combined protests of the French iron producers straight to the Minister of Marine. Nevertheless the men sailed for Quebec and their landing was the cause of a great deal of elation up and down the St. Lawrence. New France imagined it was headed into a boom.

Meantime New England was extremely interested in what was going on in her neighbour's country. By some means or other some New England agents made their way into Quebec and Three Rivers and talked persuasively to the newcomers, enticing them over the border to the New England smelters and foundrys. They succeeded in persuading Simonet's best man to go home with them, the very man who was to be the boss of the ironworkers. He made his escape from Montreal and although a company of soldiers was sent in pursuit they failed to find him. The New Englanders probably spirited him up the Richelieu and into Lake Champlain. To prevent further losses the miners were put under military guard, and forbidden to absent themselves from the plant without the written permission of Simonet.

But that was not all. Forest fires had destroyed much of the timber intended to supply the furnaces with their fuel and the company had to appeal for the right to cut trees on neighbouring lands. And then there was trouble over the subsidies the government was paying the company. The mines seemed to be a bottomless pit into which the king's golden louis were being dropped. In ten years the forges at Three Rivers had not produced as much iron as was produced in fifteen days in similar forges in France.

In 1741 the engineer, Chaussegros de Lery, proposed that the forges produce cannon for the French warships being built in Canada for the king, and to arm the batteries of Montreal and of the forts on Lake Ontario, and anchors as well. In 1742 this kind of work was begun and by 1746 the forges and foundry were showing good profits. New deposits of iron were found, too. The Company now made cast iron stoves, frying pans, saucepans, bombs, bullets, cannon balls, hammers, large kettles for boiling tar, and other such things. They also produced sheet iron for ship's plates and rudders.

By 1748 Quebec was shipping considerable quantities of iron products home to France.

So it happened that when the Swedish naturalist, Kalm, visited New France he was amazed to discover the flourishing iron industry at Three Rivers. The enterprise was of sufficient importance to be specially dealt with in the articles of Cession on the fall of New France.

When Haldimand went to Three Rivers as governor of the district, he examined the forges and the foundries and all the other property involved in the enterprise, with great care. In the days of Haldimand more than eight hundred men were employed on the project. Haldimand used the place to turn swords into ploughshares, for he organized a campaign to melt down the old guns from the Plains of Abraham and all the other metal debris of the campaign of conquest and turned it all into useful things for the rehabilitation of the life of the Canadiens.

When his term of office was over he was sent to Florida as British commandant. Later he was made a Major-General and promoted to the command in New York. There, at fifty-five years of age, he had to face the rising tide of revolution. He had little sympathy with the rebels. He thought they had prospered so well under the British rule that his tidy Swiss mind could see no sense in revolt. Yet he was shrewd enough to see that the British erred in closing the port of Boston after the "Indian caper" of tossing the tea into the harbour. In 1775 he was recalled to England because, although he was in line for a high command in the approaching war, he was not a native born Britisher and could not get the appointment. In London he was warmly received at court for the king and queen were fond of the old bachelor. He thoroughly enjoyed the lionizing. By that time he was a full general.

He was visiting Switzerland when he received word that he had been appointed Governor General of Canada to replace General Carleton who had been called to active service in the Revolutionary War. He arrived in Quebec in 1778.

In his regime the flood of Loyalists fleeing from the rebel colonies rose high. The bachelor governor again found himself acting the paternal role to thousands of distressed and war-stricken people. At the same time it was believed that under cover of the American Revolution. France would attempt a conquest of New France. So the Swiss gentleman was kept very busy, both in planning for defence and in settlement of the displaced persons on crown lands that stretched all the way from Gaspé to Niagara.

One of his chief undertakings was the building of Fort Lennox, on the Richelieu, as part of the defences of Canada against the revolutionary army.

No governor ever acted so paternally to so many people, French-speaking and English-speaking, in Canada. Yet he was a man without a family of his own, a man always trying to create a home. Wherever he found himself he set about building a house and laying out a garden, in Florida, in New York, in Three Rivers, in Sorel and Quebec. As governor, at Quebec, he added a wing to old Chateau St. Louis and he also built a country home beside the Montmorency Falls, which he called Montmorency House, but which is now Kent House. The Swiss soldier's memory is preserved in many parts of Canada with affection and respect, and the Archives of Canada treasures the long record of his life told so meticulously in his own hand. But in Three Rivers he comes alive as a man of many parts and of great heart.

12

The Island of Montreal

THE Island of Montreal is set like a giant emerald in a medallion of elaborate Florentine silver work, for there lies all about it a network of turbulent and celebrated waterways that throughout its history have been beautiful, dramatic and tragic as man attempted their conquest. Great as is the St. Lawrence river, in the days of the French regime its navigation west of Quebec was always troublesome. The ships from France were not able to sail to Montreal. Travellers and goods of trade all had to be transferred to small, specially constructed vessels which could make their way through the shallow waters between the low lying islands in the river and could be rowed, or pushed, or tugged from a towpath on the bank, up through the famous St. Mary's Current which guarded the Island of Montreal from intrusion.

Champlain tried to cope with the turbulance around Montreal as early as 1611 and while piety and mystical vision have been credited with the conception and birth of *Ville Marie de Montreal*, it was Champlain who thought out a settlement for the Island thirty years before the mission was founded.

Champlain discovered that St. Mary's Current could be navigated with comfort only when a strong wind was blowing up river from Quebec. He thought the settlement of Montreal should begin below the Current. Nevertheless, for his dealings with the Indians he sailed through the Current and sought shelter in the lee of a little islet which in time came to

be called Market Gate Island. It was the only contribution
nature made to the harbour of Montreal and all the pioneering events of the city were enacted in the vicinity of the
island. There was a little river, the St. Pierre, which flowed
from a pond not far from Lachine and emptied into the St.
Lawrence by the narrow channel at the islet. The St. Pierre
was augmented by some other little streams which flowed
out of the forest that covered the island, streams that came
to be known as Burnside Creek and St. Martin's Creek. In
due time St. Pierre River became the basis of the Lachine
canal, but the islet which gave birth to the harbour was completely swallowed up by progress. In 1830 a mole was built
to connect the islet with the main shore, so that the wharf
which then existed on the island, became the chief dock of
the city. When Montreal began its rise to wealth and luxury
in the Edwardian days, the islet was simply scooped away
altogether and the first great piers,—the Edward and the
Alexandra docks,—were built on its very site. With the dis-
appearance of the historic little islet the great modern Port
of Montreal began its fabulous history.

The waters of the Great Lakes and of the north country
tributary to the Ottawa River tumbled on towards Montreal
in many, many miles of "white water". The St. Lawrence
and the Ottawa flow towards one another at an angle, which
narrows the land between them to a slender wedge. At the
tip of this wedge the two great rivers meet in Lake St. Louis.
The Ottawa flows through the Rapids of Ste. Anne where
Moore wrote his famous Canadian Boat Song, and the St.
Lawrence through the rapids which feed power into the
dramatic Beauharnois generators. Lake St. Louis lies between Ste. Anne de Bellevue and Lachine and here the
island is devoted to pleasant country life. Many thousands
of Montrealers spend the summers here at golf and yachting
and swimming, and some live here the year round as com-
muters. Not far back from the shore is the Dorval airport.

Not all the waters of the Ottawa valley flow into the St.

Lawrence, for above the Rapids of Ste. Anne, a great part of the Ottawa flows into the beautiful Lake of Two Mountains. Dividing again they encircle Ile Jésus and cut it off from the Island of Montreal and from the Laurentian mainland. Ile Jésus is a very rich farming district, joined by several bridges to the Island of Montreal. The river between Montreal and Ile Jésus is Rivière des Prairies, and between Ile Jésus and the northern mainland is Rivière des Mille Iles, —The River of the Meadows, and the River of the Thousand Islands. There were the descriptive names the early French chose for these outlets of the Ottawa. All three rivers meet at the eastern tip of the Island of Montreal and the two lesser streams lose their identity in the St. Lawrence which flows on majestically to the sea, a thousand miles away.

The Port of Montreal is the greatest inland port in the world yet it is nearer to Liverpool than Boston, Portland, New York or Philadelphia, — nearly three hundred miles nearer than New York. It is also nearer to Central Canada and the American Middle West than any other seaport. Montreal is not a port for the show ships such as the Queen Elizabeth, but is planned for the economical ship which is built for efficiency in fuelling and in loading and unloading. There are only a dozen or so ships of the big tonnage, 35,000 tons and over, but the chief fleets of the world's commerce range from 20,000 tons downward. These are the ships for which the port of Montreal is planned.

The Port of Montreal occupies sixteen miles of waterfront on both shores of the St. Lawrence. It begins about three-quarters of a mile upstream from the old Victoria Bridge and ends at Bout de l'Ile opposite Varennes. The St. Lawrence ship channels cover two hundred and ten miles, from Montreal to South Traverse, fifty miles below Quebec City. The man-made channels represent a very important engineering feat, and provide a minimum depth of thirty feet, with thirty-five feet at high tide.

The best place to see the Port of Montreal is from the

magnificent bridge officially named for Jacques Cartier but known as Harbour Bridge. It rises one hundred and sixty-two feet above high water. It springs from a point well inland, (in a crowded part of old Montreal at LaFontaine Street and is carried high over houses and streets and rests on piers on Ile Ronde and St. Helen's Island, then on over a succession of stone piers in the shallow waters leading to the South Shore. It is two and an eighth miles long and is for vehicles and for pedestrians only. Here it is possible to imagine the river as it was in the French regime and to contemplate the enormous and wealthy industrial city that sprang from the little mission village of Maisonneuve and Jeanne Mance.

The port is open for seven and a half months every year, and for the rest of the time is ice bound. Human ingenuity and engineering skill have added a month to the usefulness of the port in keeping open water by ice-breaking equipment. Montreal was never a seaport under the French; the Port of Montreal was created by the newcomers who settled in Montreal after the cession of New France to Britain, by men who came up from the other British colonies along the Atlantic and who migrated from the United Kingdom in search of opportunities. With the blood of seafarers in their veins these men began at once to plan a seaport at Montreal.

From the very heart of Montreal the way leads from Phillips Square, where a bronze King Edward in his royal robes presides over Edwardian Montreal, down famous old Beaver Hall Hill to Victoria Square, and so to the site of a gateway into ancient Montreal, the Recollet Gate, which stood at what is now the corner of McGill and Notre Dame Streets. Continuing down McGill Street it comes to Place d'Youville and turning eastward toward the harbour on Commissioners' Street arrives at the spot where the founders of Montreal, on the eighteenth of May, 1642, decorated an altar with wild flowers out of the woods and exposed the Host

throughout the day to celebrate the occupation of the Island
of Montreal. Then in the dusk the women of the party captured fireflies to illuminate the altar because they had no
lamps. The fireflies were tied by threads and must have been
a curious sight as they flashed their little lights in desperate
efforts to escape.

This open space is Place Royale, a name Champlain gave
to his post at Montreal. And here is the memorial to the
original colonists, with all their names inscribed upon it. As
we stand in front of this memorial and look eastward we can
see the old church of Notre Dame de Bonsecours and its
figure of the Virgin with hands outstretched over the harbour.
Between these two points lay the pioneer village of Ville
Marie de Montreal, facing the river.

Montreal had the most curious birth of any city in Canada.
It was the off-spring of a period of religious revivalism in the
Roman Catholic Church. The Reformation had not only
created the Protestant movement but it had so shocked the
ancient church that it roused itself to meet the storm and to
purge itself of its errors. It found its inspiration in the
past, in the mediæval Christianity of the Crusades. France
came out of the quarrels of the Reformation fermenting with
a new religious spirit. It became the fashion for rich and
fashionable ladies to endow saintly men and women and
allow them to carry on religious work in educational and
medical fields and in the care of the orphaned, the neglected
and the unfortunate. The reports sent back to France by the
missionaries in New France, usually written in a way calculated to add fuel to the fashionable mysticism of the time,
provided plenty of scope for imaginative people. The savages
were souls to save. As Stephen Leacock puts it, "the name
Montreal, still inexact, indefinite, came to mean a place in
the wilderness where there was dire need of Christ. There
began what we might call in our current language 'a Montreal movement'. This presently took on all the aspects of the
miraculous".

94

At the time there was such an outburst of enthusiasm for religious service to those in need, in what we might today call the social sciences, that any number of new orders of monks and nuns were founded, and many who did not actually enter religious orders, lived a strictly religious life "in the world", nursing, caring for "fallen women", the aged, and in education, even the education of Indian children, when the education of children in Europe was something only for the upper classes. The background of the "Montreal movement" was one of mystical and psychic experience, clair-audience and clairvoyance.

In the midst of this time of psychic sensitivity and religious mysticism, a young priest by the name of Jean Jacques Olier de Verneuil, then only twenty-eight, founded The Company of Montreal. This was in 1636 and its object, of course, was to send missionaries to the Island of Montreal. Four years later, while the society was still merely a name, he became the parish priest of St. Sulpice in Paris. One day while at prayer he heard a voice telling him to found an order of priests to serve at Montreal. Olier was steeped in the reports of ex-plorations and missionary efforts in New France and he longed to go there himself. He was in delicate health and knew he could not be useful there. He decided to create a seminary, The Seminary of St. Sulpice, to train men who could go.

Meantime a very pious collector of taxes at La Flèche in Anjou, named Jerome de la Dauversière, one day had a vision. He saw an island, called Montreal, and was told that he should create an order of nuns who would go there to found a hospital. When he began to make inquiries about this mysterious Island of Montreal, he learned there was no settlement there. He was so impressed, however, with the authenticity of his vision, that he set out for Paris to learn more about Montreal. On his way he stopped to visit at the Chateau de Meudon. It was here that Dauversière and Olier met for the first time. Instantly they recognized each other and embraced warmly like long lost friends. Then they compared notes. It did not take them long to decide that at Montreal, the most dangerous spot in Canada, they would establish a trinity of effort,—a community of priests to convert the savages, an order of nuns to nurse the Indians and the soldiers who must fight to defend the mission, and an order of nuns to teach the youth of the new land. Neither Dauversière nor Olier ever saw Canada but their vision materialized. In fact, before many years had passed the Sulpicians became the feudal lords of the entire Island of Montreal, and to this day they own some of the original lands granted to them in the mid-seventeenth century. The order is a rich and powerful one and has oftentimes used its wealth to encourage enterprises of other orders. Their walled gardens lie along Sherbrooke Street and two little stone towers, relics of the seventeenth century, can be seen from the street still standing amid the trees.

As the story of the founding of Montreal is told by its first historian, the ex-soldier and Superior of the Sulpicians, Dollier de Casson, writing in the very years of its infancy, it has all the elements of a religious mystery play. Somewhere outside of this mundane world a plan was laid for the creation of the mission of Montreal as a shield for New France, "a dyke against the Iroquois, to hold in check their fury and impetuosity". Great men and wealthy women were moved about like puppets to embody this other-worldly planning. Reports of the missionaries in New France fell mysteriously into the hands of the right people, and all sorts of strange encounters, visions and flaming convictions combined for the conception of Montreal.

The meeting of Olier and Dauversière was a critical point in the development of the plan but the plan required women and exceptional women, as well as a leader or governor of extraordinary qualities and characteristics. There was to be no accident about Montreal, no casual landing of a few fur traders. Montreal was to be uniquely visualized and brought down into being as a complete working unit. But where

were these exceptional men and women to be found? "Some
one full of grace was needed," writes Casson, who knew most,
if not all of the founders of Montreal, "to come into this country so distant, so wild, so rude." Also, "it needed the extreme
protection of the Almighty hand always to preserve her purity
unscathed from scandal, real or falsely surmised, living thus
among military men".

Meantime, while waiting for the right women to turn up,
Olier and Dauversière acquired another recruit. Baron de
Faucamp was a very wealthy aristocrat who had heard of the
pious tax collector. He went to La Flèche to stay at the tax
collector's home, "as to a school of piety". Faucamp, too,
was a spiritual puppet, having read the same narrative as
Dauversière,—probably one of Champlain's books. Learning of Dauversière's vision and the assurance of the Jesuit
confessor that the vision was authentic, and not of the devil,
Faucamp decided to throw in his lot with Olier and Dauversière.

The first step was to acquire the island. They discovered
that it belonged to Governor Lauzon of New France, a self-
seeking, blundering misfit. He was very reluctant to part with
the island, now that it seemed to be acquiring some importance.

Meantime perhaps a little of the mystery is dispelled by
the fact that a famous Jesuit missionary had returned to
France and was living in Paris. Charles Lalemant was one
of the first three Jesuits to go to New France at the invitation
of the Recollets who found themselves unable to cope with
the situation in the colony. Lalemant became the superior
of the Jesuits when they established themselves in their own
monastery in Quebec. He had written some of the famous
Jesuit Relations, describing life in New France and picturing
the spiritual glory to be won by winning the Indian tribes for
the Church. After the death of Champlain, he returned home,
in 1636, the year of the founding of the Society of Our
Lady of Montreal. In Paris he became head of the Jesuit

order in that city. It was to Lalemant that the three pious
founders turned when they wanted to acquire the Island of
Montreal. Lalemant went with them to Lauzon, who was on
a visit to Paris. It was Lalemant, also, who chose Maisonneuve as the governor of Montreal.

Lauzon was persuaded to hand over the island to the
society of mystics, one of the few good things we hear about
him, for he was a land-grabber on a grand scale. He sold
them the island in August of 1640. However, even before
they had acquired the island or found a governor, or discovered the lady "full of grace", the founders had acquired
considerable funds, had purchased supplies and sent them
off to Quebec to be held pending the arrival of the colonists.
In fact, they shipped out so much stuff that the governor at
Quebec was embarrassed in finding storage room in the little
town of Quebec.

By some means or other, Lalemant had heard about a
certain "gentleman of Champagne" who had, it seemed to
him, the very qualities that he desired in a leader for the
founders of Montreal. Maisonneuve was a soldier who had
fought through the Thirty Years War which the dictator,
Cardinal Richelieu, had kept at the boiling point to serve
his many purposes,—now to destroy the Huguenots, then to
weaken the French nobles or to humiliate France's neighbours so that France might become a great world power. For
some reason or other, Maisonneuve, who was a gentleman of
independent means, was at this time an unemployed officer,
living in a little country inn. Lalemant knew all about him
and advised Dauversière to make an oblique approach to
him. As a ruse, Dauversière went down into Champagne,
found the little inn where Maisonneuve was living and
engaged a room as though he intended to live there for some
time. Then he sat about talking to anyone who would listen,
about the Island of Montreal and the mission station that
was to be planted there. As the days went by Maisonneuve
heard about the project and his curiosity was aroused. He

joined the circle around the loquacious Dauversière and began to ask questions. At last he asked Dauversière if he might have an opportunity to talk with him in private.

Dauversière must have tried to hide his elation and excitement under a nonchalant air but the two withdrew and had a long and intimate talk together. If only we could have a report of that conversation, how much we might learn of the life of Maisonneuve, of which we know so little! Maisonneuve said, among many other things, that he was tired of the idle life he was living, that he had sufficient income to support himself and that he would be glad to go to Montreal and place his services at the disposition of the Society of Our Lady of Montreal. Dauversière returned in triumph to Paris with one of the major problems of the society very neatly solved.

Maisonneuve is one of the mysteries of Montreal. We know very little about him except at the age of thirteen he was with the French armies in Holland. How old he was when Dauversière sought him out in the country inn we do not know but apparently his usefulness to the army in France was over. Dollier de Casson says he had preserved the purity of his heart in the midst of heretics and libertines! He was obsessed by fear of a Day of Judgment and was so strait-laced that in order to have some pre-occupation which would prevent him from "seeking the company of the wicked for recreation" he learned to play the lute. He had become a solitary, turning in upon himself after the gregarious life of the army and the garrison he had lived so long.

It is an interesting psychological picture that Dollier de Casson paints for us in his history of Montreal. He tells us that as Maisonneuve grew older his "apprehension of divine justice" increased and that to escape a wicked world he was anxious to become an exile even in the Iroquois country where the chances were a hundred to one against longevity. After Maisonneuve read the reports on life in New France written by Lalemant he decided that in the French colony he would escape the wickedness of the world by living a life

of danger and privation and service to the cause of his
religion.

It is this psychological distress coupled with the high-ten-
sion religious fanaticism of the day that explains the birth of
Montreal, as it explains so much more of the story of missions and martyrdom throughout the French regime in
Canada. The readers of the reports and books of travel published in the capital in the early days of the seventeenth
century were not many, for literacy in those days was limited.
In the fervour and ferment of the religious revival, news of
what was afoot in New France circulated throughout the
literate circles. Maisonneuve had read Lalemant's *Relations*
before Dauversière had gone to seek him out. After reading
them he had gone to Paris to talk to Lalemant. So it was that
Lalemant, the Jesuit missionary-author, held the ends of
many strings, and these were the strings that moved the
puppets into activity.

The scenes that introduce Maisonneuve into the pages of
our history make him seem like a prig and a fear-ridden
neurotic. But Maisonneuve was far from either of these
things. For a quarter of a century he was governor of Montreal, living blamelessly, working tirelessly, winning for himself the loyalty and affection of the entire community. It was
a frontier village in which life was rough and ready; it was
life lived out in the open, under the eyes of everyone, where
everybody knew everything about all the neighbours. In the
white light of that village life Maisonneuve stands out in the
round, a great individual.

But there is as yet no Montreal except in the imagination
of half a dozen people only one of whom had so much as seen
the island itself, except in visions. But they already had collected considerable funds and so they set about preparations
for the founding of the mission colony and engaged transportation in two ships from La Rochelle. Faucamp and
Dauversière went to La Rochelle with Maisonneuve to look
for colonists. It is only in the light of the poverty and despair

in France that we can understand why it was comparatively easy to pick up forty men who would accompany Maisonneuve on his venture. Thirty years of war had reduced France to a sort of social inertia. The whole country had been taxed two or three years in advance to pay for the wars, and life was, indeed, bleak and hopeless.

So it seems that Maisonneuve had little difficulty in picking up forty men, some of them artisans, some old soldiers like himself, all willing to face the Iroquois on the island of Montreal. What unwritten history lies in this episode! From some of these colonists sprang long lines of good Canadiens, among whose sons and daughters were many who became famous. One of them was to be the "first ancestor" of Sir Wilfrid Laurier.

At last Maisonneuve and his associates had all the men they needed. They had their supplies, including ammunition, stowed away aboard ship. But they were still in a dilemma. They had need " of one thing they could not find and which their purses could not buy them, a girl or a woman of character sufficiently heroic and of determination sufficiently masculine to come to this country and take charge of all the supplies and merchandise, while at the same time acting as a nurse to the sick and the wounded".

But of course the angels,—and Father Lalemant,—were busy pulling the strings of just the right human puppets for the time and the place. So another great Canadian pioneer moves onto the stage of history, unknown, inexperienced, to become the heroine of Montreal.

In the town of Langres a certain canon talked a great deal about a certain Madame de la Peltrie who had gone to New France and introduced the order of the Ursulines to Quebec, and of the Duchesse D'Aiguillon, the niece of Cardinal Richelieu, who had established the hospital nuns in the same little town. Among those who heard the canon was a delicate young woman by the name of Jeanne Mance. She was a person who had a small private income, sufficient for her own needs, and she was also caught up in the same tide of religious fervour that had swept through the upper classes. The example of other gentlewomen who had undertaken what we now call "social service" in the colony, fired her imagination. She discussed her problem with the canon and he advised her to go to Paris and seek out Father Lalemant and some of the other Jesuits. The upshot of her visit to the Jesuits was that she was declared to have a vocation for work on the frontier and she was advised to go to Quebec. Jeanne Mance did not belong to any religious order. She was setting out alone to do something to help along the fortunes of New France, and she wasn't at all certain what that something would be. We can scarcely realize now the sensation her decision created. News of it even reached the court. The Queen and her ladies were very curious about this provincial woman who was going to *Canada,*—for in telling of this matter Dollier de Casson says Jeanne Mance was going to Canada, not to New France. There was a touch of the mystical about this too, for she could not say why she wanted to go to Canada, only that she was deeply moved by the need to cross to this outpost of France. She was ordered to court to be questioned by the Queen. This was the Queen Anne who had dressed a doll and sent it to the Indian chapel at Tadoussac to be used as the Christ Child in the Christmas creche.

A priest from her home town came to Paris and she told him the whole story. He approved of her surrender to the impulse to serve in Canada, but he said shrewdly that it was up to others to take charge of the practical aspects and to provide the material help. Presently he took her to visit a very wealthy widow, Madame de Bouillon, whose husband had been superintendent of finance for Cardinal Richelieu. The rich widow was interested, and as she turned the matter over in her mind she sent again and again for Jeanne Mance, to talk things over with her. Finally on one visit she asked her if she would take charge of a hospital if she, Madame de Bouillon, would endow it. Her benefactions were to be anonymous. Jeanne rapturously agreed to the plan and was so excited over the prospects that she wanted to set off immediately, although she had no idea where that hospital was to be located. All this time, according to tradition, Jeanne Mance had not heard of Montreal. The benefactress entrusted her with a considerable sum of money and bid her Godspeed.

Her friends in Paris wanted her to go to Normandy to seek a ship that might be sailing for the St. Lawrence, but the pioneer was so impatient to be on her way that she did not want to take the time for farewells with friends who wanted to accompany her to Normandy, so she slipped off to La Rochelle instead. We do not know but it might not be too much to suspect that Father Lalemant had something to do with indicating to her advisers that La Rochelle might be a favourable point of departure. Some one did tell her that some missionaries expected to sail from La Rochelle and she hoped to have their company on the long journey across.

We can at least try to imagine the courage it took to face not only the journey across the seas, but even the journey from Paris to La Rochelle, for a woman entrusted with enough money to found a hospital travelling alone over the bandit infested highways of France in 1641.

Here, of course, again with something of magic about the encounter, she met Dauversière and Maisonneuve and was told of what they were about to do. What Maisonneuve thought of this miraculous appearance of the woman full of grace and modesty and heroism, we would like very much to know. But by now all the pieces of the puzzle were falling into place. Dauversière begged her to choose Montreal as the place for her hospital. And since she had no plans and it seemed as though the angelic puppet masters were trying to show her the way she should go, she agreed to join the Society of Our Lady of Montreal in its adventures. It was a good decision. For thirty years, until her death, Jeanne Mance was a tower of strength to the colony. To this day her's is one of the most honoured names in the long history of Montreal. The hospital she founded with the gold louis entrusted to her is a great institution for healing and for the training of nurses; great beyond the wildest dreams of the delicate young woman from Nogent-le-Roi.

Jeanne Mance and Maisonneuve did not sail in the same ship. Her ship had a fair voyage and reached Quebec in good time. Maisonneuve's ship was unfortunate, ran into storms and was delayed so long that in Quebec they despaired of his arrival. Indeed, it was so late when he sailed up the St. Lawrence that the colonists could not reach their destination that autumn. The party stayed in Quebec for the winter,—a divided and hostile Quebec. There were only two hundred Europeans in all New France at the time. They lived in fear of the Iroquois and were jealous and resentful of the new project for the settlement of the Island of Montreal, which they called "The Foolish Enterprise". Governor Montmagny begged Maisonneuve to change his mind and settle on the uninhabited Island of Orleans if he wanted an island to himself. But Maisonneuve would have none of it. If every tree on the Island of Montreal was an Iroquois, he declared, he would still go there and carry out the plans of the Society of Montreal.

Nothing could stand in the way of such determination so Montmagny made the trip up the river with Maisonneuve in the pleasant autumn weather so that he would see for himself the place where he was to plant a little civilization in the wilderness. By the time he returned to Quebec the colony had won some rich and influential friends and the leaders of the expedition found a home waiting for them. The house offered to them was that of M. de Puiseaux, at the Sillery. There they were joined by that very Madame de la Peltrie of whom Jeanne Mance had heard and whose example had sent her off to Paris. Madame de la Peltrie deserted the Ursuline nuns whom she had brought to Quebec, to take a hand in the new and exciting settlement on the Island of Montreal, one hundred and seventy-five miles up the river.

Monsieur de Puiseaux is one of the mysteries of New France. When Maisonneuve went to Quebec in 1641, Monsieur de Puiseaux was at least seventy-five years old and the wealthiest man in the colony. He did not live in Quebec with the rest of the colonists, but had one house, "the jewel of New France", at the Sillery several miles away, and another at St. Foy. He was an emotional, impulsive old man. When he met and talked with Maisonneuve in the autumn of his arrival, he immediately took sides with him against the rest of Quebec and not only offered him the use of his houses, but in an out-burst of generosity, he turned over him everything he owned, on condition that he was to accompany the colonists to Montreal and there make his home with them. It was in the house at the Sillery that Jeanne Mance and Madame de la Peltrie, and her maid Charlotte Barre, settled down for the winter, along with Maisonneuve and Monsieur de Puiseaux. At St. Foy the workmen were housed and set to work building boats to carry to Montreal all the stores which had come to Quebec during the two or three years of preparation. There was great excitement and the vivacious Madame de la Peltrie apparently thoroughly enjoyed the ferment caused by the tensions and resentment,—and the gossip,—in the little backwoods society. The newcomers were exalted and self-willed, buoyed up by their visions and their determination to seek glory and, if necessary, martyrdom, on the island dedicated to the Virgin.

What an experience for the newcomers! To watch the great river freeze over, to see the country blanketed in drifts of snow such as they never saw in France, to learn the alertness necessary to the colonists who hoped to escape attack by the Indians from up the river or across the ice.

At last came spring, the warm, sweet winds of April and May, the sudden, gaily exuberant unfolding of tiny green leaves on the naked trees, the violets and trailing arbutus and a hundred other wild flowers pushing their tender little stems up through the fragrant brown earth. Little wonder that they called May *The Month of Mary*, for its blue skies and tender promise of renewed life were as gentle as the Virgin to whom their thoughts turn more often, it seemed, than to the Christ Himself.

Fifty people accompanied Maisonneuve and Jeanne Mance when they set out in the two new boats, carrying the supplies to build shelters and provide for the colonists while they built the town. There was a third boat, for Governor Montmagny decided to accompany them and to formally transfer possession of the Island of Montreal to Maisonneuve with the rituals of feudalism, on the land itself. How impatient they must have been on that slow journey up the St. Lawrence! It took them ten days to travel the hundred and seventy-five miles from Quebec to Montreal, camping each night. How impressed they must have been with the isolation that awaited them in the wilderness of the upper St. Lawrence!

On the 17th of May they were within sight of the island, but it was the 18th before they could land. They had the wild St. Mary's current to navigate first. Once beyond it they came to the lee of a little island where the Rivière St. Pierre flowed out of the forest. Here was a little shelter and a friendly shore. Maisonneuve was the first to land, the light of spiritual victory in his eyes. Like the fleeing slaves who, two centuries later, made their escape into Canada from the southern States, he fell on his knees to give thanks that he had arrived at his destination.

Actually, the place to which they came was not unknown. It had been a trading camp for thirty years. The man who first came here to trade with the Indians,—after Jacques Cartier's discovery of the island,—was Samuel de Champlain. He called this spot Place Royale and urged the establishment of a trading post here. He came frequently and was aware of its advantages and its weaknesses. He had an experimental palisade built in order to discover what would happen to a walled fort when the floods came down in the spring. His men had cut many trees and built some of them into a piece of wall. When Maisonneuve and his colonists arrived these timbers were still lying about. They used them for the construction of the first walled encampment they established to protect themselves in the summer of 1642.

When the colonists, priests and the ladies had landed, their first task was to put up an altar, probably one of the portable altars used by missionaries. It stood in the open under the cloudless sky. Jeanne Mance and Madame de la Peltrie gathered bloodroot and hepatica, and whatever other wildflowers grew in the edge of the woods along the river banks, to decorate the altar.

In the clearing which Champlain's men had made in the forest they began the building of a little stockaded fort. Champlain has never been given credit for his more practical vision of Montreal or Place Royale, and perhaps there was some curious reason for it. The religious fervour of the Society of Montreal was rooted in a hate of the Huguenots and all their works. Champlain had been friendly to the Huguenots. It seems strange that Champlain did not receive more honour from the people of New France. Even his grave went unmarked and forgotten and now no one knows where it was. The Father of New France was dead only six years when Maisonneuve founded Montreal, yet neither his foresight, nor his published works are ever credited with setting in motion the dreams of a colony at Place Royale. Even in Laurier's youth the subject of Huguenots was a delicate one in Quebec. Laurier debated in the affirmative, in his college at L'Assomption, on the subject that Huguenots should have been allowed to settle in New France to populate the colony. But that was the last debate at L'Assomption in Laurier's time. The priests put an end to the debating society. Yet France might still be on the St. Lawrence if Huguenots had been allowed to settle in New France. Instead, as "displaced persons" they went to England and contributed greatly to her wealth. Being non-Catholics, they would have won the sympathy rather than the suspicion of New Englanders, who were fanatically resentful of the French Catholic colony to the north. We might have had less history of Iroquois war horrors and of raids on enemy towns by both French and English, if the religious intensity of the times had been moderated. As it was, the colony of Montreal was the most fervently religious enterprise in North America, and nothing would divert its men and women from their proclaimed purpose. Maisonneuve had only twenty soldiers with him to defend the little fort against the Iroquois terror. Imagine the courage it required to establish themselves on that wild and lonely island, and to do it in the gaiety of spirit that found time to pick trailing arbutus for an altar and catch fireflies to illuminate it.

Meantime, it was spring, verging on summer and everyone was full of hope and expectancy. The first problem was to erect a palisaded fort into which everyone could retreat at night for safety. The colonists lived in tents, while storehouses were built and houses planned. Now as the Montrealers began building houses and defences they were completely at the mercy of their friends at home for supplies to keep them in health and comfort. So, while they transported the supplies already in Quebec, to their new home in the spring and summer of 1642, they also waited anxiously for news from Paris, to discover just what their supporters at home had done for them.

It is here that we come upon the first member of the famous family of Repentigny, for so long associated with the community of Montreal and indeed with all of New France. It is Admiral de Repentigny who made a hurried trip from Quebec to Montreal, as soon as his ship docked after the voyage from France. He had news for Maisonneuve and Jeanne Mance. The Society of Montreal had consecrated itself, "through the Holy Virgin on the Day of Presentation" and had invested forty thousand livres in supplies to be shipped to Ville Marie. Also the Society was sending Maisonneuve twelve more men, one of them a very excellent carpenter who could take charge of the workmen. His name was Gilbert Barbier,—he came to be called "La Minime", probably because of some habit of speech. The carpenter was bringing with him four cannon, the gift of Dauversière. These are doubtless the very cannon commemorated on the memorial to Maisonneuve in Place d'Armes.

There were now forty-five associates of the society, including the Duc de Liancourt, Madame de Villesavin, Madame Sequin and Madame de Bouillon. What a contrast! One part of the enterprise living in tents in the wilderness, the other part in the luxury of the Louvre.

The work went slowly and it was spring again before the little fort was finished and the cannon mounted on it. It was the greatest good luck,—or was it angelic intervention?— that the Iroquois simply knew nothing about them for the first year of their life on the island. They had come within a few miles of Montreal, but perhaps the little party of Frenchmen who met such a cruel fate down river served to divert the Iroquois from paddling up to the clearing in the woods at Montreal. The colony had not been on the island three months before a war party of Mohawks came down the Richelieu,—the river of the Iroquois,—in August, and lay motionless in the weedy waters at its mouth, while twelve canoes approached, paddling up the river from Quebec. In them were some Hurons accompanying four Frenchmen on their way to the the Huron Missions. The leader of the party was Father Jogues, carrying with him sacred vestments, chasubles, vessels for the mass, bread and wine for the Eucharist and other things for the mission church. At the western end of Lake St. Peter they had to approach the shore to avoid the currents. They came quite unaware within reach of the two hundred waiting Iroquois, screened by the leaves of the trees overhanging the banks. Some Hurons fled and one Frenchman escaped to tell the tale. All the others was eventually dragged off to excruciating tortures and most of them to death. Father Jogues was eventually rescued by the Dutch on the Hudson River and sent home to Paris, crippled, ill, mutilated, almost unrecognizable. Montreal learned the rest of his story when he returned to New France only to again become a prisoner of the Iroquois, this time to be tortured to death. How often, as the heroic handful of men and women huddled together in the fort that first winter, must they have wondered what happened to Father Jogues, and what might happen to them in the years ahead.

By June of 1643, the Iroquois discovered them. They collected on the outskirts of the island and watched the colonists as they worked. In that summer the Iroquois killed or captured six men at work near the fort.

By July the colonists were so terrified that when a boat came up the river with messages from France and cast anchor some way below the town, no one would go out to meet it but Maisonneuve himself. He brought back cheerful news. Madame de Bouillon was giving Jeanne Mance twelve thousand livres for the building and furnishing of the hospital, the Hotel Dieu.

Presently Indian refugees fleeing from the Iroquois began crowding into the settlement in such numbers that Maisonneuve could not afford to support them. The priests baptized them and sent them off to forage for themselves. In 1643, the first gardens were planted as an experiment, but still food had to be brought from France.

Meantime old Monsieur de Puiseaux had come to live in Montreal surrendering the comfort of his home at the Sillery to share the discomfort and anxiety of Montreal. Eventually he became paralytic and senile, and regretted very much that he had handed over all he owned unconditionally to

Maisonneuve. He wanted it back again, saying that he wanted to go to Paris. We still do not know who he was before he appeared in Quebec with a fortune to spend. Some say he made his money in the West Indies or in South America, perhaps as a pirate. He was nearly eighty when Maisonneuve sent him back to Paris to be cared for by the Society of Montreal.

Madame de la Peltrie had already had enough of it and decided to go back to her Ursuline nuns at Quebec, where she was welcomed with open arms.

By autumn the fortification was complete, with new bastions to replace the old palisade of Champlain. Once the four little cannon were stoutly bolted to the wooden walls, the men of Montreal became restive, in a natural reaction to the fear under which they had lived all summer. They played with the idea of going out after the Iroquois and gaining some glory by giving them battle. They pestered Maisonneuve, although he explained that the Iroquois didn't fight as Frenchmen fight, that the Frenchmen knew nothing of the warfare of the forest. Some of the more hot-headed among them, however, hinted that Maisonneuve was afraid to risk his own life, and hearing the rumours, he decided it was better to take a risk than to see discontent grow into disloyalty. He promised them that when the opportunity arose he would lead them against the Iroquois.

One of the most useful citizens in Montreal was a dog named Pilotte. She had taken upon herself the command of all the other dogs in the settlement, and she had trained her own pups to make an inspection of the surroundings of the fort every morning. She also expected every other dog in the colony to do the same.

One March morning Pilotte, after her first excursion into the woods, began to howl dismally. She was soon joined by all the other dogs, all pointing in the same direction. "There they are," said the disgruntled men, "are we never to go after these Iroquois?" "Yes," said Monsieur de Maisonneuve, "make ready and we will set out. I trust you will be as brave as you say you are."

There were few snowshoes in the post so most of the men had to set out on foot in the deep March snow. The gate was opened to the west and thirty men in all marched out. Maisonneuve left the fort and the little chateau under the command of Monsieur d'Ailleboust. The monument to Maisonneuve in Place d'Armes commemorates this fight, for it took place in this vicinity. As the Frenchmen moved into the woods in search of the enemy they found two hundred Iroquois in ambush. Each Frenchman got behind a tree and all fought valiantly until their ammunition gave out. They made little impression on the forest-wise enemies. Three men were killed or wounded before Maisonneuve ordered a retreat. He slowly drew his men towards a road that had been cut through the woods for the transport of timber. It was a track leading directly to the gate of the fort. They went home much faster than Maisonneuve wanted them to go, for by now what each man wanted was to get behind the wooden walls under the shelter of the four little cannon.

Maisonneuve undertook to keep the way open while they all made off for the fort carrying the wounded with them. Once on the road most of them gave way to panic and fled homeward. As they approached the fort, the man in charge of the cannon pointing directly up the road, lost his head completely and fired it. "But fortunately," says Dollier de Casson, "the priming was so bad that the gun did not go off."

Coolly and slowly Maisonneuve moved backward along the road, with a pair of pistols in his hands. As slowly the Iroquois followed him. They did not want to kill Maisonneuve. They preferred to capture him. Moreover, they deferred to their chief and gave him the right to make the capture of this great white soldier. We can picture the two men, Maisonneuve, grim, determined, moving slowly backward through

112

the snow, while a few paces from him stalked the Iroquois chief with his tomahawk in his hand, closing in for the blow that was to make Maisonneuve insensible.

Maisonneuve fired one shot, when he had come near the fort, but the chief anticipated him and ducked out of the line of fire. But with the other pistol—and his last shot—Maisonneuve killed the chief.

The Indians had let their chief move on ahead in deference to his right to make the capture. Now that he had fallen in the snow, the distance gave Maisonneuve an advantage of seconds to outdistance his pursuers. But when the Iroquois reached their dead chief they gave up the pursuit and fearing that the French might sally out and seize the body they raised him to their shoulders and turned back towards their camp.

In these few moments Maisonneuve got back to the open gate of the fort. We can only imagine what happened. The terror, the remorse, the grief, the confusion, and the humiliation.

Meantime the Hotel Dieu was being built with the funds provided by the modest and wealthy Madame de Bouillon who would not have anyone know that she was the benefactress. No sooner were the doors of the hospital opened than it was filled with patients, and Jeanne Mance became the first lay nurse in Canadian history. She established a tradition that is honoured to this day. The little log hospital was succeeded by new buildings made to accommodate the advances in the art and science of healing, until today the enormous Hotel Dieu that stands on Pine Avenue in Montreal is the memorial to her pioneering courage.

Maisonneuve did not escape family responsibilities and difficulties by going to Montreal. He was hardly settled before he had to go home to attend to his father's estate. The next year he was called back again. His brother-in-law had been assassinated and his mother was about to make a disastrous second marriage. It was ten years before Maisonneuve had a suitable home for himself. By then there was a little street running from the fort by the river to the Hotel Dieu on higher ground to the east. Half way between the two places Maisonneuve built a two-story log chateau where he could live in the dignity befitting the governor of the colony. The chateau stood for exactly two hundred years and then Montreal, in its brash Victorian prosperity, simply pulled it down to make room for some other building.

How much there is that we would like to know about Maisonneuve in those days. Did he have a garden? Did he keep a diary? Did he write many letters home telling his friends what he was doing on the Island of Montreal? Who kept house for him, and how did he live? We know so little of the man who lived behind the mask of the religious fanatic, the many little inconsequential things that make up the sum total of character and quality.

The facts of history are too often as dry as sawdust, and, like sawdust, may be only what remains after men and women have shaped their lives out of the raw materials of their times. The bare facts of an episode may be easy enough to come by, but what is so difficult to reconstruct is the mood, the attitude, the motivations and the rewards that were the living factors behind the facts of history. Sometimes it is the little inconsequential asides in our records that send a sudden flash of light into the darkened pages of too sober archivists. There are many of these little asides in Dollier de Casson's history of Montreal, such as the anecdote about a strange intruder into this community of hand-picked devotees, for apparently even the Montreal of Maisonneuve and Jeanne Mance had certain ribald moments. In the staid writing of the Superior of the Sulpicians we get this glimpse into the life in Montreal:

"When summer came there arrived from France Sieur de la Barre with a good many people, part of them belonging to a

*I*t is fortunate for Quebec that A. Y. Jackson worked in the Laurentian
country in the years before the industrial expansion began forcing a
change of character on the Habitant life in the ancient province. The sunny,
cheerful, APRIL, PETITE RIVIERE shows a Canadian farm with its red-roofed
barn yawning for a new harvest.

company which the queen sent this year to Canada under his direction. . . . Remarkable here is the hypocrisy of the Sieur de la Barre who hoodwinked so many people in France and in Canada. At La Rochelle he wore at his belt a large rosary with a big crucifix which he had almost continually before his eyes, so that he entered this country as a man of apostolic piety to whom had been entrusted this command. In this way, under a cloak of virtue, he had a wicked way of living, which has since caused him to end his days under a bar heavier than that of his name. . . . This person, looking like Virtue herself, stayed in Montreal all the following year, but he was finally discovered through the frequent walks that he took in the woods with an Indian whom he made pregnant, thereby making clear the falsity of his fine pretences."

What happened Captain de la Barre we do not know but apparently he came to a bad end for Dollier de Casson thinks that "the manner of his death was for the good of his soul". What else developed in Montreal we do not discover but we do know that in the following year, when Maisonneuve heard of the death of his father and had to return to France to settle the estate, he was loath to leave Montreal before he had sent Captain de la Barre packing, "who he had realized possessed nothing of the saint save his rosary".

To little Ville Marie de Montreal in 1650 came the petrifying news of the martyrdom of Brebeouf and Lalemant. Charles Le Moyne, whom we meet so often on the pages of the history of New France, had been sent up to lend his help to the Hurons in preparing their campaign of defence against the Iroquois, but on his way he encountered the fleeing Hurons, hurrying for shelter with the French. When Le Moyne returned with them to Montreal, the colonists faced sheer terror. The Hurons numbered thirty thousand people when the Iroquois attacked them. The French were a few hundred.

The news came shortly after Jeanne Mance had left for France. She received news that the Company of Montreal was losing members to the Levant Company, that Dauversière was ill and nearly bankrupt, and that Father Rapin, the intermediary between her and her benefactress Madame de Bouillon, was dead.

This was a time of testing for the colonists of Ville Marie. They realized that, unless very considerable help arrived from France, the French would have to abandon the St. Lawrence. With the refugees from Huronia hurrying by on their way to Quebec, feeling that Montreal was not safe enough to shelter them, the soul of every man and woman in Montreal was tried to the uttermost for courage and loyalty. From that time onward the Iroquois turned their fury on Montreal and it environs. Without even the unstable Hurons as allies, every tree on the Island of Montreal might just as well have been an Iroquois.

Jeanne Mance returned to report that Monsieur Olier, Superior of the Sulpicians in Paris, and their founder, was now director of the re-organized Company of Montreal. Presently the Gentlemen of St. Sulpice would become the Seigneurs of Montreal. But that still lay in the future. When Jeanne Mance learned all that happened in New France, she sadly turned over the money ear-marked for her hospital and its development, to Maisonneuve to be used in the defence of Montreal. She had to leave her little hospital and return to the chateau where the colonists could huddle together for defence.

Throughout the pioneer history of Montreal the name Le Moyne stood for courage, initiative, vision and loyalty. Charles Le Moyne was the son of an innkeeper of Dieppe. He arrived in Quebec in the very summer that Maisonneuve and Jeanne Mance reached the little capital. He was apparently one of the lads sent out with the Indians to learn their ways and language in order to be useful in the fur trade.

He must have returned home to France a few years after his first arrival, for by 1646 he is being sent out again to New France to act as an interpreter in the negotiations of the French with their enemies. Presently he must have been recruited for the colony at Montreal, for we find him back again in France to take charge of the company's storehouse there. Probably they needed some person with practical experience in order that the Company of Montreal would send out only useful things to the settlement at Montreal. From that time onward the history of New France is studded with tales of Charles and his fabulous family.

In the winter of 1652 Le Moyne's future mother-in-law moves into focus in a story that is one of the most curious in that dignified history of the colony written by Dollier de Casson. The cultured Superior of the Sulpicians tells the incident in these graphic words:

"A woman of virtue . . . the good wife Primot, was attacked by Iroquois within two gunshots of the chateau. As soon as she was attacked she shouted loudly; at this three hidden bodies of Iroquois appeared. Three of these savages threw themselves upon her to kill her with their hatchets. At this the woman defended herself like a lioness, but as she had no weapons but her hands and feet, at the third and fourth blows they felled her as if dead. Immediately one of the Iroquois flung himself upon her to scalp her and escape with his shameful trophy. But as our Amazon felt herself so seized, she at once recovered her senses, raised herself, and more fierce than ever, caught hold of this monster so forcibly by a a place which modesty forbids us to mention, that he could not free himself. He beat her with his hatchet over the head, but she maintained her hold steadily until once again she fell unconscious to the earth and so allowed this Iroquois to flee as fast as he could, that being all he thought of at the moment, for he was nearly caught by our Frenchmen, who were racing to the spot from all directions. In addition

117

this episode was followed by a very amusing thing. When these Frenchmen who came up to help her had lifted up this woman, one of them embraced her in token of compassion and affection. But she, coming around, and feeling herself embraced, delivered a heavy blow to this warm-hearted helper, which made the others say to her; 'What are you doing? This man but wished to show his friendly feeling for you with no thought of evil; why do you hit him?' 'Parmanda,' she answered in her patois, 'I thought he wanted to kiss me.'

"The depths of the roots which Virtue implants in the hearts of her chosen is indeed marvellous; her soul was ready to leave her body, her veins were emptied of blood, and yet the virtue of her chastity was still unshaken in her heart."

Madame Primot had an adopted daughter whose name was Catherine Thierry, and who became the bride of Charles Le Moyne. Madame Primot lived to a great old age and to her dying day was called affectionately *Parmanda*. It was this vigorous old grandmother from whom the Le Moyne boys must have heard many a tale of adventure as they grew up in Montreal.

Even in 1660 there were not more that five hundred people in Montreal, and only four or five times as many in all New France. That was the year that Dollard and sixteen young colonists went out from Montreal to stop the Iroquois at Carillon. It was five years later before the king seriously set about doing something to aid the colony. In 1665 the Marquis de Tracy and the famous Carignan regiment, fresh from the wars with the Turks, arrived on the St. Lawrence.

If only we knew a little more of what was going on in France at this point we might understand a little more of the history of New France. For twenty-three years Maisonneuve had been working in Montreal as its governor. But as soon as the King sent the Marquis de Tracy to New France, for some curious reason, Maisonneuve was invited to go to

France, from which he never returned. There is no explanation as to why he was withdrawn, nor why, after returning to France he lived in poverty and obscurity, the forgotten man. He died in 1676.

He moves out of our history as mysteriously as he moved into it. What were his thoughts in that lonely retirement? Did he write letters to Jeanne Mance? And did she answer them, telling him intimate news of the colony? Did he take his old lute back to France to some obscure little country inn, and play it to ease his heart of its ache for his old comrades?

Montreal was no longer a sacred city. It had become a frontier town of trade and war and exploration. Duluth, the king of the coureurs de bois, had built the palisades thirteen feet high on the St. Peter's River side of the town; Marguerite de Bourgeoys was teaching French and Indian children to read and write; the Iroquois prowled about the environs, killing and torturing whenever they could. Yet out of this embattled village went heroic Frenchmen to preach, to explore, to trade and to fight across the continent. The days of its infancy were over. The monastic flavour of its earliest life was gone. Now the coureurs de bois riotously celebrated their return to Montreal each summer in moods anything but pious. The first act of the drama had ended.

13

A Seigneury on the Ottawa

ON THE journey from Montreal up the Ottawa in the days of the French regime, the first tribe of Indians encountered was that of La Petite Nation, so named by the French because they were a small and comparatively peaceful group who tended their own affairs and traded with their French neighbours to their mutual satisfaction. They were Algonquins who used the River of La Petite Nation as a highway into the north country where their hunting grounds lay.

It must have been because of a vision of French expansion westward that Bishop Laval appealed to the Company of One Hundred Associates for the grant of a seigneury on the Ottawa where the River of La Petite Nation emptied into it. This was an area used by the Indians as a camping ground when they came down out of the north in the springtime with their furs. In a quaint old deed drawn up in Paris, the Company agreed to give this stretch of wilderness to the Bishop as a seigneury "along the road of the Ottawa". He was to have full feudal rights of justice and seigneury, mines and minerals, water and game and fishing privileges. In return the Bishop was to render faith and homage to the Company every twenty years, either in the Chateau St. Louis in Quebec, or in Paris, with a golden link attached to a golden louis "having the value of seven pounds". He was to begin clearing the seigneury within four years unless prevented by "war or any reasonable cause". All this was nearly three hundred years ago, in 1674.

Probably Laval had the idea of founding a little settlement there and a school for Indian children attached to a mission. He did not clear the land or settle anyone on it as it would have been little short of madness to leave men and women unprotected in the path of the Iroquois. In 1680 the Bishop transferred the seigneury to the Seminary of Foreign Missions. A hundred and twenty-five years later the seminary used the deed to the seigneury to cancel off a debt for legal services to Joseph Papineau, a man of humble origin who had settled in Montreal and who by means of his vigour and enterprise became a prosperous notary.

It is one of the tricks of history that only in recent years have the seigneurial fishing and hunting rights been developed in the Seigneury of La Petite Nation. Some years ago what remained of the seigneury was purchased from the Papineau family and the estate was used to develop The Seigneury Club. The seigneurial lands then comprised a hundred and four square miles of Laurentian country with four streams and twenty-nine lakes. There is a road fifteen miles long running through the property of the Club, leading northward to Lake Commandant, named for an old Indian, Chief Commandant. If Laval did not make use of the monopoly of fishing and hunting rights, his successors have certainly done so. The Club has a private hatchery where an average of two hundred thousand speckled, brown and rainbow trout are raised annually for restocking the lakes and streams of the old seigneurial estate. The Papineau Manor House was carefully restored and its character faithfully maintained. For the club itself a great log chateau was built not far from the manor house, on the shore of the Ottawa. On it walls are murals recalling some of the chief incidents in the life of Louis Joseph Papineau, the patriot, hero and scholar.

The acquisition of this patch of wilderness on the Ottawa gave to the Papineau family a new seigneurial dignity and in 1812 Joseph Papineau was elected a member of the Legislative Assembly at Quebec. Even more significant, however, was the fact that his handsome twenty-six-year-old son was elected to sit in the same Assembly at the same time. Louis Joseph Papineau was already a captain in the militia and no sooner had he been elected than he went off to serve his country by defending it against the invasion of the Americans in the War of 1812. The war ended in 1814 and by 1815 Louis Joseph Papineau was back in the Assembly at Quebec where, at the age of twenty-nine he became Speaker of the House.

Papineau was one of the most remarkable men of his age and his story awaits the coming of a novelist who can make use of the material he provided for a great tale of early Canadian life. The struggle for self-government, the conflicting racial interests, the influx of immigrants, all provided the background against which this amazing personality moved so dramatically. Papineau was intelligent, brilliant, charming and endowed with the silver tongue that distinguished so many Canadiens. His love of his own people, his passionate devotion to the idea of freedom, his scholarly interest in history, all combined to make him an unforgettable character.

In *The Canadians: The Story of a People*, George M. Wrong says of Papineau:

"As late as in 1820 he praised the happy lot of the French under British rule. He had a fine presence and eloquence so marked that 'to speak like a Papineau' is still in Quebec high praise for an orator. It is a dangerous gift. Papineau, ardently French in spirit, could sway the crowd. As time passed, his rash and arrogant temper alarmed even prudent friends and enraged those whom he lashed. Though, under British custom, unlike that of the United States, the Speaker takes no share in party politics, Papineau in the chair became a violent partisan. It was startling to have the governor denounced as an alien despot, and his circle as the ruthless minions of the tyrant. Real grievances were few. The press was free. The farmers were lightly taxed. The church was free and the bishops formed a ruling hierarchy content with their privileges, but, at the same time, not untouched by racial feeling. The parish priest was entirely free in his religious work, with privileges equal to, and even greater than those enjoyed under the former Catholic king. Every child in most of the rural parishes was reared in the Catholic faith. Where there was a school, the teacher was a Catholic and religion was the basis of the teaching. In proportion to the population, there were many monasteries of monks and nuns, and the nuns especially gave girls a culture that often brought to a log house a note of refinement that the man, more roughly trained, not infrequently lacked. The French Canadian village with the curé to guard religion and, in some cases, a watchful seigneur to guard secular welfare, was a well-ordered community."

Nevertheless there was a real grievance shared by Upper and Lower Canada alike: those elected by the people to the popular chamber were constantly foiled by the appointed members of the other house. The two-chamber form of government meant that the people's interests were focused in the lower house, and the interests of the official classes, the military, those appointed to office by the royal will, and the ex-army officers settled on huge grants of land, were all focused in the upper house. Upper Canada rebelled just as did Lower Canada. But in Lower Canada the conflict was largely racial, though there were many English-speaking people involved.

In twenty years of agitation against the existing conditions Papineau "matured a notable gift of invective". However, his followers were few compared to the population of Quebec, for Papineau was suspected by the church because he was regarded as anti-clerical. Since he was himself a seigneur, he did not attack feudalism under which the habitants were growing restless. He was confused, too, over whether he wanted Canada to be a republic, or a state of the United States union, or whether he merely wanted the British crown-appointed officials ousted.

The violent resolutions which Papineau succeeded in passing through parliament grew in number,—ninety-two in one year:—and were sent on to the king, the old sailor, William the Fourth, who polished up many of his old navy oaths on them.

Meantime the Seigneury of La Petite Nation was slowly being developed. Joseph Papineau built a manor house, on Arosen Island in the Ottawa River, opposite the site of the present Papineauville. Just before the rebellion, the manor house burned down, but the censitaires who had little interest in the political affairs of Louis Joseph went on with their work of colonization undisturbed. Other little villages grew up along the shore of the river on seigneurial lands, and presently the whole area prospered.

But a political climax was reached at a large meeting at St. Charles in the autumn of 1837. The followers of Papineau raised a liberty tree, and placed a cap of liberty on it, at which each man who touched the pole swore that he would be free or die. The audience was told it was time to melt spoons into bullets.

With this too spectacular display the British troops went into action. Warrants charging high treason were issued against the leaders of the movement.

Many of the habitants suffered in the campaign to suppress the rebellion and some villages were burned by the British troops. Papineau and some of the other leaders fled to the United States. He was probably appalled by what had happened for he declared he had never intended physical rebellion, hoping to secure what he wanted short of armed revolt. But he left behind him prisons filled with rebels or those suspected of supporting the rebellion. At least a thousand were arrested, about a hundred condemned to death. Only about a dozen were actually executed but it was a dozen too many. Many more were shipped to penal colonies and only a few of these ever returned.

The leader of the uprising in Upper Canada was also an exile in the United States. His name was William Lyon Mackenzie. His grandson, William Lyon Mackenzie King, was Prime Minister of Canada longer than any other man had held such office in the history of British parliamentary institutions.

What curious thoughts the exiled Papineau must have had in the years he was forced to live away from the land he loved so well. For twenty-two years he had been Speaker of the Assembly until the very eve of the Rebellion. Now suddenly he was homeless and without responsibilities or occupation. He went to France, although France was as alien to him as any other country, for republican France had little in common with the royalist France from which Quebec had sprung. But in Paris he turned all his restless energies into historical research. At the Archives and other great libraries of Paris he studied the historical problems of the Canadian people. He was one of the first Canadian students to mine that rich vein of history.

In 1845 he returned to Canada and went to the quiet life of the seigneury where he prepared to build himself a new manor house. He chose a spot farther up the river than the old manor house and named the place Montebello. It was not the manor house of old Quebec that he built, but a chateau of modern France, a sunny, spacious house in which the Papineaus lived graciously. The wall of one room, that looked out upon the shore of the Ottawa, was almost entirely of glass.

Beside the house Papineau built a square tower that looks as though it was intended to defend the seigneury against the Iroquois. Instead it was a library where he could protect his books from fire while he carried on the research work which had become his vocation.

It was a very beautiful estate. Near to the tower he built a museum and a chapel amid the gardens. Farther along the road near the gates he built a mortuary chapel where at last he was buried, and where he is now surrounded by three or four generations of Papineaus. In spite of his radicalism, Papineau was one of the last exponents of the feudal spirit and he preserved the remnants of the seigneurial tenure long after its customs had lapsed elsewhere. In one of the round towers of the manor house he sat to receive his censitaires. There is still a small bell hanging there with a rope such as the censitaire pulled to notify the seigneur that he had come to pay his rent and render homage. The democracy that Papineau had preached came flowing in like a tide and engulfed him. Feudal tenure was abolished and although his tenants, like a great many Canadiens went on paying their ancient tributes, showing their respect and tolerance for the lord of the manor, they were no longer censitaires, but tenants, with the legal right to buy the land they occupied.

Papineau was the last glamourous figure of the old regime on the Lower Ottawa and he carried on the tradition in his home until long after Confederation. He was a celebrated host and his guests often travelled long distances at his invitation to enjoy the hospitality of Montebello. Nowhere in the history of New France was there a man more definitely of the seigneurial type. Tall, handsome, distinguished, he presided over his secluded home like an overlord of romance.

14

Tales Along an Old Road

WHEN we return along the shores of the Ottawa and reach Calumet, we must watch for a road that turns south of the highway and leads to the village of Grenville. We shall come to a countryside so sleepy and neglected that it is difficult to imagine that a century and a quarter ago it was the talk of two continents. The road is seldom travelled now because Grenville doesn't realize that it is a spot that could be turned into a showplace. There is a village square in Grenville, surrounded by old houses and inns, that might, with imagination and ingenuity, come to life and bring prosperity to the district.

This was the western end of the Grenville canal, as Carillon was the eastern end of that visionary project. The canal lies separated from the miles of white water of the Long Sault by only a strip of land wide enough for a roadway. Under the right kind of direction, this road by the Long Sault would bring thousands of visitors to enjoy the beauty and the romantic history of this part of the country.

Once upon a time this was a hustling town right in the heart of the trade routes of the 18th century, founded by the Royal Engineers who built the canals. The roadway from Grenville to Carillon, the old Portage Road, was the route of stage coaches that carried travellers from below the rapids to the docks at Grenville, whence there was fair sailing to Hull and Ottawa.

This was the site of a dramatic engineering dream, conceived and nourished by the great Duke of Wellington, who

127

was then chief of all the British armies. He wanted a way to transport men and munitions to Upper Canada, safe from the border warfare that had marked the War of 1812. In response to his demands, the Royal Engineers devised a system of canals which would link the Atlantic ocean with the headwaters of Lake Superior. The canals on the Ottawa were part of that plan. Officers and men of the Royal Engineers, those "scientific soldiers" of the 19th century, settled at each end of the project and the towns of Carillon and Grenville flourished as military money and soldiers' families poured into the district. Work began in 1819.

Meantime, Upper Canada was growing fast, with Loyalists and retired army officers and their families taking up crownlands in the new colony. They looked to the canals for help in developing the economy of the settlements.

The canals, including the Rideau canal, were no sooner opened for traffic than they swarmed with immigrants of the terrible 'thirties, 'forties, and 'fifties, bearing with them the horrors of cholera, typhus and smallpox epidemics. The swollen tide of human beings, who in spite of their misfortunes, were to create modern Canada by their deep instincts for home building and political freedom, surged up these canals, running against the river's currents, and in time to come, fertilizing and enriching the whole country which was in the making.

Here the story could be told. And at the other end of the white water, the story of Dollard and his companions lies waiting to be told.

Since the story of Dollard is the first great tale, in point of time, in this area, we may as well call it up in imagination now and let it serve as a back-drop for the events which began with the red-coated Royal Engineers and ends with the magnificent functional beauty and immensity of the Beauharnois hydro-electric development a few miles away.

Adam Dollard des Ormeaux was a French officer who at

the age of twenty-two went to Montreal to join the garrison under Governor Maisonneuve. We know almost nothing about him except a rumour that he had left France under a cloud, that his honour was in some way in question and that he hoped while in New France, by some act of distinction, to clear his name and earn a bright return to Paris. He arrived in 1656 and had lived for four years in the little settlement which was still in its infancy.

Ever since Champlain had gone to war with the Hurons against the Iroquois, in 1609, the Five Nations Indians had been the unrelenting foes of the Frenchmen. They had never known what it was to be free of fear of an attack by the Indians. But in the late winter and early spring of 1660 terrible rumours reached Quebec, Three Rivers and Montreal of the Indians' intention to launch a campaign that spring which would wipe the French completely off the map of the St. Lawrence. Then one day word reached Montreal that already two hundred Iroquois were encamped at the mouth of the Richelieu River, as part of the attacking forces. Terror, real and justified, engulfed the colony, and preparations of every sort were pushed for the defence of the settlements.

Although it was April the rivers were still covered with ice and snow for spring does not come early to Montreal. The French knew that as soon as the ice was out of the rivers, more Iroquois would descend on Montreal from the west, by way of the Ottawa.

At this point Adam Dollard went to the Governor, the ageing Maisonneuve, to suggest a plan. The young man saw in the crisis the kind of opportunity he had so long sought. He told Maisonneuve that he was willing to go up the Ottawa with a company of volunteers to stop the Iroquois.

What he proposed was to make a stand at the foot of the portage around the Long Sault, where the French might prevent the Iroquois from making the descent on Montreal. At first the Governor and the soberer minds in Montreal tried to persuade Dollard to give up the idea, or at least to postpone his plans until more men were free to join him. But Dollard was adamant. He had already recruited sixteen young men who were willing to risk their lives in the attempt to save Montreal and New France from slaughter.

Finally Dollard had his way. His little company were given all the help the town could afford, supplies, guns, ammunition,—and advice. At the last moment forty Hurons joined the party.

They left Montreal on the nineteenth of April, embarking at Lachine in their canoes and paddling along the icy shores of Lake St. Louis until they came to the Rapids of St. Anne. It is not clear what happened there to delay them, but the men did not reach the foot of the Long Sault until twelve days after their departure.

When they pulled their canoes out of the water on the river shore, they discovered the remains of old palisades which Huron or Algonquin Indians had used long before in a defence against their enemies. It was merely a square enclosure of timbers, without a door and without bastions. Many of the logs were rotted and broken, but this they decided to use as their fort.

Perhaps the gentleness of May days on the river banks lulled them into a false sense of security, for a few days after their arrival they were cooking a meal in the open on the river bank when two hundred Iroquois suddenly appeared and immediately attacked.

For five days the Iroquois kept up the assault and for five days the handful of young Frenchmen and their few Huron allies, returned the fire of the enemy. Meantime scouts had been sent off to call the Iroquois party waiting at Sorel. While food and water and munitions ran low, and the embattled French tried to dig a little well within the palisades for water, the unequal struggle went on. Then five hundred more Iroquois arrived and made the odds against the little garrison twelve to one. Every device of savage warfare and strategy was attempted. The end was inevitable. The Iroquois decided to burn down the miserable fort and at last the French, sleepless for eight days, starving, exhausted, tried one last effort to postpone the end. They tied a fuse to a barrel of powder and attempted to drop the barrel and its lighted fuse over the palisades upon the Iroquois who had piled brush against the walls to start the blaze. But they were too weak, for the barrel fell back amongst the survivors and exploded inside the fort. Even then four or five Frenchmen survived and as many Hurons. The howling Iroquois charged the broken walls, while one last Frenchman with a hatchet despatched his wounded and dying comrades. Only one of the whole party escaped, a Christian Huron named Louis, who was tortured but managed to escape in the darkness of that horrible night. From his lips alone the story of Carillon was told to the French on the St. Lawrence.

Some writers have called this the Canadian Thermopylae, but even this synonym for courage which has come down to us from the history of Greece is not enough to describe the sacrifice of the Seventeen who died at Carillon. At Thermopylae fourteen hundred soldiers, Spartans, Thebans and Thespians, held the Pass of Thermopylae against the Persian army of Xerxes. At Carillon seventeen young men, none over thirty-one, not soldiers but pioneer citizens who had left their fields and work benches, faced seven hundred fierce and ruthless savages, knowing full well that there could be no hope of survival, that indeed survival would mean only torture in the camps of victorious enemies.

Some historians say that many of these men were the idle and rebellious youth of Montreal, that they were reckless and troublesome. It is quite possible that some of them were, but any young men who could frankly face the odds that these men faced, and set out in canoes in the cold and wet of April to put themselves in the way of hordes of Iroquois, because their sacrifice might halt the aggressor and give their people time to prepare their defences, must be remembered with honour and with pride.

What was the result of their reckless, sacrificial service?.

Those that remained of the seven hundred Iroquois took counsel together while they licked their wounds. They had counted the dead within the palisade. They had seen for themselves how low and inadequate were the supplies. Seventeen Frenchmen had worked all this havoc with seven hundred Iroquois, in the wilderness behind a few tree trunks. What would happen, then, in attacks on fortified posts mounted with guns? The Iroquois decided to call off their campaign. We can only guess what might have been the history of Canada if there had been no Seventeen at Carillon. Next year, Pierre Boucher of Three Rivers went to Paris to tell the story to the king. In 1665 came the Carignan regiment, not only to break the power of the Iroquois, but to build new homes and found new families, so that ten years after the death of Dollard and his men, Bishop Laval could report to the king that all the cradles were rocking and there had been a thousand christenings in one year.

Twenty miles east of Carillon we come to a monastery bearing an Indian name,—Oka. All round the world it is the name of a famous cheese. But in Canada, Oka means the Trappists. The great monastery that lies astride the headland that divides the Ottawa River from the Lake of Two Mountains is an institution that combines mediaevalism with scientific modernity. Here white robed monks live in silence and women may not enter its walls.

Just inside the gateway is a whitewashed habitant log house that was the birthplace of the monastery in 1881. A little farther on are the terrace and flower gardens that overlook the Lake of Two Mountains and the Ottawa Valley from a great height. This is one of the finest views in the province. Today Oka is the foremost agricultural school in Quebec, affiliated with the University of Montreal, and here thousands of young Canadiens become scientific farmers.

The little party of Trappists who came to Canada in 1881 came from the Abbey of Bellefontaine. They were welcomed by the Gentlemen of St. Sulpice in Montreal, who gave them a piece of property in the hilly country at Oka. These men live, it seems to the outside world, in incredible austerity. Their entire life is lived in common and in silence. They sleep in a common dormitory, eat together in the refectory, study together in a common workroom, pray and meditate together and labour together in the fields, in the dairies and in the barns. They go to bed at seven and rise at two. Generally speaking, each Trappist spends eight hours a day in public prayer and six to eight hours in labour. They never speak except in cases of absolute necessity and then almost entirely by the use of one hundred signs of traditional use. Yet their researches, their educational methods, have made them famous. In many ways they are as modern as the great Beauharnois power development we shall see next along the way.

We leave Oka by an old-fashioned ferry that chugs its lazy way across the Ottawa to the shores of the old seigneury of Vaudreuil. We follow the south shore eastward to the tip of land between the Ottawa and St. Lawrence Rivers at Cascades Point where the military canal was built in Haldimand's day. The road crosses the St. Lawrence into the territory that was the Seigneury of Beauharnois and is now the site of the great Beauharnois power development. The original owner was the Marquis de Beauharnois who was the uncle of Josephine de Beauharnois, the unfortunate wife of Napoleon.

We pass the pioneer hydro-electric development at St. Timothée and ride through a habitant countryside until we come to a place with a wide open view of the great rapids that provide the power for the turbines at Beauharnois. There is a potential power development here of one million three hundred thousand horsepower. Altogether, between

Prescott, up the river, and Beauharnois, there is a power potential of five million horsepower.

Most of Canada's big power plants are in the wilderness, but here we have one in the heart of a heavily populated territory, just at the back door of Montreal. The functional beauty of such an impressive engineering project, overlaid with the significance of its part in social history, is profoundly stirring. A little time looking over the site and its magnificent structures, is well spent. As we near the power house we pass a little whitewashed house, all that is left of the quiet days of old. It is enveloped in power lines like a fly caught in a cobweb.

15

The Old Seigneuries

WHEN we leave Beauharnois behind us we are on the shores of Lake St. Louis and ahead lies Caughnawaga, an Indian village that began in the seventeenth century as a mission to Christian Iroquois. Just beyond are the Lachine Rapids spread across the wide LaPrairie Basin and we can see Montreal across the water.

Just as the St. Lawrence and the Ottawa converge around a thin spearhead of land to meet at its tip, so the St. Lawrence and the Richelieu converge in the same way at Sorel. From LaPrairie overland to Chambly on the Richelieu, the base of this spearhead, is a distance of only fifteen miles. But to ride around the river shores from LaPrairie to Sorel, and Sorel to Chambly is ninety-five miles.

The Richelieu was also an Iroquois travelway from the home of the Five Nations in New York State. One of the parties that engaged in the siege of Dollard's little fort came down the Richelieu. The Iroquois portaged across this strip of land when they were headed directly for the vicinity of Montreal.

When the Carignan regiment was disbanded many of its officers settled along these vulnerable river shores, so a good deal of the seigneurial story is written in this vicinity. The old Indian trail from the St. Lawrence to the Richelieu became the first important French highway. In the nineteenth century it became the site of the first railway in Quebec and there is a memorial at LaPrairie to commemorate it.

135

The French missionaries hoped that by settling Christian Iroquois here on the LaPrairie Basin at Caughnawaga they would attract converts from the Five Nations and at last bring all the fierce warrior tribes under the civilizing influence of French culture and the Roman Catholic Church. Out of this mission we have a curious tale which will end in the canonization of a Mohawk girl as a saint of the Roman Catholic church. Kateri Tekawitha is now the Venerable Kateri, with men and women all over the world asking her intervention in their lives. Kateri, the Lily of the Mohawks, was seen in Poland during the war, so her devotees say. In 1939 Pope Pius sanctioned the introduction of her cause and the campaign to prove her right to canonization has gone on ever since.

Kateri's mother was an Algonquin girl who lived in the mission station at Three Rivers. Her name was Kahenta. On one of their invasions of New France, the Iroquois carried Kahenta prisoner to Ossernenon. She was a Christian and the story goes that her gentleness and modesty attracted the attention of a Mohawk chief. He married her and became a Christian convert. When Kateri was four years old her father and mother both died in a smallpox epidemic. Kateri recovered from the disease but was badly pockmarked.

For some years the Jesuit Blackrobes were prevented from living with the Five Nations by the campaign of the Carignan regiment against the Indians. In the peace that followed, the treaty forced upon the Iroquois the return of the missionaries.

In 1670 the Mohawks were preparing to celebrate the Feast of the Dead, and in accordance with the rituals, the bodies of Kateri's parents were exhumed. The Jesuit then living with the Mohawks preached against the ancient tribal customs and persuaded them to abandon the plans for the festival. Kateri became one of the most devoted of the missionaries' converts. At the mission to which she was attached the priest set up a Christmas Creche, the first Crib and

136

Infant Jesus seen among the Iroquois. It was decorated with fir and hemlock and alight with candles. The Indians were so entranced with the Creche that they kept it intact until Easter.

Although Kateri was sought after by many Indian youths she would not marry. She went to the mission on the St. Lawrence with her Christian uncle and it was there her piety became a legend. In Holy Week of 1680 she died and as soon as she had expired those around her tore her clothing into tatters so that they might have relics of the saintly girl. She was buried first of all at LaPrairie and has been moved several times. Today her bones are in a little glass topped box in the Presbytery at Caughnawaga. Pilgrims carry away handfuls of the earth from her grave at LaPrairie. But as Alexander Angus says in "Old Quebec": "Kateri Tekawitha has aged with the centuries, so much so, in fact, that only an experienced osteologist could re-construct the framework of an Iroquois girl from the little pile of brown bones in the box on the Presbytery table."

As we round LaPrairie Basin we come to the famous old Victoria Bridge, spanning the St. Lawrence, and a little farther on the spectacular Harbour Bridge. Just beyond it we come to the ancient Seigneury of Longueuil and the story of the Le Moynes.

The Le Moynes were the most spectacular family in the history of New France. It was flamboyant in its sudden emergence in the fresh, fertile social soil of the colony and all its sons were endowed with extraordinary vitality and initiative.

In the seventeenth century New France was a place where young men of intelligence, who might have passed unnoticed in old France, suddenly found scope for their abilities. Such a man was Charles Le Moyne, the son of an innkeeper at Dieppe. In 1641, at the age of fourteen, he was sent out to Quebec as one of the boys who lived with the Indians in order to become guides and interpreters for the French. By 1646, when he was nineteen, he settled down in the infant colony of Montreal.

Le Moyne married in 1654 and his wife bore him eleven sons and two daughters. To distinguish themselves, the sons each took on an additional name, when their father was ennobled, so we know them as Iberville, Maricourt, Bienville, Serigny, Chateauguay and so on.

Le Moyne was an excellent father and passed on to his boys all his forest lore and pioneering skills. The grandsons of the Dieppe innkeeper wrote their names quite literally from the Arctic Ocean to the Gulf of Mexico and from Newfoundland to the Mississippi.

Le Moyne built himself a fine house in Montreal, and when Louis the Fourteenth granted him a seigneury on the south shore of the St. Lawrence, he named it for a village near his birthplace in France, the Seigneury of Longueuil.

He was a successful and an ambitious man and amassed a great fortune. Part of that fortune was invested in a fortified chateau at Longueuil. It was the greatest feudal stronghold on the St. Lawrence in all the history of New France. Its towers were impressive, the walls built to withstand siege, and it had a manor house, a chapel, store-houses and quarters for an armed garrison. It became part of the defences of Montreal against the invading Iroquois.

Later when Fort Chambly was built, the road from Fort Chambly to the Chateau of Longueuil was the highway by which men and supplies could be transported quickly to the Richelieu to defeat the enemy as far as possible from the city itself.

The old chateau is gone, destroyed by the vandalism of men who had no sense of history. It became a quarry for those who went about their short-sighted business in the village of Longueuil some generations ago. On the site of the chateau today stands the Church of St. Antoine. Into the

138

building of the church went what remained of the stones of the chateau. Beside the church runs the Chambly Road.

In the parlor of the old convent that stands near the church, is a drawing of the Chateau of Longueuil, the only remnant of the ancient glory that remains to the modern town.

Le Moyne D'Iberville, whom his biographer called The First Great Canadian, entered the French navy but his heart remained in Canada. When two renegade Frenchmen went to England and helped the king's cousin, Prince Rupert, to found the Hudson's Bay Company, d'Iberville came home to Longueuil and, with two of his brothers, Ste. Helene and de Maricourt, raised an expedition to travel overland to fight against the English on the Bay. They captured three forts and made all the English captives. Next year he seized an English ship full of furs, a rich prize. He left de Maricourt in command on the Bay and sailed with her to Quebec. Then the English angrily sent two ships to oust the French. On his return to the Arctic, d'Iberville found the two of them ice bound. He burned one and captured the other, the *Hampshire*. With the ship loaded with furs and prisoners, too, he sailed again to Quebec. On the journey he met another English ship, but quick of wit, he raised the British flag, saluted them, and passed them by.

The English still held a fort on the Bay, and next year d'Iberville, with his young brother, Le Moyne de Chateauguay and a company of adventurers, set out to take it. The first stroke of tragedy fell on the Le Moynes that year, and young Chateauguay was killed in the assault on the English fort. D'Iberville renamed it Fort Bourbon.

Meantime d'Iberville had been reading all the old tales of La Salle on the Mississippi. La Salle, going overland found one of the mouths of the river, but he was murdered on its banks. D'Iberville dreamed of finding the mouth of the river from the sea. He thought if he could find the way to the Mississippi he could found a colony at its mouth and so have a way to keep his life-long foes, the English, out of the west. He worked hard at court to get support for his plan. Finally in 1698 he was given four ships for an expedition to the Gulf of Mexico. Later they were joined by a French warship.

On the shores of the gulf d'Iberville discovered a tribe of Indians encamped. He had learned from his father how to get along with Indians and so he won their confidence and learned from them how to reach the great river that he sought.

He set out with two small boats and a handful of men to coast the shores. Then one day he noticed a swift current in the water. The water was much lighter in colour than the sea water. He thrust in his hand and then he put his tongue to it. It was fresh water! D'Iberville turned the prows of his little boats into the current and followed it until he discovered the entrance to the Mississippi.

After this still another Le Moyne comes into the story,— Le Moyne de Bienville, the founder of New Orleans and of the French colony of Louisiana. It was d'Iberville who called it Louisiana for his king. D'Iberville died a few years later at Havana, but de Bienville spent the rest of his life as governor of the colony and he died in New Orleans at the age of eighty-eight.

The road along the river leads next to Boucherville, the village that grew up around the manor house of Pierre de Boucherville, whom we discovered as Governor of Three Rivers. On through historic countryside, settled under the laws and customs of the feudal age, we go to the village of Varennes, whose name commemorates another officer of the Carignan regiment, Lt. Varennes. He married a daughter of his neighbour at Boucherville, Marie Boucher, and one of their sons was La Verendrye, the first white man to see the Rocky Mountains from the prairie. This is the road that follows the old shore highway of the French regime, the road that linked seigneury to seigneury and habitant farm to habitant farm. It was along this road that the gregarious Canadiens sat on their narrow verandahs generation after generation. Many of these old houses still stand, and in the sunny afternoons, or the cool and quiet evenings, they still sit there, two, three or even four generations, in their rockingchairs, watching the life of today move by, just as they have watched it since the days when the shaggy horse provided the fastest means of travel.

Finally we come to Vercheres, a typical, drowsy old French village. Le curé, le docteur and l'avocat are still the chief men of the town. It is neither modern nor antique, neither rural nor urban, a sprawling village that has lost its habitant character and hasn't yet become a town. But down near the water's edge stand the remains of an old mill and a memorial. This is historic ground; it is, in a sense, sacred ground, for here was lived out a story that is familiar to every school child in Canada, a story that will some day, we can hope, prompt the rebuilding here of a replica of an old seigneurial manor house and fort, with palisade, chapel, mill and oven. Some day, that is, when the people of Vercheres awaken to the quality of their heritage and develop more than a careless interest in their traditions. Some of the villagers will tell you that part of the old manor house still stands, converted into a dwelling house, but no attempt has been made to verify the claim or to preserve the relic, if it is an authentic one. So Madeleine de Vercheres seems a little lonely as she stands on her bastion, a sturdy bronze figure, windswept and courageous, an old musket grasped in her steady hands.

Madeleine's father, Francois Jarret de Vercheres, was born of the noblesse of Dauphiny in France and became a soldier when he was a boy. Later he received a commission in the regiment of the Prince de Carignan. He was twenty-four years of age and a veteran of the wars against the Turks when

141

his regiment was ordered to Canada in 1665. When the campaign against the Iroquois ended, he was one of the officers who decided to stay in Canada and accept a land grant and the obligation to colonize it. Mademoiselle Marie Perrot was living on the Island of Orleans with her parents when he settled down in Canada and she was only fourteen when she married him. The retired officer of 28 and the child-bride went off to build themselves a home on the banks of the St. Lawrence, in the uneasy peace that followed the campaign against the Indian foes. Three years later, in 1672, Vercheres was granted the land on which he had settled as a seigneurial estate,—it became the Seigneury of Vercheres.

Part of his duty in return for the very considerable area granted to him with all the feudal rights then established in New France, was that of defending the land on which his tenants settled. So Vercheres, with the help of his tenants, surrounded his manor house with a palisade of timbers sharpened into points. There were four bastions to the wooden walls so that its defenders could enfilade the walls if they were closely besieged. In addition there was a stone redoubt in which arms and ammunition could be stored and in which women and children could take refuge in time of danger.

As the years passed, confidence increased and the tenants cleared more and more land, farther and farther away from the manor house. All this time Governor Frontenac had been in Quebec and kept the Iroquois subdued. But when he was recalled and stupid men sent to replace him, the Iroquois again decided to descend on New France to accomplish the purpose they had relinquished in 1660,—they would wipe out the French colony.

In their first terrible raids on the colony they inflicted the Massacre of Lachine upon the unfortunate colonists and about the same time one party from the Richelieu attacked Vercheres. Madame Vercheres was alone with her children.

Madeleine was twelve years old. The little family put up such a stout defence that the Iroquois, who had been told that the men were away, were afraid they had been tricked. After two days' siege, the Iroquois withdrew, humiliated at having been defeated by a woman.

This little girl who had helped her mother in the defence of Vercheres, was steeped in the traditions of fortitude and ingenuity that were bred in the early life of New France. The stories on which she was brought up were not the kind of stories the 'teen age girls of today would enjoy. News that a great company of Iroquois had come down the Ottawa and were encamped at its mouth, started the flow of tales of terror, of the fearful things that had happened to the habitants who had to harvest their crops under armed guards and whose wives and children had to flee to the seigneurial forts all along the rivers. Madeleine knew all the stories of the attacks on Le Chesnaye, Repentigny, Boucherville and Longueuil. An older brother had gone up to LaPrairie to help drive the Iroquois off from Montreal. His young body was brought down the river to Vercheres in a canoe when the fighting had ended. Madeleine's sister, Marie Jeanne, had married at the age of twelve, and in the following year, at the age of thirteen she was a widow. Her brother, Francois, had been killed by the Iroquois when he was sixteen. The eleven children who were born in the manor house at Vercheres had "supped full on horror" by the time they reached their 'teens.

But they were all quite literally imbued with the idea that the French nobility were born merely to serve God and the king. This was no idle chatter, but a belief that coloured all their actions. Yet these children of the nobility were poor in everything but their pride. Sieur de Vercheres, in spite of his seigneurial rank, could not have lived in the fort at Vercheres without a pension from the king, like so many of his fellow seigneurs. Yet, if it hadn't been for his poverty, we would

never have known the story of Madeleine de Vercheres, and
we would have been the poorer for the lack of the tale of her
almost legendary resourcefulness. For the events of that time
at Vercheres went by unnoticed, perhaps because there
were so many similar episodes on the St. Lawrence. The
story lay hidden for two hundred years before it was discovered in the Archives in Paris in 1896. It was there only
because at one time Madeleine was desperate for help. Her
father had died and she was living with her mother and helping to establish her younger brothers and sisters. When she
could manage no longer on the little pension the king continued to her mother, she wrote to the Comtesse Maurepas
and asked her if she could induce the king to grant either a
commission to a young brother, or a small pension for herself.
She told the Comtesse a little of why she felt she had the
right to ask for help. The Comtesse was interested and a
message went out to the Marquis de Beauharnois, the Governor of New France, to ask him to investigate the story that
Madeleine had told. As a result of this Madeleine set down
the account of her adventure and Beauharnois sent it to Paris
to the Minister of Marine. Madeleine got a little pension and
the paper was filed away with the report on the situation. It
went into the French archives, and was entirely forgotten
until a research worker in Paris came upon it by accident, two
centuries after the incident.

In October of 1692 Monsieur de Vercheres was in Quebec
where he had been called on business affairs, and Madame de
Vercheres had gone to Montreal. The crops were in, the time
seemed quiet and beautiful. At Vercheres, fourteen year old
Madeleine was left in charge of the family and servants. The
fort was in bad repair. In the manor house were two young
boys, Madeleine and an old man of eighty, two soldiers and
two servants. The habitants were busy in their fields with the
last farm chores before the freeze-up, killing pigs, cutting
firewood, banking the cabins against the cold.

The fort was a hundred and fifty feet or more from the water's edge, and there on the morning of October twenty-second, Madeleine and the soldier, Laviolette, were standing, probably discussing drawing up the buoys that marked the channel to the dock, before the freeze-up. Into the quiet routine of autumn life came the raucous war cry of the Iroquois and a random shot from a musket. The girl and the man flew up the path to the fort. Madeleine saw forty or fifty Iroquois running across the clearing towards the fort and "within pistol shot". In fact, before she got to the gate an Indian clutched her shawl. Fortunately it came off in his hand. The girl and the soldier got through the gate and those waiting within slammed it in the face of the pursuers.

Madeleine hoped that the shots would bring neighbours to her aid, but the habitants had already been dealt with, probably during the night, for a score of the settlers had been murdered.

Then began Madeleine's heroic preparation for defence. We may wonder now that the men in the fort did not take over from the girl, but we must remember that they were living under feudal conditions, and since the girl was of the nobility, the men about the fort did not question her right to take command. First of all she inspected the fort and put everyone to work repairing the inadequate walls.

"After the breaches had been repaired," she says in her own story of the siege "I betook myself to the redoubt which served as guardhouse and armoury. Here I found the two soldiers, one lying down and the other with a burning fuse in his hand. 'What are you doing with that fuse,' I demanded. 'We want to fire the powder and blow up the fort,' was the craven reply."

Madeleine's rage must have been impressive as she stood in that little stone redoubt for it had an electric effect.

"You miserable wretches," she said, stamping her foot, "begone, I command you."

145

"I spoke so firmly," writes Madeleine in her memoir, "that they obeyed forthwith."

Out of the stores she picked a soldier's helmet for herself, and muskets for herself and her two brothers, and for the old man of eighty. Then returning to the bastions she ordered the little cannon to be fired, partly to impress the Iroquois but also in the vain hope of warning someone who might come to her aid.

Already some of the wives and children of the habitants had reached the fort. Their cries of grief and screams of terror were so great that Madeleine quickly realized they would encourage the Iroquois. So she gathered the little company around her and told them soberly what the situation was and how their cries were contributing to their danger. She was in the midst of her appeal to the tenants when to her horror she heard a canoe approaching the dock. In the canoe was a colonist named Fontaine with his Parisian wife and several children. Madeleine asked the soldiers to go to the dock and warn the Fontaines to be swift in getting into the fort, but she saw that the soldiers were reluctant. So, acting instantly, she told the gathered company that she would go to the dock and that if she did not return, they were to keep up the defence of the fort to the very end. Then she opened the gate and walked boldly down to the dock, hurried the Fontaines out of the canoe and marched them all ahead of her back to the fort, before the Iroquois fired a shot. She had shrewdly figured that the Iroquois would think the episode was a ruse to lure them out of the woods into the open where they could be fired upon, and she was right.

That night there was a fierce snowstorm and a northeast wind howled around them and bitter cold enveloped them. Knowing from all the old tales of Iroquois warfare that they would choose such a time to attack, she made her military preparations. She sent the two soldiers, whom she no longer trusted, to the redoubt to look after the women and children

*T*he Quebec spring, with its warm, fragrant days and its clear cold nights, starts the sap running. Jackson painted THE EDGE OF THE MAPLE WOOD on canvas, in the open, where he could feel the grip of winter relaxing. This was the first of Jackson's canvases to be recognized as significant. It was painted in 1910 in the Eastern Townships.

huddled there. The two boys and the old man she set on guard on three of the bastions and took the fourth herself. They had not a moment's sleep but stood their ground in the snow and wind all night long, exchanging their cries of "All's well" with a courage and endurance that to this day rouse our sense of poignancy of their situation. If only the old man had set down his memories of that night! How strange an adventure for him, to find himself under the command of a 'teen age girl.

"One would have thought," said Madeleine when she told the story years later, "that the fort was crowded with warriors".

The Iroquois were thoroughly deceived. They had been told the fort was empty of its defenders. Later on, some of them who were taken prisoner in another incident, told the Governor of Montreal that they held a council that stormy night, and decided that from the losses they had already sustained from gunfire from the fort and the vigilance that was displayed, that they would not risk an attack on the palisade.

Within the fort, in the middle of the night, Madeleine heard the sound of steps approaching the walls and just as she was expecting to see the enemy emerge out of the snow, a sentry at the gate cried out to warn of the approach of something in the storm. Madeleine went down and peered through a loophole. There, to her immense relief she saw a forlorn herd of horned cattle approaching. Still she feared that this might be a ruse and so she cautiously waited for developments. But when they bawled pitifully and she was certain they had come of their own volition, she opened the gate and let them in.

They were all so cheered by the fact that they had survived the first night that they spent the next day in good spirits. The wind dropped, the storm was over and everything was fresh and green under a brilliant October sun.

147

Yet into this loveliness a new note of despair was sounded, for above the trees they could see the smoke of ruined habitant homes, and hear the cries of captives being tortured in the Iroquois camp.

At midday, Madeleine suddenly remembered that yesterday morning she had spread a big washing of household linen down on the rocks by the riverside. Linen was precious, hard to get in New France, and Madeleine was horrified at the thought of losing it. Again she asked the soldiers to sally out for the laundry, and again they refused. So she called her two brothers and they made the sortie, gathered up the linen and flew back to the fort, while the soldiers fired the cannon towards the woods to discourage the Iroquois from emerging.

For eight days the Iroquois hung about in the vicinity, reluctant to give up their plan of campaign and also reluctant to take a chance on what might meet them at the palisade. After days of tension and fatigue even Madeleine's brave little body was worn out. She was dozing at a table with her head lying on the butt of her musket when she heard a commotion on the river. She was up in an instant and climbed the steps to the top of the bastion, peering through the dusk.

"Who are you?" she cried, and heard the happy word in reply "French".

It was Lieutenant de la Monerie and forty soldiers from Montreal, only eighteen miles away. The gate of the fort was thrown open and the young commander sallied forth, her musket still in her strong young hands. She saluted the officer formally.

"Sir, you are welcome," she said. "I surrender my arms to you."

She held out the musket to him. In spite of eight days of fatigue and strain, in spite of the fact that she must have been crumpled and untidy, she was a figure of such dignity that the officer, deeply moved, gave her a courtly bow and said quietly: "Mademoiselle, they are in good hands."

She invited him to inspect the fort and he found a sentry on each bastion, and the Iroquois, watching from the shelter of the woods, decided it was prudent to call off the siege. They withdrew as silently as they had come. The siege of Vercheres was over.

Then Madeleine made one request of the relieving force. "Sir," she said to Lieutenant de la Monerie, "kindly release my sentries that they may take a little rest, for they have not left their posts for eight days."

We can imagine Madeleine returning at last to her own room in the manor house, discarding the heavy clothing she had worn on duty, and creeping into her own bed to fall into a dreamless sleep of utter fatigue. Let us hope she slept around the clock.

16

The Richelieu River

THE Richelieu is not a long river. It flows from Lake Champlain, just south of the United States border, and crosses southern Quebec to the St. Lawrence. It was the River of Death, the quick route of the Indians to the French settlements, and along its course, Americans, too, invaded Canada. Montgomery came this way with his army to force the "fourteenth colony" into rebellion, and in 1812 the Americans were turned back from Montreal in a famous battle that ranged all the way from Chateauquay to St. John.

The first fateful episode on this river was the journey of Champlain and his men with the Huron Indians to make war on the Iroquois, of whom he knew little. Hurons and Algonquins, the friendly tribes he knew best, persuaded him to take his European arms to support them in their rivalry with the Five Nations. He had to keep the friendship of the Indians with whom he wanted to trade and explore, but he pulled a hornet's nest down upon the French by his action.

In July of 1609 he and his men set out from Quebec in a pinnace with the Hurons. When they came to the mouth of the Richelieu, most of them suddenly decided to go home. Several hundred paddled off with their kettles and knives for which they had traded their furs. Only about sixty were willing to see the campaign through.

When he got to Chambly Basin, Champlain discovered his allies had lied in order to induce him to go with them. He could not sail on to the Iroquois country with his pinnace. He faced the rapids and the portages that altered all his plans.

He sent the pinnace and some of the men back to Quebec and his party went on in canoes. The lake into which he sailed must have impressed him very much, for it was the only spot to which he gave his own name,—Lake Champlain.

Finally they met with the Iroquois and the two sides spent the night howling defiance at each other. Next morning Champlain put on a plumed helmet and shining breastplate, and chose two Frenchmen to accompany him with muskets. The Hurons, at a signal, were to open their ranks, and the magnificent Frenchmen were to walk through and astound the Iroquois.

All went according to plan and at the appointed time Champlain walked through the ranks of the Hurons and came face to face for the first time with the enemy. As a matter of fact, both French and Iroquois were so enthralled with the sight of each other that nothing happened while they merely paused for time to look each other over. Probably Champlain regretted that the fine, well disciplined Iroquois warriors were not his allies, rather than the nondescript and undisciplined Hurons. Then Champlain raised his musket and fired a single shot. Two of the Iroquois chiefs were killed and a third mortally wounded. The Hurons shouted, the other two Frenchmen emptied their muskets, and the Iroquois, except for a dozen or so who were captured, fled into the woods, and the campaign was over.

From that day dated the implacable hate of the Iroquois for the Frenchmen and their allies.

Today as we travel up the Richelieu through the old seigneuries we find a busy industrial city on the site of the Seigneury of Sorel, named for one of the officers of the Carignan regiment. There were only about two thousand people in New France in 1665, and it seemed, after the arrival of the regiment, that there were as many soldiers as there were settlers. The campaign against the Iroquois was laid on the Richelieu. The first fort they built was on the site of Fort

Chambly at the foot of the rapids. They threw "a bridle of forts" along the valley.

The men were veterans of the wars against the Turks, and the Indian war was their last campaign. Intendant Talon induced the king to disband the regiment in New France so that he might persuade officers and men to settle by the offer of grants of land. The king even provided them with brides and sent Bride Ships sailing the Atlantic, carrying the mistresses of new homes.

The seigneurial system was already far in decline in France and had become mere absentee landlordism. But transplanted to New France it took on new life and extended its history for two centuries. The colonists were glad of the leadership of the seigneurs and the seigneurs enjoyed the unexpected sense of importance in their new feudal rights. Although there remained a strong sense of rank, there was, nevertheless, through the sheer facts of daily life in the wilderness, a unity of interest that robbed the system of some of its evils.

Most of the settlers were young and many of the brides were 'teen age girls. With so much youth and vigour unleashed in the colony, Talon could see his plans flourishing under his very eyes. The fields spread, the flocks of sheep and fowls multiplied, while the farmers learned to grow flax and their wives to spin and weave it.

Priests for the settlements were appointed by the Bishop of Quebec, and the whole colony was treated as a mission, with the focus of religious life at Quebec.

Yet among the seigneurial rights was that of building a church and appointing a priest of the seigneur's own choice. This entailed the creation of a parish. Many seigneurs were anxious to have this system established so that they could have a parish priest friendly to their interests and permanently established among the tenants. But this meant, to the Bishop, a chipping away of his authority. In order to postpone the evil day, the Bishop decreed that he would not sanctify any seigneurial church not built of stone. And as few of the seigneurs could afford to build a stone church, they found themselves frustrated.

Since the church owned and controlled so much territory in New France, the lay seigneurs grew restive. The church was the bulwark of feudalism and worked hard at its development and extension. It is true that the religious orders were, generally speaking, much better seigneurs that the ex-officers and court favourites who so often acquired grants of land. The church farms were the best in the colony and the habitants who were tenants of the church usually had a higher standard of living than those on the lay seigneuries. But nevertheless the Jesuits, so the colonists thought, owned too much land, for they had all the best land in the colony and by the time of the Cession owned one-eighth of all the granted land in New France.

It was only when Intendant Begon insisted on it that the church reluctantly agreed to the laying out of the parish system. Finally, in 1722, only a generation before the fall of New France, the colony was divided into forty-one parishes.

Usually a parish was coterminous with a seigneury, since the seigneury already formed a unit of settlement, with a chapel, mill, bake oven and manor house, as its centre. Sometimes a very large seigneury became two parishes, and sometimes two or three small seigneuries became one parish. The seigneurial church now became the parish church.

Sometimes, of course, there had been no other place of worship than a room in the manor house and then the new curé would have to set about the building of a church.

Under the new parish system the curé often lived with the seigneur and sometimes became his very close friend, sharing his interests, political and cultural, economic and religious.

So the manor house became the center of the social and

religious life of the community. The church and the manor house were the indivisible centre of the parish life.

The habitants were, however, by no means the helpless serfs of feudal Europe. In 1663 Bishop Laval ordered a tithe of one-thirteenth of the produce of the farm to be paid to the church and the Sovereign Council made it law. But the habitants put up so good a fight for a lesser tithe that the Council cut it back to half,—one twenty-sixth. The struggle between the two interests went on for years until in 1679 the king confirmed the lesser tithe. That tithe law remained in force down to the twentieth century. The tithe was intended in the first place only against grain, but when the habitant took to growing flax, tobacco and root vegetables the church attempted to impose the tithe against all of these. There was another campaign of stubborn resistance and again the habitants prevailed. The habitant could and did appeal against the church to the king and frequently the king decided in his favour.

When a parish church was built by funds contributed by benefactors or by the people themselves, the bishop had the right to appoint the curé, but if the seigneur built the church he had the right to choose the curé. The bishop might refuse to consecrate a wooden church, so that he could keep the right of appointment in his own hands, but he could not refuse to bless a stone one. As late as 1700 the bishop had to get a ruling from the king that he might build a stone church in any seigneury in which no stone church had already been built.

Among the officers of the Carignan regiment demobilized in Quebec was Jacques de Chambly. Seven years after he had helped to build Fort Chambly he was granted a seigneury on Chambly Basin and settled down to colonize. Sorel also settled on the land he had helped to defend and brother officers settled along the Richelieu,—Countrecoeur, St. Ours, Hertel de Rouville and many more. The St. Ours family still live on some of their seigneurial lands and maintain a way of life imbued with memories of the past.

Chambly and de Rouville married sisters and when Chambly died without heirs his lands were bequeathed to de Rouville, one of whose sons adopted the name of Chambly. It was Hertel de Rouville who, with four of his brothers under his command, led the infamous raid on Deerfield in New England.

The first Fort Chambly had wooden palisades fifteen feet high. It was burned down by the Iroquois in 1702 and was rebuilt. But the building of the present stone fort at Chambly is a story worth telling because it concerns one of the very earliest citizens' movements in Montreal.

The rebuilt Fort Chambly was so small and inconsequential that the council at Quebec decided to abandon it altogether and sent orders up to Montreal to demolish the fort.

Now for more than a generation, for forty years in fact, Fort Chambly had been a symbol of defence and safety to the people of Montreal. The idea of abandoning it and leaving the old Iroquois portage from Chambly to LaPrairie Basin open again to the enemy, roused the citizens of Montreal to a fever of excitement. A town meeting was called and the people met in the seminary of the Sulpicians, who were seigneurs of the island. They declared that Fort Chambly was the great keep of the city and that hostile English were not many miles away. The town meeting decided to rebuild the fort on its own initiative and make it a massive stone fort adequate to its purpose. Montreal sent a delegation to the Sovereign Council in Quebec with the counter-proposal and asked its consent to go on with the work. Also, they sent representatives to Paris to urge the project and to ask the king for help.

Getting help from the court at Versailles was always a slow business and the situation was urgent, so while the delegation went about the slow process of asking for help, the rest of the city went straight ahead and built Fort Chambly. If ever there was a community project, it was the building of the stone fortress on the other end of the long portage.

It took the king and the government of France three years to make up their minds about Fort Chambly. When they got around to telling Montreal that their project was approved and that they might go ahead with their plans, the new Fort Chambly was already in use.

In the War of 1812 Fort Chambly was one of the points of defence against the American invaders. The hero of Chateauguay, Colonel de Salaberry, made his home in Chambly where his house still stands and he is buried in the cemetery of the parish church.

In 1852 Chambly was abandoned as a military post. It had fallen into bad repair when it was handed over to the Canadian government. There was another proposal to destroy the fort and it was a Canadien who spoke out: "There is a vandalism more dangerous than that of time," he said, "it is that of man and it must be resisted." The federal government decided to restore the fort and it has become a national shrine, well worth a visit for the memories it evokes.

There is a strange story associated with this fort which seems incredible but it is sober history. Father Rale, a missionary to the Abenakis, and the aristocratic Governor, Marquis de Vaudreuil, conspired together to incite the Christian Indians to deeds of pure atrocity. The Jesuit historian Charlevoix leaves us in no doubt of the facts. Rale lived with the Abenakis on the frontiers of New England for many years. The conspiracy brings into focus Hertel de Rouville and a Calvinistic preacher, Rev. John Williams of Deerfield.

In midwinter of 1704 Vaudreuil sent off a party led by Hertel, for the purpose, as he wrote to Paris, of keeping the Abenakis stirred up to prevent them going over to the English. The fifty Frenchmen and two hundred Indians snowshoed three hundred miles across country to Deerfield, which comprised forty-odd houses. Williams, a Harvard graduate, was the town's minister. He was married and had eight children, one of whom was away visiting. The story is too long to tell in detail but Hertel's starving company reached Deerfield one night and lay in deep snow until the village settled down to sleep. Then they fell upon it. Bursting into the Williams home, the Indians killed two children and their negro nurse and took all the rest of the family prisoners. By sunrise the whole village was in flames and one hundred and eleven of the living were driven off into the snowy woods. About fifty others had been killed. Nearly a hundred and forty had escaped in the darkness to the surrounding woods. A door marked with the hatchet cuts is one of the relics now in the Deerfield museum, according to Parkman who tells the whole story. The captives were driven up a hillside from which they could look down upon the burning homes, and before they moved out of sight of it, one child was despatched by tomahawk because the Indians decided it was too much trouble to take it along,—even though the children had a cash value when they got back to New France, for many of the Canadiens redeemed the little prisoners and brought them up in their own homes. Even the Marquise de Vaudreuil adopted such a child.

Mrs. Williams had had a child just a few weeks before the raid and apparently this infant was one of two killed before the rest were made prisoners. Mrs. Williams was ill and the shock weakened her. The Indians would not let her walk with her husband but sent Williams on ahead. A day or two later they had to cross an open stream knee deep. She had barely been able to make the crossing when she sank exhausted on the bank. An Indian clubbed her to death because of her weakness. Her body was left on the snow, and a few days later a pursuit party found her there and carried her back to Deerfield. Through freezing or thawing weather, through snow and ice and slush, the party plodded on over those three hundred miles to Montreal. As they neared New France the party broke up into small groups and the Williams family was completely separated. Only half the captives ever saw Deerfield again.

At last the party in which John Williams was included reached Fort Chambly,—not the stone fort of today but the wooden one of an earlier date. Here, by way of contrast with the brutality of the weeks of travel, he was received with respect and kindness. He was taken into the home of one of the leading colonists and welcomed at his table. Later, when he was taken down the Richelieu to Sorel in an Abenaki canoe, a Frenchwoman came to the shore as he approached and called the party ashore. She took Williams into her home and set a table for him, serving him the best she could produce, telling him that she, too, had once been a prisoner of the Indians. The Abenakis she served in the chimney corner.

Presently, the Marquis de Vaudreuil, who had ordered the raid, sent for Williams and invited him to visit Montreal. Williams was the guest of Vaudreuil who was extremely kind to him. Vaudreuil ransomed one of Williams' daughters, and tried to ransom another who was in the hands of the Caughnawaga Indians. But they refused to give her up.

Great efforts were made to convert Williams' children. Williams himself was offered a pension for life from the French king if he would adopt Catholicism and settle down in Quebec. They feared his influence so much that he was not allowed to talk to the English captives, not even his own children.

Vaudreuil genuinely liked the stern, sad Calvinist and remained consistently kind to him in his captivity but he would not set him free. He told him that he would exchange him only for a pirate named Captain Baptiste, a noted buccaneer that the British were holding in Boston.

Deputies came from Boston again and again to treat with the French for the redeeming of the prisoners and to make an exchange of those they held in New England. The French throughout were reluctant to give them up. They went back, a few at a time, but at least a hundred remained permanently in New France.

Many of those who remained married French men and women. It may have been that in some cases the contrast between the dour and highly disciplined life in New England, and the gay and light-hearted way of life of the colonists in New France proved enlightening to the captives. They had never experienced that kind of a life before. Probably some of them didn't want to go back to Puritanism and Calvinism in New England. In one curious case a captive boy named Gill married a captive girl, but their hundreds of descendants, who still bear the name of Gill, were French and Abenaki. One captive girl lived to become Superior of the Ursuline convent in Quebec. She always maintained a correspondence with her family in New England and exchanged gifts with them.

Three years after he had become a prisoner, Williams was released and two of his children were released with him.

To get to Fort Lennox, the finest historic site on the Richelieu, requires an effort on the part of the traveller, because he must find a boatman to take him across the water to Ile aux Noix. It is worth the effort because the site is beautiful and the fort very interesting. Ile aux Noix is only ten miles from the United States border. During the Second World War Fort Lennox was a concentration camp for enemy aliens, but in peace time it is used as a camp for university and community groups taking special courses in leadership and public services. The Fort is under the management of the National Parks Bureau and was renovated and put into excellent condition after a half century of neglect.

Ile aux Noix is the island that Champlain discovered covered with nut trees. The first settler on the island paid his rent with one bag of nuts gathered from the island each year. It is three quarters of a mile long and covers about two hundred and ten acres. It was at one time the centre of naval activity and there was a shipbuilding yard on the Island.

It was only in 1758, a year before the fall of Quebec, that New France decided to make its chief frontier defence at Ile aux Noix. The island was fortified and two thousand men of a famous French regiment were established there. It was so strongly defended that the British did not even attack it until 1760. It was commanded by Comte de Bougainville, a soldier and a scientist, who became so famous that he was buried in the Pantheon in Paris. Actually the fort was never besieged. The commander played a hoax on the British.

The war was almost at an end and when the British appeared and established themselves on three sides of the fort, Bougainville decided it was wiser to retreat and save his men for the defence of Montreal. So one moonless August night he withdrew all but fifty men, who were left to carry on as though nothing had happened. The next morning the British began a bombardment in response to some shelling from the French troops within. A little later the French offered to surrender if they were allowed the honours of war. The British gladly accepted the offer, in order to avoid bloodshed. Officers were named by both sides to carry on negotiations for the transfer of the fort. All this took time, for the formalities were carefully observed. We can imagine the chagrin of the British when they finally entered the fort to discover the size of its garrison.

In the British regime Ile aux Noix was an important point of defence against the Indians, and presently against the Americans. In 1776 the British took out the old French plans and dusted them off. They decided to complete the project begun by the Marquis de Montcalm. Even before the American Revolution had ended the erection of the present fine stone fortification was begun.

Today Fort Lennox is a park for visitors and picnickers.

From the highway we approach through the village of St. Paul, on our way to the Island where Canadians and Americans mingle together with rarely a thought for the time when their forbears fought each other for possession of Ile aux Noix. There is some fine architecture in the buildings of the fort and some magnificent views of the country round about from the earthworks. The fort is surrounded by a moat sixty feet wide. Once there was a drawbridge but that has given way to a more prosaic approach to the main gateway. There are still parts of the sally port by which the French escaped under the noses of the surrounding British troops. The walls in some of the buildings are eight feet thick.

Some of the trees on the Island are so old that they saw the wars of French against the Iroquois, English against the French and Americans against the Canadians. It might even be that the ancient tree in the courtyard, the tree that has escaped damage in all these campaigns, was there, a slender sapling, when Champlain named the Island.

17

The Eastern Townships

QUEBEC can be divided roughly into three parts, like
Gaul. Each of these parts is so distinctive that it
gives character to the geographical areas involved
and dictates the economic and social life of those territories.
There is, first and foremost, the Laurentian Plateau area which
comprises the whole northern region of the province from the
St. Lawrence and Ottawa valleys to its northern and eastern
boundaries. Then there is the Appalachian Region which
covers the entire south-eastern territory of the province including Gaspé and all the land east of a line drawn from the
southern tip of Lake Champlain to Quebec city. Finally
there is a triangle that lies within a line drawn from Quebec
city to Hull, from Hull to Lake Champlain and again, from
the southern tip of Lake Champlain to Quebec city. This
triangle comprises all the rich, lowlying, agricultural territory
of the province.

Quebec is the largest province in the Dominion and we can
get some notion of its magnitude when we realize that ninety
per cent of the province lies within the Laurentian Plateau,
and its famous cultivated areas total only about five per cent
of its territory.

The highest mountains in the province are in the Appalachian range, in those areas of Gaspé that were never covered
by the Labrador Ice Sheet. But in the low-lying triangle of
agricultural territory there are eight very interesting and curious mountains. These hills are called by the geologists "plu-
tonic intrusions" and they represent the "substructure of vol-

canoes" which were once in active eruption. Mount Royal is the most westerly of these hills, and Shefford Mountain the most easterly. It is just west of Knowlton. They vary from seven hundred and fifteen feet, (Mount Royal is seven hundred and seventy feet) to seventeen hundred and forty-five feet. As we drive through the Eastern Townships we see these "intrusions",—that word is quite descriptive,—such as Mt. Johnson, Mt. Rouge, Mt. St. Hilaire, near the Richelieu, Mt. Yamaska, not far from Granby, and Mt. Brome, not far south of Mt. Shefford.

Orford Mountain, in the Orford National Park, is something else, for it is a part of the Appalachian range and lies at the entrance to the lake country. South-eastward of the plain area is a beautiful lake and mountain country, stretching as far as the United States border and into the Chaudière Valley.

Except for the lands settled by the French along the St. Lawrence shores and in the valley of the Richelieu, this territory is known as the Eastern Townships. They are a social and political contrast to seigneurial Quebec and cover thirteen counties. Along the river lands we see such names as Iberville, Rouville, Vercheres, but inland from this fringe of ancient French settlement, we see the names of counties such as Drummond, Sheffield, Richmond, Sherbooke and Brome. Here in the placenames are clues to the history of the countryside.

In the French regime this was a land of terror, a great wilderness in which lurked death and torment. There was plenty of good land along the rivers for as many French as came to the colony, so they were content to leave this buffer wilderness unexplored, between them and the English in the Atlantic colonies and on the Hudson River. It was originally Algonquin country but the Jesuit missionaries who worked among the Abenaki Indians in what is now Maine, induced their semi-Christianized converts to move northward to the shores of the St. Lawrence, just as the Mohawks had moved to Caughnawaga. They settled down at the mouth of the St. Francis River and were called the St. Francis Indians and exceeded anything the pagan Indians could conceive in brutality. They moved from their Mission Village down the rivers of Connecticut to prey on the English. Consequently the French very wisely stayed out of the land given over to this terrible border warfare. The forest and lakeland that comprised this wilderness was the Abenaki hunting ground. The furs they trapped here they sold in Montreal and Quebec and often took along English scalps as well, for they were paid a bounty on them. The whole area was referred to in French times and early British times as the St. Francis Country, and as such was made into a court district after the fall of New France.

It was through this country that hundreds of English captives were brought by the Indians. Some of these captives who returned home eventually, knew the country and its travel routes, and it was probably due to them that in the British regime there was an immediate urge to open up this wilderness.

There were three well known routes from the American colonies to New France. One of them was by way of Lake Champlain, and then either up the Richelieu, or by way of Missisquoi Bay across country to Lake Yamaska, (now Brome Lake,) and by the Yamaska river to the St. Lawrence. The second was the Indian Road, as it was called, all the way from the Atlantic by way of the Black river and its portages to Lake Memphremagog and so to the St. Francis.

The third route was into the Chaudière Valley and this was the route that Arnold took with his army attempting the conquest of Quebec in 1774. This is now the Kennebec highway.

In the Seven Years War these Abenakis were so active in their guerrilla warfare against the British that Col. Rogers, of Rogers' Rangers, finally was assigned to an expedition to punish them.

Rogers had a debt of his own to settle with the Abenakis, for his wife and children had been murdered by them. He was assigned two hundred provincial troops most of them men who, like Rogers, had bitter personal quarrels with the Indians and their French masters, for the same reasons,— raids, massacres, the taking of white prisoners. Rogers and his men moved up from Crown Point in batteaux to Missiquoi Bay, where he hid his boats and supplies for the return journey. Then he set off across country to the St. Francis river. He had not gone very far when scouts caught up with him to tell him that three hundred and fifty French and Indians were in pursuit of his party. However, the Rangers moved on and reached the vicinity of the village of St. Francis just about three weeks after the fall of Quebec to General Wolfe. He was not concerned with what was going on in the capital of New France on the other side of the St. Lawrence. He had just one objective, the village of the barbaric Abenaki Christians.

Disguised as an Indian, Rogers crept up to the vicinity of the village in the darkness. He discovered that the Indians were having a wild celebration and that most of the warriors were away from home. His men lay low until the feasting and dancing ended at four o'clock in the morning. Then, as soon as the village was quiet, they fell upon it with gunfire and tomahawks. Of the three hundred people in the village, they killed two hundred and took many of the others prisoners. The Americans found the village decorated with several hundred scalps and there were also some living prisoners whom they rescued. Then the invaders quickly turned and began their dangerous journey homeward.

While the Loyalists were settling in the Richelieu and St. Lawrence valleys, after the American Revolution, and the St. Francis Country remained a great wall of forest between

Quebec and the American republic, the people of New England were looking yearningly northward into the virgin country with its water power and forests and rich uncleared land. The land was not open to settlement but there seemed little to prevent an enterprising man from slipping across the vague borderline and settling down on a nice piece of land, trusting to good fortune that in time he could make a claim for it and get a deed.

Hundreds of families did just that. These people were nearly all Puritans or Quakers. There was nothing to follow but blazed trails and they depended on flint and steel and a little "punk" to start fires to cook as they travelled or to keep animals off at night. If they travelled in summer they sometimes ran into moose flies so savage that their bites could drive a horse so frantic that he became unmanageable. On the portages they sometimes had to fell trees to make bridges to cross creeks and streams. If they came by winter, which was considered a wise thing to do, travel was easier along roads that were merely "brushed out". At night they cut hemlock boughs which they laid on snow around the fire, and then the travellers laid down in a circle round the fire and rested as best they could.

Those who came up by Lake Champlain and Frelighsburg often travelled for two weeks to get to their destination, for it took seven days to get from Frelighsburg to Lake Memphremagog alone.

However, the first settlers came by way of Lake Memphremagog to what is now Stanstead and Bolton. After news of the granting of Responsible Government to the two Canadas in 1791 there was a considerable migration northwards and one case may illustrate how the Eastern Townships came into being.

Nicholas Austin, of Somersworth, New Hampshire, was a Quaker and a royalist, although he did not take an active part in the revolution. Early in the war, however, Austin

166

learned of a plot to seize Governor Wentworth as part of the plan for getting control of the colony. Austin rode for hours during the night to tell the Governor what was afoot and then returned to his own home before daybreak. The plot, he told the Governor, was to be put into effect at nine o'clock the following morning. Sir John Wentworth and his wife could not believe the news and took some time to think it over. However, before dawn they left their home and set out for Austin's house and stayed there until they were able secretly to leave New Hampshire and sail up to Quebec. Consequently when Austin decided to move to Canada he had friends at court in Quebec and he was made warmly welcome in government circles.

Austin had a curious history. He was born a Quaker but he fell in love with a very charming and cultured woman who was not a Quaker, and when he married her he was expelled from the community. Perhaps it preyed on his mind that he was excommunicated, because he worked very hard to win the right to return to the Quakers. Eventually, by dint of severe self-discipline, he induced the community to receive him again. He wore their garb and spoke the speech of the Quakers all his life.

Yet he was certainly not a Quaker by natural inclination. He was ambitious to be a large land owner, he became famous for his litigations, and though he had a strict sense of justice he was extremely tenacious about what he considered his rights and could fight his enemies with their own weapons. In Somersworth he lived in great dignity but became obsessed with the desire to trek north. In part he was anxious to leave because he was being persecuted for what his neighbours believed to be his royalist sympathies. They never caught him out aiding the royalists but they had their suspicions. At one time all his papers were searched but no proof was found of his loyalty to the king. By his reticence about his loyalty Austin had saved his property intact.

Austin was an obstinate, self-willed man, and a family tyrant. When he decided to leave the community in which he was being made to feel the suspicions of his neighbours, he set methodically about disposing of his beautiful estate. He went to the St. Francis Country over the old Indian Road into Lake Memphremagog and selected a site for settlement. Probably he had also been given some assurance that the land he wanted would be granted him by his friends in Quebec. However, Austin seems to have been driven more by angry purpose than by clear vision; he had what a writer of the time described as "an earnestness of purpose which seemed another name for obstinate perseverance."

An arm of Lake Memphremagog was known as Sargeant's Bay, a beautiful spot in a country of hills and waters. This was Austin's new home. He built a cabin and then returned to Somersworth for his family.

He had several sons and four daughters, and he compelled them all to accompany him. His gentle and sensitive wife had, of course, no choice. She had to turn her back on the comfort in which she had lived all her life and travel northward with him.

Nicholas Austin brought his party of pioneers across country in the wintertime. They had three large sleighs drawn by teams of oxen. They camped nine nights along the way. Finally they came to the little cabin Austin had built to mark his claim in the fall of 1793. The men of the party must have gone to work immediately to build extra cabins to accommodate the big party, and by spring of 1794, when the snow melted away, they were ready to go to work on the land. What life must have meant to the four daughters and the distracted mother we can only guess, but Mrs. Austin had not been very long in the log cabin in the clearing before she went out of her mind. The daughters found themselves virtual prisoners in the wilderness, with the insanity of their mother and the contentiousness of their father dominating their lives.

Some settlers had come in before Nicholas Austin and had settled east of Lake Memphremagog on the Stanstead Plain which stretched roughly from the present town of Stanstead to North Hatly. But Nicholas was the first on the west side of the lake and he opened up the land that became Bolton township. There was a high ridge of mountains between his settlement and Lake Yamaska, or, as it is now called, Brome Lake, mountains two to three thousand feet high.

The first step was the clearing of the land which was covered with forest. Austin had plenty of money to invest and went ahead with his grandiose scheme of creating another great estate in the wilderness. The first year his men cleared ninety-five acres. The timber had to be burned. They had so many fires that oftentimes they could not see the sun. It was in that acrid loneliness that his wife's mind slowly gave way before her fears. The fires sometimes got out of control, and once even the little cabin nearly went up in flames.

Some day an author will take this case history of a pioneer and turn it into a great novel. Here are all the elements of conflict and tragedy, the Quaker whose ambitions drove him nearly mad, the careful man of wealth who began squandering his fortune like a half-mad visionary. Sometimes he went to Quebec to plead his cause but he was four years on the land before he could get his title to it. Meantime, since it was not his, other settlers came and made their homes where they chose and went their own particular ways on the land he claimed.

Yet he showed great ingenuity. When he settled at Sargeant's Bay the nearest mill was Dunville, Vermont, forty miles away. The first year, 1794, Austin found himself with an excellent crop of grain, but had no market for it and no means of turning it into flour. So he contrived a mill of his own, a sort of huge coffee grinder, operated by a brook. It ground six bushels of wheat into flour in twenty-four hours. For meat his sons killed moose, from which they salted and smoked six hundred pounds of food and also tanned leather.

He grew corn and for years ground it in a mortar, like the Indians, to make corn meal.

But Austin was "better equipped to make enemies than to make friends", and as the years went by his life sank deeper into tragedy. He was constantly in litigation and so at last he lost nearly all his land and his wealth as well.

Yet in his wiser moments when he was perhaps trying to find a centre of quiet in the turbulence of the life he had created for himself, he would wander alone on Gibralter Point in a wooded patch that had escaped the axe and the flame. There the Quaker again got the better of the man of conflict, and under a great birch he may have found himself again in moments of peace, when all the illusions of his ambitions and his wealth fell away from him. He must have been a very lonely man, and in those moments of clarity perhaps he realized what he had done to his wife and his defenceless daughters. When he was close to death in 1821 he asked that his body would be buried under a great white birch tree on Gibralter Point. And so there he was buried in the only place in which he had known peace in Canada. The birch was his only monument. Then, years later, by accident, the birch tree was cut down, and there was nothing to mark the place where Nicholas Austin lay.

The way in which the land was granted to Austin was characteristic of the whole policy of land settlement when it got under way after the Canada Act of 1791. A single man or a group of associates would apply for a township. Austin was granted the township of Bolton in 1797. For his own share he got 62,671 acres. Altogether three million acres in the St. Francis Country were granted in freehold tenure and of this 1,425,000 acres went to just sixty people an average of 24,000 acres of forest land to a person.

Those who got these huge land grants had no intention of settling on them, except in rare cases. It was a landgrabbers' holiday. The consequence was a strip sixty miles wide between the settled country on the St. Lawrence and the

A Typical Laurentian Villag

settlements along the United States border, an area of virgin forest without roads or clearings, held by its owners for the increase in values that would come as the legitimate settlers developed surrounding townships and made them a source of wealth.

The Canadiens on the St. Lawrence did not want English-speaking neighbours. The British did not want Americans with their republican ideas coming into the country to share the plums in trade. So this curtain of forest had a curious effect. Just as Austin had discovered, when he had good crops, that he had nowhere to sell his produce, so other settlers discovered that no matter how much grain they harvested or cattle they raised, there were no markets except back in New York and Vermont. Finally the Canadian administrators realized it was dangerous to ignore these settlers any longer. After all, if Quebec would not recognize them, they might go over to the Americans in a body and attach their settled territory to the republic. However, the French legislature at Quebec steadily refused to vote funds for roads that would give the settlers access to the St. Lawrence country. So, as early as 1800, army engineers traced out the routes of roads to the new settlements. When Sir James Craig came as Governor General, fresh from an appointment in India where he need not concern himself with democratic processes, he decided to over-ride the legislature. He set the army to work to cut the roads that had been surveyed. The first road ran from Levis to Shipton where it linked up with a road the settlers had made for themselves. It was known as Craig's Road.

It was opened in 1810 and fortunately for Craig, it happened to be a year of famine in Quebec, and the criticism and hostility faded as droves of cattle arrived in the markets from the farms behind the forest curtain. The price of beef that had soared to the fantastic price of fourteen cents a pound, dropped back to the normal six cents.

The country beyond the barrier of the forest was so little

Church of Ste. Famille, Island of Orleans

known in Quebec that when Joseph Bouchette went in to make a survey, he was amazed to discover twenty thousand people living comfortably and prosperously beyond the land-grabbers' forest. They had saw mills and grist mills, orchards, asheries and workshops of many kinds.

While the New Englanders had been coming in to settle in the vicinity of Lake Memphremagog, there had been another stream of newcomers moving in from Lake Champlain. We come into the area they settled as we drive from St. Jean into the Eastern Townships. These people, like the Quakers, were excellent settlers, good farmers and husbandmen. They established the character of this beautiful and prosperous countryside. They were free, ambitious and independent and well able to work the machinery of democratic government.

The Lake Champlain route led into Missisquoi Bay. Frelighsburg took its name from one of the earliest settlers. From here many made the slow and arduous journey toward the Sutton Mountains which stood between them and the settlers from New England. At Farnham we come to the Yamaska river, along whose shores many of the newcomers settled. Cowansburg and Sweetsburg are today prosperous communities that began in this way. The Yamaska is one of four rivers that cross the Eastern Townships and empty into the St. Lawrence between the Richelieu and the Chaudière whose banks were settled by Canadiens. The Yamaska has its source in the Sutton Mountains in Brome.

Knowlton is one of the best known towns in the Eastern townships, a famous summer resort around Brome Lake. Its founder was Col. P. H. Knowlton who set up an ashery, for the handling of potash made in the clearings when the settlers burned the trees cut from their homesteads. Potash was the first cash crop and of very great importance to the settler. To encourage business in Knowlton, the Colonel built and maintained a road from Sweetsburg, twelve miles to the west, and to Magog, nearly twenty-five miles to the east.

The Sutton Mountains were still a barrier between the settlements to the east and those to the west, and the only way was by the long roundabout way to Magog. The mountains were an impenetrable wilderness. Then one day a settler named Lester Bell was out in the forest setting sable traps when by sheer accident he discovered a pass that opened the way from the vicinity of Knowlton to the shores of Lake Memphremagog. Today we ride through Bolton Pass on good roads and find it hard to imagine what a tremendous event it was to the Eastern Townships to find the pass. A road was cut but even in 1820 it was fit only for horseback riding, and was a very dangerous journey especially in winter or icy weather. The new road led to Knowlton's Landing on the Lake. Across the Lake was Copp's Ferry.

By 1826 the road was greatly improved as part of a travelway from Stansteal Plain to Montreal. The highway was built from Stanstead to Copp's Ferry, (now Georgetown) and boats operated on the lake to carry travellers to Knowlton's Landing. Then the road ran on to Knowlton, Farnham and so to Montreal.

The Eastern Townships were firmly integrated into the life of Quebec.

The industrial heart of the Eastern Townships is the city of Sherbrooke that has grown up at the junction of the St. Francis and Magog rivers. This was The Big Forks of early days. Not far from Sherbrooke, with its hundred factories, at a spot once known as The Little Forks, is the town of Lennoxville which began as the site of an ashery and came to be best known for its famous Bishop's College. It was founded by a native of Vermont, Dr. Lucius Doolittle, who opened a school in his own home in 1842, and by 1843 had brought the first college into being. It became a university in 1853 and will soon be celebrating its centenary of educational history.

Throughout their early history the Eastern Townships proved their faith in education as the groundwork for democracy by building schools for its children. It was this very urge for education that in time altered the whole nature of the region. When the Canadian west began to open up, many of the families of the original settlers in the Townships felt "the call of the west". Ambitious young people began moving out where free homesteads of fertile prairie land could be had for the asking. As the older farms in the Eastern Townships were put up for sale, French farmers moved in and bought them. There are no vacant or abandoned farms in French Canada. The Canadian of British or American descent was quite willing to sell his farmlands if by so doing he was improving the future prospects of his children. But the Canadien regards the land as a trust. Profit is secondary to his love of the soil and of the social ties of rural and patriarchal life and the parish. Peace and a growing prosperity, a higher standard of living all contributed to a steady increase in the number of Canadiens and the need of more farmlands. So with the west attracting the English-speaking farmers and the French-speaking drifting in to fill the vacuum so created, the balance in language groups began to change. Even those English-speaking farm families who wanted to stay in the Eastern Townships found the educational problem becoming more difficult. As the population changed there were often not enough English-speaking families in a community to support an English language school. If these families wanted their children to attend schools conducted in their own tongue then they had to move along to communities that provided English education.

In 1837, 90% of the people settled in the Eastern Townships were English-speaking, and 10% French-speaking. Fifty years later, in 1887, only 41% were English-speaking and 59% were French-speaking. In a hundred years the situation had become almost completely reversed, with only about 15% English-speaking, and 85% French-speaking.

18

The Lauriers at Arthabaska

AS WE drive out of Sherbrooke on our way to Quebec we shall follow the route of Craig's Road. We are now travelling through the land settled by those driven out of the United Kingdom in the vast post-Napoleonic depression era,—English, Scots, and Irish.

A great many of the original immigrants were still living in this vicinity when there came to live in the little village of St. Christophe, a young lawyer in very delicate health. His name was Wilfrid Laurier. In time it was the votes of the pioneers who started him off on the most spectacular political career in our history.

St. Christophe is now Arthabaska and it is there we will find the old villa which Laurier and his wife built for themselves and which is now a national shrine. Here are many mementoes, some amusing, some poignant and others romantic, like the white satin boots that Lady Laurier wore in Westminster Abbey at the coronation of King Edward the Seventh. Here, too, is the death mask of Sir Wilfrid, showing the finely chiselled features of a great Canadian, with the imprint of dignity and genius upon them. Here also is the worn despatch case, still containing the notes of the last speech he was preparing.

Laurier's story is a Canadian fairy tale. The log cabin to Laurier House progress of the great statesman is as full of significance as that of the great American, Abraham Lincoln, whom Laurier was so quick to recognize as a political genius. When Laurier was a very young man in Montreal, and civil

175

war was brewing in the United States, the sympathy of the majority was with the south, but with Laurier's clear-sighted ability to weigh facts and values, he gave his sympathy interest and admiration to the gaunt and tragic Lincoln. Several shelves in his library were set aside for books about the American president. Yet Laurier himself was a complete contrast to Lincoln, except in his innate love of freedom and justice and peace.

Here was a lad from a Laurentian village which did not even have a railway running into it. This boy from a log school in the backwoods of Quebec put himself through a famous law school at McGill University at the cost of so much labour that by the time he was graduated from the University he was close to death with tuberculosis. Perhaps the misfortune was one of those ultimately fortunate accidents, for it drove him into a backwoods village in the Eastern Townships where he made himself so respected and loved that the British and American and French farmers united to launch him upon his political career. Yet Laurier was a radical in his youth, a left wing liberal who was regarded as subversive both by the older politicians and by the Roman Catholic church. He was persecuted by the priests of his own faith for his democratic principles. Yet he lived to be the idol of Quebec.

Laurier's Canadian ancestry goes back to the earliest decades of the history of New France. Among the colonists who came out with Maisonneuve and Jeanne Mance for the founding of Montreal, was one named Augustin Hébert. He had come from the Norman town of Caen. Four years after his arrival, that is in 1645, he married a young woman of twenty, Adrienne du Vicier. They had four children, for one of whom Maisonneuve stood godfather. Six years later, Hébert was killed by the Iroquois. He was the "first ancestor" as the Canadiens say, of Sir Wilfrid Laurier.

Maisonneuve was apparently concerned for the little fam-

176

ily, for he set aside land as a grant to Adrienne's second husband, land near the fort, which he was to hold on condition that he would provide adequately for the children of Augustin Hébert.

One of the daughters of Hébert, Jeanne Hébert, when she was fourteen, married Jacques Millot. Her husband was twenty-eight. They had ten children, and the eldest of them, Madeleine, married, when she was fifteen, Francois Cotineau.

Francois was a newcomer to New France. He was one of the men who had come out with the Carignan regiment. His full name, after the manner of the day, was Francois Cotineau dit Champlaurier,—and that translated is "laurel field". It may have been the name of the hamlet or district where he lived, or it may have been a distinguishing mark of the property on which his father was a vinegrower. Perhaps to distinguish the vinegrower's family of Cotineaus from other branches of the same family, they were known as the Cottineaus of the Field of Laurel.

Probably the farm to which the young bride and groom moved, on Ile Jesus, was a grant for Cotineau's services in the wars against the Iroquois. Be that as it may, the family were pioneers in spirit and as generations went on they moved farther from Montreal, on up into the Laurentian hills, into the Seigneury of Lachenaie. The name became, as time went by, Cotineau-Laurier, and by the seventh generation, Sir Wilfrid's father had become merely Carolus Laurier.

The father of Carolus, Charles Laurier, was a man of most unusual mental capacity and his range of interests was far beyond that of the average Canadien of his time. Among other things he mastered mathematics and became a land surveyor, and was the inventor of some very useful surveying instruments.

To his son, Carolus, he gave a piece of land at St. Lin in the Laurentians, when he married Marie Marcelle Martineau. Carolus was both farmer and surveyor in turn. Marie Laurier was a woman of exceptional intelligence and charm. Her "first ancestor" had also come to New France in the seventeenth century. She had a love of literature and of nature and of pictures, and had some skill in drawing. Eight years after their marriage a son was born, whom they named Henri Charles Wilfrid Laurier. In the registry of his christening, Carolus is then described as "gentleman" and the child's godfather was Sieur Louis Charles Beaumont of Lechanaie. His godmother was the wife of Sieur de Beaumont and her name had been Marie Zoe Laurier. Little Wilfrid's mother died when he was seven years of age, but she had already made a deep impression upon the mind of the child.

Carolus married again and fortunately the woman he brought to the little log home at St. Lin was an ideal foster mother and won Wilfrid's love and confidence.

In the nearby village of New Glasgow there was a settlement of Scotch Presbyterians. Carolus had many friends among them. He was sufficiently untrammelled in his thinking to realize how important it would be to Wilfrid to have a knowledge of the English tongue. So when Wilfrid was eleven he took him out of the parish school and sent him to live with some friends in New Glasgow so that he could attend an English-language school,—English, that is, with a broad Scottish accent.

Part of his stay in New Glasgow was spent living with the family of John Murray, a Scottish merchant and also Clerk of the Court. It may have been here that Wilfrid got his first insight into the working of the laws of the country and certainly here it was he also learned tolerance and understanding of other faiths and ways of life. The Murrays had family worship every night and Wilfrid expressed a desire to join them in it. In school he met boys and girls of all creeds. Moreover, here he learned to love English poetry, to which he was introduced by a Scottish schoolmaster who always kept a glass of whisky on his desk. All his life Wilfrid recalled him with affection. He not only learned to speak the English tongue but he knew how Canadians lived and thought, where they resembled the Canadiens and where they differed from them. From those days stemmed his power to bring the two peoples within his country closer together.

At the age of thirteen, Wilfrid Laurier was sent to L'Assomption College, then and now a famous French classical school. Here he became acquainted with French and Latin literature. Latin he always read for pleasure. He loved history, and he also loved the courts that sat in L'Assomption. Sometimes he was punished for leaving school without permission in order to attend court or political meetings. He had already acquired very liberal political views from his father and had heard a good deal about Papineau and his cause. Moreover, he had read Garneau's history of Canada, which Garneau had written to disapprove Lord Durham's charge that Canadiens had no literature. All these things fired his incipient political instincts. His liberalism,—then considered "subversive" and "red"—survived the conservatism of L'Assomption.

In 1861, at the age of twenty, he went to McGill to study law. It was his first experience of city life.

When the young student went to Montreal he knew no one in the city. But neighbours at St. Lin reminded him that the village doctor, who had been a friend of his mother's, —and who probably brought him into the world,—had gone to Montreal to live. So the young man called on Dr. and Mrs. Gauthier, and they liked him so well that they invited him to live with them, and there he stayed for two years.

Fellow guests in the Gauthier home were Madame Lafontaine and a daughter, Zoe. Zoe was a pretty and capable girl who earned a living for herself and her mother as a music teacher. She was a very frank young lady but her kindliness and graciousness made her frankness charming. Her love of music captured

young Wilfrid's heart. He was shy, reserved, intro-
spective, courteous, but these are not the qualities to make a
successful public man, and we can only guess at how much
we owe to Zoe Lafontaine and her wit and friendliness for
transforming the shy country lad with his radical ideas into
the great and beloved personality who was to play so significant a role in Canadian life.

In order to support himself in Montreal, Wilfrid Laurier
became clerk in the office of a very brilliant lawyer who was
also "a very aggressive Rouge". The infant Liberal movement was the "red" movement of the times and anyone who
supported its ideology was looked upon askance by the conservative elements in society, who gradually came to be
called the "blue" element. Both French and English-speaking
lawyers taught in McGill law school and so Laurier was well
grounded in both French and English law traditions in the
province and in the points of view of the two language
groups. When he finished his three-year course, Laurier was
chosen Valedictorian.

With his diploma in hand he started out on his career. He
was in love with Zoe Lafontaine. She returned his love, but
it had not been discussed between them because he had
nothing to offer her. However, now that he had joined a law
firm, he felt some hope. But at this moment his world
crashed. He had serious hemorrhages and found himself a
tubercular case with both throat and lungs involved.

That was when he sought refuge in St. Christophe, a community of mixed tongues and the seat of a law-court. There
was an interesting group of writers and artists and two of
his neighbours were Suzor Coté and Phillippe Hébert.

Meantime Zoe Lafontaine had been waiting for Wilfrid to
claim her. She was attractive and there were many young
men in Montreal who were anxiously hoping she would decide to marry one of them. Her mother and friends were
pressing her to marry and the years were passing by. Wil-

frid was still reluctant to ask Zoe to marry him, for fear she would find herself with an invalid on her hands, so he was silent and stayed away in St. Christophe.

At last Zoe decided to marry a prominent Montreal doctor. She worked at her trousseau, perhaps with a heavy heart. Old Dr. Gauthier, who was so fond of the young people who had lived under his kindly roof, decided to act. He telegraphed Laurier, asking him to come to Montreal on a matter of urgent business. Wilfrid, of course, responded to his old friend's plea and took the train promptly and arrived one morning asking anxiously what was amiss.

When the two young people met they knew without prompting what was amiss. Their carefully concealed feelings for each other burst into flames. Laurier could act with despatch when the occasion demanded it. Perhaps it was the knowledge that her wedding dress was made, that the marriage ceremonies were only ten days away that lent wings to his feet. Zoe decided she could not marry her doctor and Wilfrid decided he wouldn't give her a chance to change her mind. He hurried off to the proper authorities and got a special license and they were married that very day. Zoe thought that perhaps her married life would last only a year or two, for Laurier was still a very sick man, but since she loved him she wanted to bring him happiness and care and comfort for as long as their life together might be. As soon as the wedding was over Wilfrid had to rush back to St. Christophe, for he had to attend court next morning. Zoe packed away the wedding dress she would never wear and put her trousseau into her trunk. Wilfrid came three days later to claim her.

The romance of Zoe and Wilfrid Laurier is one of the great love stories of Canadian history, for it remained a romance throughout the long and well-filled years of their life together,—fifty-one years of the closest companionship of heart and mind.

The house in Arthabaska is the home they built together shortly after their marriage. The great double row of maples that grow on the circular driveway leading to the door, were maple saplings planted by the bride and groom. They lived quietly in the house for thirty years before Laurier became Prime Minister of Canada and moved to Ottawa to make his home.

They had no children. Zoe devoted herself entirely to caring for Laurier's health and the skill and persistence of her nursing restored him so fully to health that four years after marriage he ran for a seat in the provincial legislature. The Scots in his constituency backed him and he won the confidence of so many, Canadiens and Canadians alike, that his entrance into the political field was a turning point in our history.

So far his life had been not merely simple but almost puritanical, with his good friend, Dr. Poisson, and Zoe standing guard over all his activities. Certainly we may be sure that when he decided to enter politics, Zoe approved, for from the outset they worked together as one. A few years later he entered the federal field and was elected to the House of Commons. Later still he became leader of the Liberal Party and that post he held until he relinquished it only to William Lyon Mackenzie King.

For twenty years after Confederation the Conservative Government was in power in Canada. Canadians had looked forward to a great regime of expansion and prosperity when the colonies united in the great political experiment of national union. Instead it was a period of depression, internal strife, political ineptitude, graft and corruption. The country was so large and unwieldy, its people so inexperienced, the national problem it faced so colossal that the new Confederation bent under the weight of its responsibilities. There was the difficulty of reconciling the divergent interests of tongue and creed, the problem of land grants and of railway building, complicated by ignorance of the country, geographically and economically. It is little wonder that some serious mistakes were made in government and development.

One of the most serious of all conditions was the exodus of young Canadians to the United States, where expansion and prosperity combined to fascinate ambitious young men.

When Laurier's party came to power in 1887 everyone was saying that Confederation had failed. Canada was unknown and unappreciated, seething with discontent at its slow growth which was less than half the rate below the border. In those years one out of every four native-born Canadians moved to the United States, and three out of four immigrants did the same thing. By 1890, one-third of all the Canadian-born were south of the border. During Laurier's regime as Prime Minister, two million people immigrated to Canada, and not only did the Canadian exodus fall off remarkably, but Americans began immigrating into Canada instead.

As Laurier grew older he became an astute conciliator and even when he stood his ground firmly in some public issue he always made out his case in such just and reasonable terms that he earned the admiration even of his opponents. During the Riel Rebellion he had been a vigorous opponent of the Conservative policy. In July in 1885 there had been a long day of speeches and then a night session. Sir John A. Macdonald had planned a sudden coup to end the debate and put the issue to a vote while the house was nearly emptied after two long dull speeches. The question was about to be put to the house when Laurier rose to meet the emergency, without any preparation. As soon as he was on his feet and speaking in English the house began to fill with the bored members of parliament. For two hours he held the house silent and spellbound so that "not a sound but the orator's voice and the ticking of the clock could be heard in the chamber".

It was the greatest speech of his career and put Laurier in the forefront of Canadian politics, marked for greatness. One of his opponents, a Conservative cabinet minister rose in the house next day to say: "I think it is a matter of common pride to us that any man in Canada, can make, on the floor of parliament, such a speech as we listened to last night." One of the leaders of his own party said next day that "Laurier, not content with having for a long time in his own tongue borne away the palm of parliamentary eloquence, had invaded ours and in that field has pronounced a speech which, in my humble judgment, merits this compliment, because it is the truth, that is the finest parliamentary speech pronounced in the parliament of Canada since Confederation."

Laurier became in time "not a personage, but an ideal". In 1895 he became Prime Minister of Canada and the honour so conferred upon him was the result of his unerring loyalty to his own principles, his love of humanity and his faith in the rule of law. The guiding principles of his life were individual liberty, collective prosperity, racial and religious harmony, and, for Canada, growth towards nationhood. In politics he stood for universal suffrage, freedom from feudalism, separation of church and state, and in his own province, he urged full participation of the Canadiens in the working out of Confederation's potentialities.

When he became Prime Minister he had to make his permanent home in Ottawa. But the home of their youth remained for the Lauriers always a retreat for summer time and holidays and at the end of her life, Lady Laurier retired to it to live out the years remaining to her as a widow. The home they made in Ottawa is also now a national shrine. Lady Laurier left Laurier House to Sir Wilfrid's successor and protegé, William Lyon Mackenzie King, and he in turn has left it to the nation to be not nearly a national shrine but also a working library for students of Canadian history.

Meantime in the year following his elevation to the highest

political post in the land, Laurier went abroad for two months
to participate in the great imperial celebrations for the diamond jubilee of Queen Victoria's reign. Zoe Laurier, of
course, went with him. The Canadian couple made a most
significant impression on European society. Laurier's distinguished personality, his memorable speeches, his dignity and
nobility of mind, did more than all the statistics that Canada
could produce to impress the people of Europe with the fact
that Canada was no longer a colony, but a young nation.
The little music teacher had become the great Canadian lady,
charming, wise and witty, moving through the most brilliant
Victorian society with a brilliance of her own. In the impressive imperial pageant which had been planned in honour of
the aged queen and which suddenly made the world realize
the power and extent of the British Empire that Victoria and
Disraeli had created, none moved with greater poise and
distinction than the handsome Laurier, so kingly in his own
right. For the first time Britain was impressed and even
affectionate towards Canada. The great Canadian was not
an offspring of Britain. He was French as well as Canadian.
When Victoria mounted the throne as a girl of eighteen, Canada was in rebellion against the handling of colonial affairs.
Before her reign ended Canada was the senior partner in the
association of British Dominions. Before Laurier left London
he was knighted, and from that time on the good companions
were to be known as Sir Wilfrid and Lady Laurier. Zoe had
married a sick, perhaps a doomed young man, in order to
take care of him. She little dreamed how far she would go
with him.

At that time Britain and France were drifting towards war.
The arrival of Sir Wilfrid in Paris filled the French with curiosity. Here was one of their own breed, one of the lost
colonials of the ancient French dream of empire. Yet he
came to them as a Prime Minister of a new nation in which
their own people were, obviously, to play a dramatic part,

and he came bearing a title from the British Queen. Laurier and his wife were perfectly at home in Parisian society. He observed a good deal in French life, while the French were observing and evaluating him. When he was the speaker at a French gathering he said: "I have noted upon many a public building the proud device that the armies of the Republic carried through Europe,—Liberty, Equality, Fraternity. Very well: all that there is of worth in that device we possess today in Canada."

Sir Wilfrid Laurier was one of the most distinguished Canadians the country has ever produced. When he died in 1919 the nation mourned for a very great gentleman.

Lady Laurier survived him for several years and on her death, the Arthabaska house was purchased by Noah Timmins and Kirk Cameron and some associates in Montreal so that it could be opened to the public as an historical shrine. Madame J. E. Perrault, as a labour of love, collected Laurieriana. Seventy-five items for her collection she retrieved from the attic of the old house.

Today several of the rooms are much as they were in the days the Lauriers, for instance the drawing room, and the bedroom on the ground floor. Some of the others have been turned into a museum. Here we can see Laurier's inkwell, his familiar red tie and horseshoe tie pin and a thousand and one things to recall to mind the private and public lives of the Lauriers. In front of the house is a figure of Laurier by Alfred Laliberté, a tribute to Laurier's memory from his neighbours and friends. In one of the rooms is a large unfinished portrait of Laurier, by Suzor Coté, showing him with the famous red tie. The house has some important art collections, such as the cartoons and sketches by Henri Julien, the drawings of Suzor Coté for the illustration of Louis Hemon's *Maria Chapdelaine*. There are many sculptured figures by Laliberté illustrating the life of the habitants, pieces such as "First Boots", "Butter Making", "The Water Carrier", "The Spinner", "The Log Driver" and "The Hem-

lock Barker". Here also there is a pleasant little sketch of
Laurier's birthplace at St. Lin by Robert Pilot.

Many a grey headed *grandpère* in Arthabaska today can
recall the lively children's parties Zoe Laurier used to give in
the garden behind the old villa, for she loved children, and
they knew it. More Canadian children of today should be
taken to the old house and told the story of the man who
lived in it and of the great career he created out of the
thoughts and visions that were nourished under its historic
roof.

187

19

The Sugar Maple Country

AS we drive northward we come into the Land of Maple Sugar. This area is known among Canadiens as Les Bois Francs,—The Hardwoods. It is a land with a character of its own, the syrup-making countryside of March and April and the flaming, flashing country of the maple woods in their last autumn dress.

The maple leaf is the Canadian emblem, familiar to all the world through Canadian trade and as insignia on the uniforms of the armed services. It has a good deal of significance. The maple tree grows at its best and most useful fruition in eastern Canada. It belongs almost exclusively to the northeastern area of the North American continent. It is a gracious tree, wide-spreading, its heavy foliage providing broad shade. Whether it is *L'Erable* of the Canadien or the *Maple* of the Canadian, it plays an intimate part in the common life and consciousness of eastern Canada.

It does not adapt itself to life in other lands but needs the climate of Canada to be at its best, for its sweet sap only runs under special climatic conditions. It requires marked changes in seasons, a cold winter, a prolonged, frosty spring, in which the days are hot and sunny and the nights are cold and the temperature falls below freezing. It needs the snow around it to harden every night until it disappears and the ground slowly thaws out.

The maple leaf has a symbolism entirely suitable to express the ultimate dream of the Canadian people and the pattern of their way of life. For when the maple leaf is reduced to its basic abstraction, it is a five pointed star,—the symbol of Man,—the creative, spiritual Man, the soul behind the personality.

All who call themselves Canadian today, except the native Indians, of whatever race or tongue or creed they may be, are here because their ancestors, near or far in time, came to this country imbued with a dream of greater freedom, of a better way of life, to be created here by their own efforts, for themselves and their children and their children's children. Here they could help to build a greater humanity, a more just society, a more democratic culture, than they had ever known before.

The maple tree is not merely beautiful, although it is one of the most beautiful trees in the whole vegetable kingdom. It is a very useful tree. Maple wood is one of the important hardwoods for building and for furniture making. But the maple tree can live for a hundred years and be useful every year of its life in providing man with sugar for his needs. The art of making maple syrup and maple sugar was a skill of the Indians. The sap was taken from the "wounded maple" in the Sugar Month.

There is an old Indian legend that explains why maple sap takes so much boiling. It seems that long, long ago Nokomis, the Mother Earth, created maple syrup as a treat for her children. She bored holes in the maple trees, and behold! when she put vessels below the holes, thick maple syrup poured out, all ready to eat. But she had a very mischievous grandson named Manabush. He came along one day as she was filling her birch bark vessels and he said to her: "It is not good for man that syrup should come this way. If man finds it so easy to gather maple syrup, he will become lazy. Men and women must be made to work. To get the syrup they must cut down trees to make fires and make pottery bowls to hold it. They must spend days and nights tending the fires and the syrup." But Nokomis would pay no attention to him for she thought her people deserved to have the syrup as she had prepared it for them. However, Manabush was determined to have his own way. So he climbed to the tops of the maple trees and poured water in so that the syrup would be diluted into sap. That is why, ever since, there has been only two or three parts of sugar in every hundred parts of sap. All the rest of the water in the sap has to be boiled away before men have, once more, the syrup that Nokomis intended them to have.

However, we may be thankful that he did not insist on us calling maple sugar by its Algonquin name,—sinzipikwat.

No one knows when or how the Indians learned to tap the maple trees by "wounding" them with a tomahawk, and gathering the sap in birch bark pails. They did at last make pottery bowls in which the sap was boiled. When the French came, Indians traded cakes of maple sugar wrapped in birch bark for goods the strangers brought.

In time the Indians got iron and copper pots from the French and so made their syrup-making very much easier. Also, they got axes from the French to make the chopping of firewood much easier, too.

The French were in Canada nearly a century before they learned to make use of maple sap. They owed the impetus to do so to a Dutchman who was King of England.

William of Orange was a lack-lustre, puritanical little Dutchman who was grimly determined to upset the plans of Louis the Fourteenth for making France the ruling power in the world. Louis ruled France for seventy years but in his plans for making himself world dictator, he lacked the sea sense. He had almost achieved his ends when he fell foul of the practical but quite unspectacular William of England. William opposed despotism and Louis symbolized all that he despised in autocracy and royal ambition. William decided he had been in power too long. "He was almost diminutive in stature," writes Prof. George Wrong, "a half invalid, in taste a plain Dutchman who disliked pomp and show, a silent man who loved solitude and who made little appeal to the popular imagination . . . This sickly, brave, indomitable man lived in scorn of pleasure, with the changeless aim of defeating the designs of Louis."

He made his nation ready for the war which began a few weeks after his death, in 1702. Early in the war French ships were swept from the Atlantic. New France, so dependent on the mother country for its supplies, suddenly found itself in real difficulty. There was no sugar in the country and no new supplies of cloth for clothing and bedding.

Into this situation stepped one of the most significant women in the history of New France, a woman who deserves to be commemorated by the business and professional women of today as a great pioneer woman in business. Madame de Repentigny was probably encouraged in her spirit of enterprise by her husband who came of a family distinguished by their periodic efforts to rouse Canadians to a sense of their own importance and to the need to do things for themselves.

There had been Repentignys associated with the history of New France from its earliest days. The first to settle in Canada came in 1636. He was Pierre de Repentigny who organized the Company of Habitants in an effort to induce Canadiens to defend their own interests as traders against the monopolists of old France. Since his time the family had taken an active part in the colony, always imbued with a sense of nativism. One of his descendants became a soldier and was one of those who helped to defend Montreal against the Iroquois at the time of the Massacre of Lachine. His name was Pierre Legardeur de Repentigny. He had been married just four years to a daughter of the town's notary, Agathe de Saint Père, and already they had two little daughters. After the crisis caused by the events at Lachine, the Governor of Montreal was anxious to recall the garrison at Fort Frontenac, (now Kingston,) to reinforce the defences of Montreal. The journey up the St. Lawrence through the

Iroquois infested country was an extremely dangerous mission to entrust to any man. It was Pierre Legardeur who was offered the assignment. All Montreal must have prayed for him for they knew that nothing short of a miracle would get him safely to Fort Frontenac. But he did get there and lived in Montreal until he was eighty.

His grandfather had lived in Montreal with Maisonneuve and had a seigneury near the present L'Assomption. It was here Pierre built his manor house, which still stands. But it was in their Montreal house that Madame de Repentigny became a pioneer in industry. In the winter after the supply ships were lost, Madame went into action. First of all she bought from the Indians eight New England prisoners who had a knowledge of spinning and weaving, and these she set to work in her Montreal home producing homespun cloth and blankets for the colonists. They worked for her for several years before they were ransomed and returned home. It was during that time she did research work in dyes and materials available in the country and she made use of her knowledge of the Indians to learn the methods of sugar making. She spent the winter rousing her neighbours, French and Indian, to action. A few years later she could report to the king that thirty thousand pounds of maple sugar was made annually on the Island of Montreal.

Thereafter the making of maple sugar was a part of habitant life. The work was slow and hard, but the gregarious habitants managed to turn the whole process into a festival and the "sugaring-off" camps were places of merry-making. The rising of the sap was the signal that the long cold winter was over and some deep-seated pagan instinct in the merry habitants responded with delight. From the time of the tapping of the trees whole communities worked at the sap gathering, the stoking of the fires under the great iron kettles and the boiling of the sap to syrup and then to sugar.

Today the industry is so modernized that it is conducted

entirely on scientific and co-operative lines. At Plessisville we find the headquarters of the maple producers' co-operative and the plant to which the syrup is brought by the members for further processing and marketing.

The Indians used to travel to the hardwoods country in good time to be ready for the running of the sap. The Canadiens adopted their methods. Some farmers have their woods at the end of their ribbon-like farms, a mile or so from the house, but some have their maple groves fifteen or twenty miles away. In such a case the whole family moves off to the sugar camp, singing the traditional sugaring songs. To this day the evenings at camp are times of merry-making, of singing and dancing. Quebec still maintains its old ceremonies of the blessing of the maples and the traditional sugaring-off parties.

The best and greatest of the maple groves are in these townships around Plessisville and northward towards the St. Lawrence. Since the best results come from trees with the best crowns, the maple producers give their woods great care. The best sap tree needs a long, thick trunk and a corresponding great system of roots to support its enormous spreading branches and its heavy leafage. The soil must be good, rich and moist. Since only about three per cent of the sap is sugar, the water which is boiled away in making syrup in the natural process would be given off by the leaves in the form of evaporation in the summer season. A good large maple tree will "transpire" into the atmosphere about it a hundred and fifty tons of water in a season.

The sap pails are still carried on a yoke on the worker's shoulders as in the traditional methods, but from there on the processes are changed. The covered metal pails, the modern sugar house with its evaporator which replaces the old open iron kettle and which uses less fuel and produces a lighter syrup, are now the rule in the industry.

Although maple wood is such an important industrial product, cutting down a maple tree to make building material is false economy to the sugar producer, for the standing tree serves generations of his family. The maple woods that remain are well cared for, in contrast to the methods used a hundred years ago to clear the land when tens of thousands of acres of maple woods were slashed and burned to make potash.

Wood must still be cut in one winter to provide dry fuel for the next year's sugaring-off. It takes ten cords of wood to boil the sap from a thousand trees. Some of the big producers have private woods in which they tap anywhere from two to six thousand trees.

The co-operative movement saved the old industry from extinction and today Quebec produces between eighty and ninety per cent of all commercially handled maple syrup and sugar in Canada. The co-operative started work in 1925 with seventeen members and in the first year produced five thousand gallons of syrup and some sugar for the market. Today the production is well over two million gallons a year and the producers get about three dollars and fifty cents a gallon for the syrup. More than half the produce is sold directly to consumers and the remainder is divided between the home market and the export trade. However, much more syrup is produced for home consumption and is not computed nor offered for sale. But the co-operative enterprise alone has twenty thousand people engaged in the industry in Quebec, and more is made and sold than ever before in the history of the province. The country of Les Bois Franc is not only beautiful and significant, preserving its traditional character and culture, but it has had the initiative to add to its old traditions the most important of modern characteristics, the spirit of co-operation and the willingness to graft scientific methods onto the old ways of life and industry.

Perhaps among the busy sap gatherers on a crisp and sunny March day there moves the happy spirit of a very capable

194

and practical lady from the days of long ago, Agathe de Repentigny, watching with satisfaction the descendants of her fellow Canadiens carrying forward the industry she founded, and using the same kind of initiative and common sense she displayed when she recruited the natural resources of her community to meet a crisis in 1704.

195

aie St. Paul, Quebec

20

The Beauport Road

IN spite of the veneer of modern life that has been laid down over this countryside, the Beauport Road is still essentially Norman, although the conflict between tradition and efficiency has robbed the travelway of much of its earlier charm. However, even speed and commercialism cannot quite extinguish the character of *ancien Québec*. Nowhere is the plan of early settlement better exemplified than in these homes pressing close to the highway, with their high pitched roofs, snowy walls and narrow verandahs on which whole families,—two, three or four generations,—sit to watch the comings and goings of the neighbours and of their speed-ridden visitors.

Along the Beauport Road can still be seen some of the outdoor bake ovens that have not only provided generations of Canadiens with good, sweet habitant bread, but which are a symbol of freedom from the yoke of feudalism. Under the seigneurial tenure every housewife had to take her bread to the seigneur's oven to be baked. Often she had to walk long distances with her loaves only to find when she reached the oven that they were frozen, or that so many of her neighbours had got there before her that her bread could not be baked. It was only after a struggle for freedom from the petty tyranny of the seigneurial right to enforce this claim upon the tenants, that the Canadiens won the right to build their own ovens and bake their bread by their own doorways.

The old houses along this way are oftentimes still carpeted with the colorful catalogne that the pioneer women were taught to make in days of crisis by the great engineer Gideon de Catalogne who lived in Montreal in the time of Madame de Repentigy. Possibly he designed the looms on which the first rag carpets were made and so the gay and useful fabric was given his name. Sometimes these houses are even now presided over by women who spin homespuns and linens on looms inherited from generations of housewives long since gone. In spite of all the highways and buslines, these people are still essentially farmers and beyond the highways their inherited fields run down to the water's edge or up into the hills.

This *ancien Québec* is divided into two parts by Montmorency Falls. From Quebec to the Falls lies the area generally called Beauport, although there are several villages on the road through the original Seigneury of Beauport. The area east of the Falls is Côte de Beaupré. Cap Tourmente, raising its stormy head over the river, is the gateway to a different type of countryside with a story of its own.

The colonizer of the Beauport shore was a very young man when he first came to Quebec. Robert Giffard may have been a young man of means seeking adventure, for long before ships had to carry physicians under law, he came to the St. Lawrence as a ship's doctor with a trading expedition. While the ship was at Quebec taking on a cargo of furs, young Giffard swung his gun over his shoulder and set off on the flats along the river east of Quebec. The place was alive with game of every description, but the wild ducks were so plentiful that the place was called *La Canardiere*, a name it still bears.

Giffard liked the Beauport shore so well that he decided to stay. In order to do so, in 1627 he built himself a little hunting lodge on the banks of the Beauport River where it emptied into the St. Lawrence. In the following year he must have decided to go down the river to meet the ships coming from France in the spring, for we discover him at Tadoussac aboard one of the ships captured by the Kirke brothers. He was carried off to England as a prisoner of war.

The Beauport shore continued to haunt his memories. When the adventures of the gay young Kirkes in Quebec were over and Giffard was free to return once more, he sailed back to Quebec. He put in a plea to the king for compensation for his misfortunes in the colonial wars and for his services to the settlers as a physician and surgeon.

In the meantime, even while the Kirkes were prowling about the St. Lawrence, the King of France had hit upon a new scheme for development. For twenty years Quebec had been merely a tiny Huguenot trading post. In spite of Champlain's efforts to create a colony, very little had been achieved. The new plan was one of those hybrid schemes that often took shape when nobles were badly in need of money and traders were in need of influence in royal circles. The king created the Company of One Hundred Associates. It was made up of nobles of various degrees and twelve of the bourgeois Associates, who were to contribute the commercial "know-how", were raised to the rank of nobility.

The Associates were to be the proprietors of Canada, and were to govern in peace and war; they were to enjoy the whole trade of the country for fifteen years except for the cod and whale fisheries; they were to settle two or three hundred colonists immediately and sixteen thousand before the end of the fifteen year period. Along with the monopoly in trade the king gave the company two ships. Specifically, the fur trade was to be a monopoly in perpetuity. How easy it is to plan for a future of which we know nothing!

Cardinal Richelieu put himself at the head of the Company. As Prof. George Wrong says of him, "A sweeping title did not cure his ignorance of economic law. He knew little of commerce and had the despot's unshakeable belief in control by authority. Not one of the French trading companies of this period succeeded."

The first attempt of the Associates to exploit their magnificent charter was made in the spring of 1628 when they sent out seventeen ships and two hundred colonists to inaugurate the new regime. These were the ships, the fat prey, that the lively Kirke brothers found lying in the harbour at Tadoussac. Their loot was so great that they had to abandon their plans for an attack on Quebec and return home with ships and prisoners. They left the colony so helpless that it was ready for surrender by the time they returned the following spring.

This was the Company to which Robert Giffard appealed for land. The seigneury he wanted stretched from the Beauport River to the Falls of Montmorency, and from the shores of the St. Lawrence, far into the hills to the north. Giffard was the first seigneur in New France. He must have been a man of means, for he brought out a party of forty colonists.

When he was granted the seigneury he immediately built a manor house. It was quite an imposing place with high peaked gables and a tower for defence. It probably had also a palisade of pine trunks around a courtyard, after the fashion of manor houses in France. During the siege of Quebec, more than a century later, the Giffard Manor House was the headquarters of the Marquis de Montcalm. It stood until near the end of the 19th century.

Robert Giffard was the first of the seigneurs who had to appear before the Governor at Quebec, without spur or sword, and on bended knee declare his homage, swear fealty and pledge his military service to the king and the king's deputy. Then, with the sword returned to him by the Governor, and spurs on his heels, he withdrew, confirmed in the possession of his lands. His seigneurial homage was made just a few days after the death of Samuel de Champlain, to the deputy governor who had the flamboyant name of Marc Antoine Bras-de-Fer de Chateaufort.

Giffard married and had a family of daughters who grew

up in the manor house, but he had no sons to carry on his name through the history of New France. His was one of the most successful of the colonizing ventures of the 17th century. The lands he laid out among his people, running from the river shore and sub-divided among their sons and grandsons, transformed the seigneury into one long village along the river shore. The fields grew fair and fertile, the herds sleek, the cottages snowy and comfortable, and all lived in the neighbourly traditions of New France.

The Falls of Montmorency were once a magnificent note in the St. Lawrence country. Today, hedged in by the commercialism of contemporary life, the cataract has about it as much natural grandeur as a polar bear in a zoo on a summer day. In dry seasons its once furious waters merely dribble over the sixty foot ledge and drop rather mournfully the two hundred and seventy-four feet to the river below. In its natural state Montmorency Falls plunged over its ledge and in its leap churned to such snowy whiteness that the old inhabitants lovingly and flippantly called it La Vache,—The Cow. There are steps by which the visitor can descend to the foot of the falls and explore the spot which was once famous for its winter sports. The young and gay folks of Quebec used to drive out here in sleighs to toboggan down the sides of an enormous hump that was formed by the frozen spray of La Vache. It was so great that the 19th century equivalent of snack bars were cut into the side of the ice hill. The falls are said to have burrowed for themselves an underground channel so that the water rises to the surface somewhere in the north channel of the St. Lawrence towards the shores of the Island of Orleans.

Sir Frederick Haldimand, the bachelor governor of Canada, who came to Quebec in 1778, built himself a summer home near the falls and called it Montmorency House. He had beautiful gardens for he was a keen horticulturalist. When his term of office ended he retired to Switzerland where he died in 1791. Presently his estate at Montmorency Falls was advertised for sale. The purchaser was Prince Edward, young son of George the Third, who had come to Quebec in command of a regiment. He little guessed as he spent the pleasant summer months in the house by the falls, that an unborn daughter of his would become Queen of England and reign for sixty years. Part of the old house has now been incorporated in an inn.

The Côte de Beaupré, beginning beyond the Falls of Montmorency, reaches to Cap Tourmente. This, too, was one of the seigneuries granted by the Hundred Associates, this time to Sieur Cheffault de la Regnardière, who merely passes in and out of the history of New France. Apparently he did nothing whatever with the great seigneury that lay between the Montmorency river and the Gouffre river where Baie St. Paul grew up at its mouth. His land stretched inland for eighteen miles, and included all the adjacent islands in the St. Lawrence. Years later part of the seigneury fell into the hands of Laval and it was to him that the famous Côte owes its pioneering history.

The use of the word *côte* in Quebec is a remnant of the feudal tenure of the seventeenth century. It means in English the slope of a mountain, a coast line or side by side. In Quebec it often serves the three uses of the word, as it does in Côte de Beaupré, for the homes of the censitaires were built side by side, on the hillside along the coastline of the St. Lawrence. On the Côte de Beaupré are now five villages, Boischatel, L'Ange Gardien, Chateau Richer, Ste. Anne de Beaupré and St. Joachim. The colonists who cleared these lands were among the most prosperous in New France, for indeed to this day the lands along the North Shore in this vicinity are among the richest in Quebec. Côte de Beaupré was populated much faster than the Beauport shore, for as long ago as 1667 the number of inhabitants of Côte de Beaupré was six hundred and fifty-six souls while there were only one hundred and twenty-three at Beauport and indeed only four hundred and forty-eight people in Quebec itself.

Consequently the churches built in the Beaupré parishes were fine large churches and being well supported by prosperous farmers they did not want for rich decorations and church treasure.

The village of Chateau Richer got its name not because there was a chateau of that name in the vicinity but because there was an old bachelor named Richer living in a hut that his neighbours derisively called Chateau Richer. It was a favourite spot with the huntsmen of Quebec who killed thousands of birds there in a season. There was an abundance of salmon hereabouts, as well. Snowshoe clubs made Chateau Richer a rendezvous, especially in the sugaring-off season. For those who owned smart horses, the sixteen miles to the village made a pleasant outing.

At Petit Pré, the boundary between L'Ange Gardien and Chateau Richer, Laval built a big stone mill in 1691 at which tenants of the seigneury could have their grain ground into flour. The building of such mills was the duty the seigneur owed to his tenants, and of course, it was also a source of considerable profit to the seigneur. Laval had a room set aside in the mill in which he could stay during his pastoral and seigneurial rounds, for this seigneury belonged to the church. Here, this man to whom the courts of Europe were open, because of his aristocratic and clerical rank, lay down to sleep on a narrow, comfortless bed that he might be among his scattered sheep.

Best known of all the villages is Ste. Anne de Beaupré. Many thousands of the sick, the crippled, the troubled, make the pilgrimage to this St. Lawrence village in a spirit of faith, to seek the beneficence of good Ste. Anne.

Second only to Lourdes as a place of pilgrimage and healing, Ste. Anne de Beaupré draws scores of organized pilgrimages every year from all parts of the continent. In July, in the days preceding and immediately following the feast day of Ste. Anne, the village simply bulges with its transient population. Those who cannot find shelter, sleep in the open or in their cars, so long as they feel themselves in the spiritual shelter of the famous saint.

Since the earliest days of the colony Ste. Anne has been the special friend of *les Canadiens*. Since sailors played so large a part in the discovery and settlement of New France, the patron saint of sailors was often called upon for help and guidance. She was honored in dozens of places by having rivers, mountains, capes and villages called by her name. The mother of the Virgin Mary was believed to have a special tenderness for the men who go down to the sea in ships. The story goes that in the sixteen-fifties a vessel sailing to New France fell into distress in a terrible storm. While the sails ripped in the gale and taut ropes snapped, the crew made a solemn promise together that if they escaped with their lives they would raise a chapel to Ste. Anne. Presently the gale subsided and the ship came at last into the pleasant waters of the St. Lawrence. So in 1658 the foundation was laid for a chapel on the lovely Beaupré shore.

One of the men working on the chapel was Louis Guimont, whose home was in Côte de Beaupré. He was so crippled with arthritis that he suffered agonies while he laid the stones. One day it occurred to him to ask the help of the saint on whose chapel he was working and for whom he was suffering such anguish. He made his prayers to Ste. Anne, and then went back to work as usual. He had only laid three stones when he straightened himself and to his incredible joy, found himself a well man.

It is easy to imagine the excitement in the little white houses along the Côte de Beaupré that day. The building went on apace, everyone lending a hand in a kind of ecstacy because the chapel was so well approved by the saint.

The first chapel was built too near the shore, for in the

season of high tides it was flooded. Four years afterwards it was rebuilt on high ground. The first two churches were of wood and in 1676 a stone church was built. Even this was rebuilt twice, in 1694 and again in 1787. That church served Ste. Anne until 1876. Then a great new church was built. The miraculous statue of Ste. Anne that was enshrined in all the other churches was transferred to the new church. However, the stones of the old church were carefully preserved and rebuilt into a memorial chapel and in it all the old furnishings were restored. It still stands, this replica of the old shrine of healing.

Meantime the new church was enlarged from time to time until it was burned down in 1922. In this fire most of the relics and the treasure of the church were saved and moved to a temporary church. Then it, too, burned down and in this fire almost everything was lost, even the miraculous statue of Ste. Anne. The charred wrist bone was recovered.

It was Bishop Laval himself who procured this relic of Ste. Anne for the little Beaupré church and it was exposed to the devoted pilgrims for the first time in 1670. It was eventually set into a hand of gold, made from the jewelry left in the church as gifts by pilgrims.

Now a huge basilica has been built as the shrine for Ste. Anne de Beaupré. Its magnificence sits a little oddly on the countryside with its humble farm homes. It is in the old chapel, with its stones charged with the prayers and petitions of generations long gone that one finds the old Ste. Anne. In the splendour of the new basilica Ste. Anne may find herself sometimes a little ill at ease. It will take the prayers of many generations to consecrate the new shrine as the little habitant chapel was consecrated in the years of long ago.

Beyond Ste. Anne de Beaupré is Cap Tourmente,—Cape Storm,—rearing its dark head over the river. We have come to the eastern end of the Lowlands of the St. Lawrence, those rich and fertile lands which cradled the colonies of both Canadiens and Canadians. Technically, the Lowlands of the St. Lawrence spread over the whole rich valley territory as far west as Lake Erie. Northwards from the Lowlands spread the rich, rough country of the Canadian Shield, the Laurentian country of lakes and streams, fur and timber, power and minerals.

There was a farm atop Cap Tourmente as long ago as 1626. The land was part of the seigneury of the de Caens, the rich Huguenots who had the monopoly of trade in New France in the days of Champlain. Champlain himself built houses and barns there and kept cattle grazing on the plateau to supply meat for the settlement at Quebec. The farm was laid waste by the Kirkes on their way to take Quebec in 1629 and the herdsmen were killed or wounded.

When the Huguenots were banned from New France in the days of Richelieu, Bishop Laval took over the lands for the use of the seminary he had founded at Quebec for the education of colonial youth. Food for the school was raised on the farm three centuries ago and to this day it is still the Seminary Farm and still the property of the school that Laval founded.

This was the site of the first experiment in technical education in North America. Bishop Laval discovered that a good many of the boys in the colony who went to his school were not suited to the priesthood. Many of them had aptitudes for the arts and crafts, rather than for the classics and theology. So, wise man that he was, he transferred those with technical bents to a new school of arts and crafts at the Seminary Farm, near St. Joachim of today. He brought from France fine painters, woodcarvers, ironworkers, locksmiths, architects, cabinet makers and all sorts of other teachers. And since he could not find artists and craftsmen in fashionable Paris who would go to the colony, he searched for them in the quiet provinces, and found men working in the traditions of the renaissance. These were the teachers who came to New France and in the masonry, the carved altars, the gracious figures of old wooden saints, in silverwork and fine woodwork in old chapels, churches, houses, convents and schools, we find today the influence of this old school at Cap Tourmente.

The influence of the school is not yet ended. In the nineteen-twenties, Marius Barbeau, A. Y. Jackson and Arthur Lismer discovered at Ste. Anne de Beaupré the eighty-year-old woodcarver who was the last of those who learned their art from the masters of the old Cap Tourmente school. They found him still at work, patient and unknown, a beautiful, saintly man in a fragrant workshop where for more than fifty years he had been carving ships' figure heads, statutes of the saints, the great Madonna of the Saguenay and countless other things, all bearing the stamp of the all but forgotten traditions of the French Renaissance. In the research work that followed, the influence and traditions of the masters of the Cap Tourmente school were traced down to Louis Jobin.

Today in the art galleries of Canadian cities and in the National Gallery at Ottawa the work of Louis Jobin is exhibited side by side with the works of modern artists who welcomed with affection and respect the old woodcarver who so faithfully enshrined in his woodworking shop the values which are common to all creative souls in all ages and in all countries.

21

The Road to the Saguenay

THE old French roads ended at Cap Tourmente for the Priests' Farm and the old school of arts and crafts lay at the end of the settlement eastward along the St. Lawrence.

From Cap Tourmente to the next place of settlement at Baie St. Paul the land was so rough and wild that the French engineers and colonizers despaired of ever connecting the two settlements overland. Moreover, at Baie St. Paul there was quite a good port, and the French were not too concerned about the overland communications. The highway that now runs from St. Joachim back into the foothills of the Laurentians to Baie St. Paul is a very familiar one to all lovers of Canadian paintings, for it is the territory from here eastward that became the happy hunting ground of members of the Group of Seven and the young Canadian painters who came after them.

As late as 1832 there was no passable highway through this land which resembled in its wild and dramatic beauty parts of the Swiss Alps. There were already some settlers, but a writer of the time said that these farmers made few demands for help or betterment, for they had been so long isolated and neglected that they had slipped into an attitude of peasantry quite unlike the spirit that characterized the habitants of earlier pioneer days. As a writer of the times said: "The inhabitants being insensible to everything to which they had not been habituated" and not demanding

207

proper road communication "this interesting part of the country will remain for a long time neglected".

At last, with an aroused government taking over the development of this lovely countryside, a road was built through it at very considerable cost, for the engineering difficulties were very great. However, at the end of the road was a flourishing community which combined argriculture with porpoise fisheries. At Les Eboulements a fleet of schooners brought the small white whales into the docks where their oil was extracted. The oil, along with the produce of the Gouffre Valley, was shipped to Quebec from the docks at Baie St. Paul and Les Eboulement, but at last these Canadiens could drive up to the capital as well as sail to it. The road through the wilderness had opened up the settled country beyond and this part of Quebec is now a popular holiday area, the home of Quebec weavers and spinners whose skills have made Quebec handicrafts famous. The painters of Ontario who have been going into this land sketching for the last thirty or forty years have contributed largely to the high standards of design and workmanship put into the handicrafts. As constant visitors to the homes of the habitants they encouraged the craftsmen to develop their skills and to maintain their traditional vegetable dyes so that their catalogne, hooked rugs and homespuns would retain the character that gave them distinction. A. Y. Jackson and Arthur Lismer were among the first to discover Charlevoix County as a sketching ground and they made many friends among its people.

The highway runs from Baie St. Paul past Les Eboulements and Ste. Irénée to Murray Bay and Cap a l'Aigle, the most popular and fashionable of the St. Lawrence summer colonies. Beyond Cap a l'Aigle the road runs into very good and prosperous agricultural country, and then comes to St. Simeon. There are many more summer resorts along the way, not quite so fashionable or expensive, but many of them quaint and restful. St. Simeon is the place where the ferry that

joins the north and the south shore comes to dock. Travellers
bound for the Gaspé Road cross here to Riviere du Loup. Beyond St. Simeon the road to Baie St. Catharine and the Saguenay runs into primitive wilderness, a land for fishermen and
hunters, but there are magnificent views along the way, into
the mountains on the one hand and the massive sweep of the
lower St. Lawrence on the other. The country is criss-crossed
with streams and dotted with lakes that delight the soul of
fishermen. It is a land as wild and unsettled as it was when
Frenchmen first came to claim the St. Lawrence for their
own.

We have our first glimpse of the Saguenay in that great
amphitheatre at the the portals of the river, as the ferry car-
ries us across to Tadoussac. It was here that ships paused to
make a choice of the two routes that lay before them, the
two great travelways of the Indians. Up the Saguenay was
the route to the hinterlands and to the Arctic. Up the St.
Lawrence lay the way to the Great Lakes and the prairies,
the Rockies and the sea beyond.

The St. Lawrence was the kindlier river, with good green
foothold along the way for men grown weary of the sea. The
Saguenay was frightening in its magnificence and its mystery.
Some of that legendary mystery of the Saguenay still remains
in spite of all that has happened in its kingdom in the last
hundred and fifty years. The traveller must be very unimag-
inative indeed who feels no awe in the face of its massive and
dramatic beauty.

This strange waterway is half river and half fiord. Its navi-
gators, even up to Chicoutimi, seventy miles upstream, have
to contend with tides. It was formed, so geologists say, by a
titanic wrenching of the earth's crust that left this great slit in
the Laurentians. For centuries the awe-stricken said that
the river had no floor, that it was impossible to plumb its
dark depths between the over-hanging cliffs. This fallacy still
persists, though it is truly deep enough to be impressive with-

209

out any fable to bolster up its claim to fame. Perhaps many of the sombre traditions of the Saguenay are due to the very human attributes of jealousy and fear. Those in possession of the Saguenay country said to those who wanted to take possession: "This is a savage river. It is the River of Death. Look at its gloomy walls, look at its dark and mysterious waters. Stay out." The Indians who were the middlemen between the Indians of the far north and the Frenchmen, passed this tradition to the whites. Later on the traders passed on the tradition to incoming colonists who always pushed the Indians farther and farther into the hinterlands. Now we have overcome this legacy of fear and see in the Saguenay not gloom, but the glory of its colour and its sculptured cliffs, the rhythm of the hills that enfold it, the play of light from dawn to dusk, upon its rocks.

Without any doubt, before our recorded history, carved Viking ships sailed to the Saguenay, their long oars glittering with sea water. When Cartier came to the Saguenay he was told fabulous tales of the Kingdom of the Saguenay far up the river and of a white race that wore woollen cloth but did not eat. Indians told him that there were rocks rich in rubies and emeralds and amethysts.

One thing and another kept the Saguenay a place of mystery until about a century and a quarter ago. Even then the Indians were reluctant to tell what they knew of their hunting grounds. The government organized a commission to explore and survey the district and find out what was the truth about the headwaters of the Saguenay. So little was actually known about the country that the commissioners were looking for a volcano on the north shore of the Saguenay. The report which they made was the basis on which the future development has rested.

During the wars with Napoleon, England was cut off from the Scandinavian countries on which she depended for her timber, especially for the masts. Desperately casting around for new sources of supply she sent out to Canada a young man named William Price, to search for suitable materials. The Saguenay country was one of the areas to which young Price turned. What he saw impressed him so much that when the wars were over he came out here to settle. Realizing how richly endowed the Saguenay basin was, he went up into the little mission station of Chicoutimi and set himself up in business. William Price became the Father of the Saguenay. When the colonization of the Saguenay began in 1837, the Price lumber camps provided work for thousands of the pioneers, for he established thirty industrial centres in the Saguenay region. When he died in 1867, the year of Confederation, he left behind him fourteen children to carry on the traditions he had established. He opened up a country as large as a continental kingdom. As the virgin pine forests were cut, the country bred a hardy race of woodsmen, the natural successors of the trappers and hunters. And in the wake of the timber cutters came the steady stream of colonists who were outgrowing the lands in the St. Lawrence valley. The lumberjacks have pioneered many a stretch of Canadian countryside, for often after he had cleared the giant trees away, the lumberjack brought in his family and settled on the land, tearing up the stumps and bit by bit making fields and meadows of the forest lands. The settlers in the Saguenay Basin have been patient, frugal, contented, in their effort to conquer the wilderness and turn it into prosperous parishes.

The history of the Saguenay in the white man's era runs something like this,—fish, fur, timber and power. Fish brought the first European adventurers here, while a little later fur was the lodestone; the English came for timber and stayed to make paper. The Americans came lured by power from the cataracts of the Upper Saguenay with which to turn bauxite into aluminum.

Baie Ste. Catherine is an obscure little village but its neighbour across the mouth of the Saguenay,—Tadoussac,—is famous. Only a few hundred people make their home there, but it has for a long time been a holiday haunt. The Bay of Tadoussac is a lovely pool of water lying within a smooth beach curving like a golden sickle between two rocky headlands. If, in imagination, you can strip Tadoussac of all that is recent and modern, you can then re-create it as it was in days gone by. Beyond the yellow beach the land rises in great terraces not of rock, but of sand. There is an Indian tradition that this was the first of the world to emerge upon the face of the waters and that each of these terraces marks a pause as the sea retreated and the earth took shape. When you climb the terraces you will find them as soft and fine as a sea beach. They were known to the Indians as Mamalons, or The Place of the Great Sands, for these sand hills rise a thousand feet above the rivers that flow at their feet. They form the broad angle where the St. Lawrence and the Saguenay meet.

Tadoussac Bay was a favourite rendezvous of the Indian tribes from time immemorial. Terrific battles have been waged here on these sands between opposing federations of Indian tribes. The Iroquois made their way here from their home territory south of the Great Lakes, to make life miserable for the Montagnais and their allies.

The Montagnais and their neighbours in this part of the world, were, in comparison with the Iroquois, a gentle, good-natured people, fond of fun and laughter, living nearer to the idea of individualism than any people before or since. They had practically no government, except for a certain toleration for a leader here or there who did what little there was to do in the way of inter-tribal relations. They were true children of nature, with no fixed abode, no possession except what they could carry in a canoe, trusting to fate for food and clothing in this land so rich in game. The Montagnais were an imaginative people and every rock and stream had its legend and its traditions.

The Indians believed that it was at this place of golden sands that the red race and the white race first came face to face with each other. But they were not referring to the French, or even to the Vikings. Their traditions came from a misty past, for they said that men from the lost continent of Atlantis came here for fish and furs.

Cartier's report of the Indian story of rubies and emeralds in the Kingdom of the Saguenay sent the avaricious Jean Francois de la Roque, Sieur de Roberval, hurrying off to King Francis the First, begging for letters patent granting him the right to colonize the new found land. He got the king's consent and he invited Cartier to return with him. They found, however, that they could get no volunteers who would settle in the wilderness so the king opened the doors of the prisons to them and told them to take their choice of any men and women condemned to death. "We need not regard all such persons as degraded criminals," writes Professor George Wrong in "The Rise and Fall of New France". "Men were then sent to death for even minor lapses and heresy was deemed an offence as vile as treason. Nonetheless condemned criminals were not the best material for France's first attempts at colonization. We have glimpses of gangs of prisoners chained together, marching under guard to St. Malo. Women as well as men were to go and we hear of a girl of eighteen chained to a hideous wretch whom she was to marry."

The plan failed, but Roberval,—who eventually had a town on Lake St. John named for him,—tried to sail up the Saguenay in search of jewels, and lost one small ship and eight of his men, the first recorded shipwreck on the Saguenay.

One strange tale remains to us of that expedition. Roberval was a harsh and greedy man. When he came, he brought with him his ward, a pretty young girl who, during the long voyage, fell in love with one of the gentlemen of the party. Roberval was bitterly opposed to the match. The young

Marguerite defied him and Roberval, in a fury, decided to put her ashore on the Isle of Demons in the St. Lawrence. The ship paused while Marguerite and an old nurse were rowed to the island. When Roberval's ship sailed on again, her lover, strapping his musket on his back, jumped overboard and swam back to join her. Roberval sailed home without so much as looking back to see what had happened to them.

How they managed to live we don't know, but the following year Marguerite had a baby. The little thing died. So did the old peasant nurse. So did the lover. Only Marguerite lived on alone in spite of cold and loneliness. She killed wild animals for food and fished in the sea. Two years afterwards she was rescued by a fishing boat and taken back to France.

The Kirke brothers, three young Englishmen in search of adventure and with some curiosity about what the French were doing in America, came to anchor in Tadoussac Bay in 1628. They found a lot of French ships at Tadoussac Bay and captured several of them. They had so much loot and so many prisoners that they had to forego their trip to Quebec. So they returned the following year. Meanwhile, Champlain and his people had a bad time of it in Quebec, since none of their supply ships arrived. The Kirke brothers had shepherded them to the Port of London. Quebec was close to starvation. David Kirke stayed at Tadoussac and sent his brothers, Lewis and David, up to Quebec where, in a very nicely worded letter, they told Champlain that they intended to have Quebec and they would much prefer not to put him to too much inconvenience; would he be good enough to hand over the fort without fighting and they were his affectionate servants?

Champlain being wise and humane, took the more discreet course and surrendered the city. The first conquest of Quebec was a very simple matter. The brothers were the soul of courtesy to the older gentlemen. They would not enter his room at the fort, nor interfere with his personal belongings. They were Protestants, their mother being a French Huguenot, but they not only permitted mass but they supplied the wine for communion, the colonists having none.

About two thirds of the colonists decided to return to France, so with the priests and Champlain with them, the English sailed back to Tadoussac where all the ships were mustered for the return journey to England.

At Tadoussac the quarrels between the Catholics and the Huguenots grew hot and bitter. Indeed, one of the officers of the Kirkes, a certain Jacques Michel, grew apoplectic over the arguments and died there. The Kirkes proceeded to give him the noblest funeral that Tadoussac had seen, or has since seen. A coffin was made for him and on it was laid a drawn sword. Marine officers carried it to his lonely grave and two hundred men from the ships marched behind him in tribute to a brave officer. The Huguenot minister repeated the prayers of the reformed church over him, that being probably the only Protestant funeral service at Tadoussac. All the ships had been called from their anchorages and lay within the Bay. After a musket volley, ninety guns from the ships barked their requiem for the dead adventurer.

For a while after the French regime was restored, the trading rights at Tadoussac were auctioned off every year. After 1675 it became one of the chief trading posts of the King's Domain and the profits it made went to add splendour to the court at Versailles, to buy silver chairs and glittering crystal candelabra for a monarch whose love of luxury knew no equal.

Under the British regime Tadoussac became one of the posts of the North West Company, founded by those romantic Scottish merchants of Montreal who wrote a new and flamboyant page into the story of trade and exploration in Canada. It finally became a Hudson's Bay Trading Post and so it remained until fairly recently.

It is a modest and demure little place, the Indian chapel at Tadoussac, with its red roof and its snowy walls, its tiny turret and old iron-hinged door. There is something about it that compels curiosity and affection. White picket fences crawl down the hillside and meet at its steps. Within the rails in tangled grass and bushes stand scores of dark crosses, leaning forlornly through the long years. When we enter we find narrow, straight-backed pews, tiny framed Stations of the Cross upon its walls, pictures dark with age, and a carved and decorated altar.

This is all that remains to connect the Tadoussac of today with those adventurous times when the *fleur de lis* still floated over Canada and the missionaries and furtraders shared the trails of the Saguenay country.

The Jesuits who worked at Tadoussac for a hundred and forty years or more were men of red blood, daring anything for the propagation of their faith, men sometimes of aristocratic birth, sometimes of keen intellects, who, even in the wilderness found much on which to whet their minds. The Jesuit Relations, the reports of the missionaries to their Superior in France, are amazing documents and remain our greatest source of details of those early days of New France. These men did not make their hampering priestly robes an excuse for avoiding long and arduous journeys, for they were great woodsmen and tireless travellers, who paddled and preached their way with equal dexterity.

So we find them studying anatomy on the bodies of their slaughtered game, dissecting by the smoky flame of a torch, or jotting down botanical names, translating Indian myths, recording ethnological observations, and even sometimes admitting that they believed the Indians had the means of communicating with the Devil himself.

For many years the Jesuits had no permanent mission at Tadoussac, merely camping there while the furtrading season was on and travelling with the hunters back to their winter quarters in the interior. Father Jean Duquen, from Amiens, in France, was the first to build a chapel here. It was of cedar logs and bark, built by the sailors of a French ship, and fragrant it must have been with the natural perfume of the wood intermingling with the incense. The Duchesse d'Auigillon, niece of Cardinal Richelieu, gave him the money to build the chapel, and the King gave him a bell to hang in its turret. He had drugget of a curious weave to hang on the rough walls. The bell still hangs in the chapel today and when you hear its thin voice, you are listening to the same call that rang out into the wilderness three centuries ago to call the savages to hear the story of the Christ child. As for the drugget on the walls, the Indian had never seen anything like it and they thought the design of the weaving was some sort of magic spell.

There must have been a sort of barbaric splendour about the little chapel. Sometimes the converts brought skins as gifts to the missionaries, to be exchanged for ornaments for the altar. There is still a crucifix there that was purchased with beaver skins. There were men and women, too, up the St. Lawrence and over in France, who kept an affectionate watch over the chapel and sent it gifts. Everyone who travelled to or from France knew Tadoussac. Dozens of ladies stitched at silks and linens, making altar cloths and sacerdotal robes for the priests. The nuns at Quebec made artificial flowers for the altar, while nuns in France sent statues, crucifixes and rosaries. Madamoselle Bazire, whose father was once in charge of the trading at Tadoussac, worked for twenty years on embroideries for the chapel.

In the chapel today may be seen crudely carved candle sticks made by the missionaries for their altars and these are among the most touching of its relics.

In the sixteen-sixties, the Iroquois swept down the St. Lawrence and massacred all they could find at Tadoussac and burned all there was of a settlement. For years after-

217

wards the northern Indians would not return there to trade
or worship.

The Jesuits were more than missionaries, they were diplo-
mats and mapmakers, scouts and emisssaries. It was in 1671
that Father Albanel, who had been many years at the mission
post at Tadoussac, heard from the hunters that there was an
English ship on the Sea of the North,—that is on Hudson's
Bay. Albanel sent word to Talon. Nothing could have been
more disturbing to the Intendant, who had hoped to drive the
English out of America, than to hear that they had come in
by the back door and were in the north.

The truth was that two Frenchmen, who considered themselves badly treated in New France where they had been out-
lawed as coureurs de bois, had gone to England and by way
of retaliation, revealed the wealth of the fur trade in the
far north. Their tale was so colourful and so convincing that
no less a person than Prince Rupert, a cousin of the king,
decided to go into the fur business. The English gentlemen
who joined him were known as the Gentlemen Adventurers
Trading into Hudson's Bay. Today the company is still doing
business all over Canada as the Hudson's Bay Company. It
was one of their ships that the Montagnais hunters had seen.

Intendant Talon sent down to Tadoussac for Father Albanel. After a consultation at Quebec the priest got just what
he wanted most, official support for a journey up through the
north country in search of a route to the Sea of the North,
which not a Frenchmen had yet seen. Two other Frenchmen were sent with him and a party of Indians.

They left one day in August, 1671, travelled by way of
the Saguenay, Lake Kenogami and Lake St. John, and at its
northern side they camped for the winter with the Indians.
In the following summer they went on, discovered Lake Mis-
tassini and came finally to Rupert River and so on down
to James Bay. This was the first overland journey to the
salt water of the north. They discovered an English post from

which they hauled down the flag and substituted a *fleur de lis*.

They returned at last to Tadoussac, arriving there a year to the day from the time they had left. They had travelled twenty-two hundred miles, encountered four hundred rapids and crossed two hundred portages, though their travelling time was just sixty-three days.

In the following year Father Albanel returned to the Indians at James Bay, but the English were there and he was taken prisoner and carried off to England where he was detained three or four years. Twenty years later he died at Sault Ste. Marie, still a missionary.

The little Indian Chapel as it stands today is due to Father Claude Godefroy Coquart. He was a very busy and efficient gentleman with the keenest interest in everything that went on in his gigantic parish which stretched from the St. Lawrence to the Artic. The year in which he was to build the new chapel he was delayed in getting down from Chicoutimi "partly because I wished to conclude a marriage upon which I had set my heart". So he hurried on from his match-making episode to the mouth of the Saguenay. It was the Intendant who had given him the money for the chapel, and perhaps the timber came down from Chicoutimi, for there was a mill there. On May 16, 1747, Father Coquart himself, adding a little ceremony to the undertaking, drove the first nail and blessed the site. The building was to be ready for the coming of the Indians in June. The funds, however, ran out, and the roof had to be left to the beneficence of the next Intendant, Francois Bigot, of whom we hear very little that is pleasant.

However, it was Intendant Hocquart who was the real benefactor of the Indian chapel and Father Coquart promised in return that on every Ste. Anne's day there would be a mass in the chapel for his sake.

The tiny chapel could not hold all who came to worship there, so its doors stood open to the world. Below, on the sands, the Indians would gather in their buckskins and feathers. Beyond, some of them, floating motionlessly in their canoes, lifted their faces to the mystery under the peaked roof. Beyond them, again, at anchor, swung the trading ships from France.

To this very day the service on Ste. Anne's day continues, and the little church, called like a ghost from its silence and solitude, hears mass celebrated at its historic altar and once more the doors stand open to the people gathered outside while prayers are offered for the soul of its first benefactor.

22

The Laurentides Park

WHEN we return from the mouth of the Saguenay and reach Murray Bay,—or Malbaie, as the Canadiens still call it,—we shall turn away from the main highway and take the quiet road,—15A in the guide books,—that leads into the hills. The road follows the Malbaie River which divides two old seigneuries, the seigneury of Mont Murray to the east and the seigneury of Malbaie to the west. Two of Wolfe's officers took up these seigneuries after the fall of Quebec and although their families are no longer there, some of the traditions of seigneurial days are still maintained hereabouts. This is a photographers' paradise, a countryside that has not yet lost its original quality and character.

Here is a sparse and unhurried life in a setting of natural magnificence and a people who live while they work and spice their labour with songs and with the art of getting along together.

This is a colonization road. The official regional maps show that there was a great patch of crown lands in the interior, an irregular wedge that lay between the Seigneury of Malbaie on the east, the Seigneury of Les Eboulements on the south and the Seigneury of Gouffre on the west. When the Canadiens were looking for more land for new homes, these parishes were laid out on the crownlands and soon filled with settlers. Few travellers know what lies along this good highway into the interior but it is a land that Canadian painters discovered long ago.

The chief village on this route is St. Hilarion, set high up on the plateau. The hills, the farms, the people hereabouts have become familiar to all those who visit the art galleries of Canada from coast to coast.

Once we leave St. Hilarion we descend towards the valley of the Rivière du Gouffre, one of the loveliest bits of old Quebec left to us. There are no taverns and no tourist cabins in the community of St. Urbain which lies astride this valley. This is a community that belongs to a century gone by, a valley in which the best of the traditions of the habitant are still preserved. How long it will escape the blight of commercialism is a question, but for the time being here is a Canadian village living quietly in the bossom of a valley made lovable and beautiful by the faithful toil of pioneer hands of three or four generations ago. This is not Quebec of the French regime. It was a wilderness a hundred and fifty years ago. The families who came here to settle were crowded out of the St. Lawrence valley in the time of peace that followed the Cession.

Baie St. Paul was the community from which the parish of St. Urbain was born. Although the venturesome spirits of Baie St. Paul had known the valley of the Gouffre ever since the time of Intendant Talon, who sent his surveyors into the valley to look for iron, yet for the most part it was unexplored wilderness in the French regime. Towards the close of the French period the King of France sent a party of experts into the valley of the Rivière du Goffre to examine the tall red pines that colonists had reported could be found there. The experts found great virgin forest stands of timber ideal for masts for the French navy. The king decided to get them out. The project brought a windfall to the colonists who up to this time had lived a very limited and difficult life, far from the capital, without roads and with only the river ships to carry their goods to market. Now the king offered work to the habitants and their sons. So important was the cutting of the red pine masts that the king offered to provide all the necessary equipment, jacks, tackles, capstans and ropes, so that the men of Baie St. Paul could go far into the valley, up to the edges of the Laurentian plateau, cut the tall, straight trees and carry them to the shores of the river and float them with great care down to the St. Lawrence, so that they would suffer as little damage as possible before they reached the shipbuilders.

So began the clearing of the Valley of the Gouffre and so were established the traditions of the skills of its men with their axes. As more and more of the young men went north they came into contact with the Indians and went into trapping and trading with them, learning the arts of the Indians in forest living. Then as the forests were cut, the rich new land was revealed for settlement.

The first experiments in cutting masts were made before 1700 but there was so much jealousy and rivalry over the Canadian trade that monopolists in France became alarmed at the growth of the timber business on the St. Lawrence. Canadian masts were threatening to undersell the masts from the Pyranees. However, the Canadian timber trade eventually developed into an enormous export business. The forests of Quebec were stripped by the lumberjacks who at the same time opened up more and more land for the overflow from the crowded habitant homes. Sons of habitants moved away from the old seigneurial lands to the new homesteads and so the Valley of the Gouffre came to be settled.

The love of the soil is hard to eradicate in the Canadien. It may give him less money for his labour, but the habitant is loath to relinquish the family life that the farm gives him. He is a gregarious fellow and he likes plenty of neighbours who also have many sons and daughters and who share the festivals of the church with him.

The Gouffre is not a long river but rises in two branches from several little lakes a few miles northward. It is a winding river with deep salmon pools along its course. In the early days there was a terrible whirlpool in Baie St. Paul, which it was thought this river caused, for it was called The River of the Whirlpool. Many little ships were wrecked by the whirlpool that spun them around and tossed them on the rocks. As the settlers moved onto the new concessions, or "les Ranges" as the Canadiens call them, the community grew until it was large enough to qualify as a parish, and so it became the Parish of St. Urbain in 1827.

It is not so long since this highway running from the St. Lawrence to Lake St. John was the roughest kind of wagon trail through unsettled country. It, too, was an old colonization road, called the St. Urbain Road, and over it thousands of colonists moved into the Lake St. John country. When the first waves of settlement subsided and regular communication was set up by way of the Saguenay, the road fell into disuse. Nature tried to retrieve her own by growing trees and bushes over the old gash in the forest that the road had made. Today it is a beautiful highway and there is even a bus service over it from Quebec to Chicoutimi.

To this day there is no settlement north of St. Urbain until the road has passed through the Laurentides Park and the Lake Ha! Ha! district and comes to the new settlements in the region of St. Gabriel de Ferland. For northwest of St. Urbain lies the four thousand square miles of the Laurentides Park, the greatest game reserve in all Canada and the land of "La Truite". Here are fifteen hundred lakes and as many streams, and tens of thousands of acres of forest that will always be reserved to show generations to come what this country was like when the pioneers first laid their hands upon it.

The Laurentides Park is an enterprise of the Government of Quebec and is controlled by the Department of Game and Fisheries. But its owes its existence very largely to a son of one of the pioneers of the Valley of the Gouffre,

Thomas Fortin, the last of the coureurs de bois and a man of extraordinary personality. The Park begins a few miles north of Quebec city and stretches to within a few miles of Lake St. John. The St. Urbain Road skirts the eastern limits of the Park. The Laurentian Plateau comes to within twenty miles of the St. Lawrence and the sudden rise in the level of the country signalizes the beginning of a mountainous terrain in which rivers comparable to the Saguenay have their rise and many mountains soar to four thousand feet. Thomas was the child of this country, the foster son of its Place Spirit, and he came to play a remarkable part in its destiny.

The only road that actually crosses the Park is that which begins at Quebec and runs through the Jacques Cartier river country. In the center of the Park, in the Hell's Gate area, the road divides, one branch running northeastwards to the Chicoutimi and the other, the main highway, following the route of the old Jesuits' Road to Metabetchouan on the shores of Lake St. John.

It seems incredible now that the Jesuits once had a farm at Metabetchouan in the seventeenth century and that they proved the fertility of the country and brought their farm produce to market over the Indian trails through this Laurintian country. Sometimes they actually drove cattle to Quebec by this route. Yet even late in the nineteenth century this remained an almost impassable trail, where horses sometimes died of exhaustion. The Hudson's Bay Company had a post on the site of the old Jesuit farm, but there were traces of the Jesuit work there until comparatively recent years, even the marks of their ploughs in the furrows.

For a while this, too, was a colonization road and finally, when this had become a route into the new frontier around Lake St. John and when modern industry and the great power plants and paper mills and aluminum plants had grown up, engineers turned the old trail into a fine modern highway.

Ninety miles of this road lies within the Park, from Barrier to Barrier.

However, it is the St. Urbain Road that is the historic route into the Laurentides Park and it was the men who loved the wilderness and approached it from the Valley of the Gouffre who gave birth to the idea of this provincial Park. It was caribou that first took famous visitors into the Laurentians by this route just as it was trout that took the fishing lodges into the wilderness. Men of vision made it clear that this was a country that should be preserved unchanged for the future. To get into the secret places of the Laurentians, to follow the trails of the caribou and to fish for the bright trout, the visitors needed the skills of the men of the Gouffre. So it was that generations of the habitants have become guides to the strangers who come into the valley and made their way up the slopes into the Laurentian Plateau. And of all the guides none approached Thomas in skills and vision and in the power of his simple, personal greatness. Into the ears and hearts of those he took into the forests he poured the ferment of his love of the country, year after year for more than fifty years. Yet he was still a comparatively young man when he saw his dreams of preservation beginning to take shape and he devoted the rest of his life to the care and development of the Laurentides Park.

Only the few approach the Park from the east today as compared with the heavy traffic by the highway from Quebec to Lake St. John. All the big and fashionable lodges are in the west. But the knowing ones, who travel by the eastern road, approach directly into the heart of the Laurentians and fish from the quiet lodges where "La Truite" is undisputed sovereign.

The Gouffre Valley is only thirteen miles long and so we need only to go two miles out of the village of St. Urbain to come to a point on the edge of the Laurention plateau which opens up one of the great and unforgetable views of Que-

Gouffre Val

bec. Some day the Department of Game and Fisheries must build a log lookout on this point so that no traveller will miss it. It lies just beyond the last farm where the road makes a turn. Driving north we are almost certain to miss the view which lies at our back, and driving south we may catch a glimpse of it, but unless we are forewarned we plunge down the road and miss it entirely. Here is a view that stretches upwards in the valley towards the hills and southward all the way to the St. Lawrence, a sweep of twenty-five or thirty miles, a perfect example of a habitant community with all the familiar features of steep-roofed houses and white barns, of steepled churches and tiny fields in a patchwork pattern. Here is the very character of old Quebec unfolded like the open pages of a story book. This is a place to linger for a while and in which to store the memory with fragments of beauty to be retrieved at leisure when the Laurentian country has been left far behind. It is worth travelling a long way to that little corner of a field beside the St. Urbain Road, from which the whole Valley of the Gouffre can be comprehended at a glance.

The transition from the valley to the Laurentian Plateau in a sharp and dramatic one. As soon as we leave the site of the lookout we come immediately into untenanted land and the road twists and turns through the woods between mountains. Presently we come to the Barrier and ahead of us lies thirty miles of roadway through the Park to the northern Barrier.

To keep this land free from forest fires and from the poachers who would commercialize its fish and game, requires of the government an elaborate, protective program. At the Barrier we must prove our right of entry and our good intentions.

Those who intend to fish must have their permits from the Department and their reservations, and these reservations had best be made six or eight months ahead of time. The

227

ower Dam, Shipshaw

casual traveller going through to Lake St. John country is also passed through the barrier but he is given a travel permit stamped with the time he enters the Park and he must account, at the northern Barrier, for the time he spends along the way. There is no loitering in the Park for picnicking or poaching.

As part of the protective policy the government leases private camp sites all around the edge of the Park to individuals or to groups who usually organize fishing clubs, but each holder of a lease is required to engage a guardian who must be approved by the Department and who must be a competent and responsible person. The result is a ring of native forest rangers all the way round the Park, pledged to protect the woods and the wildlife and to prevent poaching. When any private camp fails to live up to its agreement it loses its license.

In this Park of four thousand square miles there is accommodation for only two hundred guests. There is no way to cross the Park from east to west except by canoe. Much of the interior is still practically unknown. There are waters no canoe has ever riffled, brooks in which no fly has even been cast, animal trails that no human foot has followed and mountain sides that have never been scaled.

The basis of the policy that governs the Park was developed by the guides and fishermen and huntsmen of generations gone by, for there are very good reasons for all the strict rules applied to life in the Park. From time to time the government leases timber rights, but the camps came under the laws of the Park while the forests are being cleared, because one of the fundamental reasons for the Park is to preserve the flow of the many rivers that rise in the Park. On their lower reaches some of these rivers provide power for local industries. Forest fires at their source could destroy their usefulness to the towns that have depended on them. They are part of the economic life of the province. Outside of their economic purposes, these rivers and the network of lakes and streams that feed them, provide shelter for wild life of all kinds, in addition to fish. Quebec once swarmed with salmon which were fished commercially by anyone who chose to do so, although the Hudson's Bay Company claimed the monopoly of the fishing rights at the King's Posts. But the big company fished "unmercifully" as one old writer put it and destroyed the salmon fisheries before the government stepped in and retrieved its fishing rights. The Laurentian trout would be destroyed in the same way if protective action had not been taken.

As it is, the Laurentides Park is one of the most famous trout fishing areas in the world today. The fifteen hundred lakes are stocked by nature. There has never been a fish hatchery in the Park nor any re-stocking of its waters. The *fontinalis*, as the lovely fish is called, belongs to the great family of charrs and its local name of brook trout is really only a courtesy title but one so well established that the millions of lovely little creatures will always be known as Laurentian brook trout. There are many variations of them created by their individual *locale*. There is no livelier fish of its size, and no better eating than trout out of the cool, brown waters of a Laurentian lake.

The water of these Laurentian lakes is not blue or green as it is in other places, but takes its colouring from the "peaty soil" and it ranges all the way from "the mere tinge that gives a dusky uncertainty in the deeper places, running through many shades to the profoundest blackness" as W. H. Blake, who fished and hunted in this country all his life, has told us. "Dearest to the fisherman's heart," he wrote, "is the honest brown water, natural and proper home of the trout, turning the sands beneath to gold." Blake knew that there are no rules and regulations for catching Laurentian trout. "The weather for catching fish," he wrote, "is that weather, and no other, in which fish are caught . . . They may come at any hour of the day or night, without wind, or with it."

There are so many variations to trout in the Park that there is a perennial discussion as to whether or not they all belong to one species. They vary in size and slightly in formation, and in colour. It is one of the most beautiful of all fish as it is one of the liveliest, and sometimes plays for as much as half an hour before giving up to the fisherman in its struggle for freedom. Blake says that where food is plentiful and the conditions good, a trout will weigh three pounds in three years. The natural food washed down into the lake is not enough for trout, and at some times of the year, big trout live on little trout.

In the old days those who loved this countryside and were working for its preservation sometimes took the time to put little trout into empty lakes. It happened that sometimes, because of a waterfall too high to jump, or a beaver's dam, there would be a little lake without trout. When the woods- men found such a lake they would go to the nearest fishing ground and hurriedly scoop up some tiny trout in whatever would keep them alive for the journey, and then take them to the empty lake. Then year by year the fishermen or the guide would go back to the little lake to fish. In this way it was learned that the trout will gain a pound a year under ideal conditions. But no one knows why some will grow large and some will not, under ordinary natural conditions, nor whether some of the little ones are as old as the big ones, but just never got a chance to put on weight in the proper period of growth. Food conditions vary greatly and also the height of the water from year to year affects the migratory condi- tions. One authority on fishing has said that it is impossible to tell whether a big trout is ten or two hundred years old. One fisherman, in forty years of fishing in this area, never once saw a fish dead of old age. Some other kinds of fish live indefinitely and so perhaps *fontinalis* do also.

Those who like to be alone with nature in her big moods and who have the peace of mind and the art of serenity will seek out the little lodges of the St. Urbain area of the Park. These lodges are maintained by whole families from the Valley of Gouffre. The father of the family will be the guardian, the mother, the cook, the girls will wait on table and keep the lodge in order, while the boys will act as guides. For the most part, the fishermen who come to these camps are regular visitors. While on the Quebec side of the Park the big lodges are run more like inns in any resort country, these lodges are reserved for parties who have the sole use of them. The camps are simple and comfortable and manage to retain an atmosphere of genuine remoteness from the mechanical and commercial life of our times.

Camp Lac Ste. Anne is perhaps the most beautiful of the camps. It is on an island a mile from shore in the middle of a lake which is unbelievably untouched by man. The slopes are covered with tall, straight spruce woods and around the rim of the shoreline the bushes lean over the water in unbroken green, reflected in the shallows where the young trout find the clean, cold and shadowed waters that they need. From the island the visitor is quite likely to see a great moose standing in these shallows where he has emerged from the woods, his great antlered head held proudly and confidently while he inspects the harmless intruders, for there has been no hunting in the park for thirty years.

The road beyond Lac Ste. Anne leads all the way to the famous old Chemin des Canots and is the original route of the caribou hunters for generations past and of the pioneer fishermen who came into this country long before the Laurentides Park was conceived. Today it is still a rough road, but quite usable for the motorist headed for the camps high up in the interior of the Park.

The old hunters walked this way with their packs on their backs; and Lord Grey, the wise and beloved Governor General who was so warm a friend of Thomas, was also a true "man of the north." It was up this route that the Blake family travelled as far back as 1875 to their camp at Lac La Roche where W. H. Blake wrote so many of his essays and mulled over the translation of *Maria Chapdelaine*.

On the way up to Chemin des Canots we cross part of Les Grands Jardins, the great moss barrens where the massive herds of caribou used to graze before civilization drove them away. Here at Lac La Roche was the first and most celebrated of the lodges, Chateau Beaumont, whose guests were often very famous men of two continents.

Les Grands Jardins were vast areas of the high plateau which were not wooded but had something of the character of Labrador and were covered with shrubs and wild flowers and the thick mosses that caribou seek. The mosses are characteristic of this high land, and where we come upon barren and rocky land, without moss, we can guess that there has been a forest fire across the territory, for it takes a generation for a coat of moss to restore itself to the cold and windy land. The establishment of the Park probably came too late to save the caribou for this part of the country, for they have not been seen hereabout since 1920, yet in the hunting literature of the world are many stories of the enormous herds that crossed these barrens.

When the caribou no longer came here to be hunted, Chateau Beaumont was abandoned until it was taken apart and transported down the road to its present location on Lac Turgeon. There it stands today, still one of the most famous lodges in the Park and treasuring its long traditions of hospitality and good sportmanship.

But it is around the Blake camp at Lac La Roche that so much of the early tradition of the Park still lingers. For long before Murray Bay became fashionable the Blakes of Toronto went down each summer to the old St. Lawrence village. It was there in 1875 that an older Blake invited the young lad,

William Blake, to go with him on a fishing trip up the Malbaie river. They were to have as guide another young lad, the eighteen-year-old Thomas Fortin of St. Urbain.

Thomas was a lad with the blood of coureurs de bois and of voyageurs in his veins. He came of that great breed of guides and woodsmen who combine in themselves all the virtues of the habitant with the skills of the Indian. Blake used to say that the great guide must have "a relish for hardship" in addition to all his woodland knowledge and skills, and this Thomas had in good measure. One of the earliest stories told about him concerns a time when he was working in the bush as a lumberjack. He drove an axe through his foot and *hopped* an incredible number of miles back through the March snows to St. Urbain, to get medical treatment. All the way he sang old familiar folk songs to keep himself from groaning with pain.

For a long time the Blakes wanted to explore the upper reaches of the river which divided the two old seigneuries of Mont Murray and Malbaie. Thomas already knew the region and so the Blakes explored with him one of the most magnificent river courses in Quebec. Some who have travelled that wild country say that there are parts of it more spectacular than the Saguenay itself. Blake, years later, wrote of one spot where the river comes to "stupendous and unscalable precipices" and falls hundreds of feet, "like silver poured from a crucible, pausing and falling again" at a spot called Décharge de la Mine d'Argent.

It was on that journey that young Thomas endeared himself to the Blakes for life. For seventy-five years, the Blakes and the Fortins have maintained a relationship of mutual affection and respect. As for the two youths, Thomas and William, the journey began a rare and intimate association that remained unbroken until, half a century later, William Hume Blake was laid to rest in the cemetery of the little Protestant church at Murray Bay.

It was Thomas who persuaded the Blakes to buy the fishing rights to the upper Malbaie river and establish a camp at Lac La Roche. Every year young Blake would spend some days in Thomas' home in St. Urbain, planning the summer's expeditions. And in these years together in the Laurentian wilderness, the two men talked over the need for a reservation to maintain the character of the country. Thomas talked from the point of view of the habitant and the coureur de bois who loved the land. Blake could look at it from the point of view of his family who were famous in law and education and politics, for the Blakes were foremost in the progressive thinking of their day. And so the two lovers of the wilderness talked around their camp fires and slowly recruited supporters for the idea of a provincial park to protect the forests and the wildlife.

Meantime Thomas became guardian of Camp La Roche and after him came his son, Louis-Thomas Fortin, and after Louis-Thomas, a third generation of Fortins has become guardian of the old camp, although now there are no Blakes fishing on the Malbaie river. The camp is in other hands, but it is the only privately owned fishing camp in the Laurentides Park. When the Park was created, in recognition of W. H. Blake's services in promoting the project for a reservation, the property was left in his hands. So today the old camp is still haunted by the warm spirits of the two men, Canadian and Canadien, who sat so often before its fire-place and exchanged tales of adventures and themes of their philosophy of life. Perhaps it was here, too, that Blake talked over with Thomas the new novel by the Frenchman, Louis Hemon, *Maria Chapdelaine*, in which he immortalized a family so much like the Fortin family. For tradition in the Park says that it was Thomas who frequently came to the aid of Blake, when he undertook the translation, explaining idioms and activities of the Peribonka pioneers whose life Thomas could so sympathetically interpret. Though Blake was

234

at home in the French language, the native can always extract from the narrative of his own countryside the bits and pieces of localism which give a book like *Maria Chapdelaine* its character.

It was in 1895 that the first reservation of twenty-five hundred square miles was made and the Laurentides Park created. Later more territory was added to it to make its extent almost four thousand square miles. It was only after it became a reservation that the Montagnais Indians withdrew from the territory into the north, for they could no longer hunt and trap and fish in the protected lands. There are still traces of their camping places and of their trails.

Along this road into the interior we can see parts of the tortuous Malbaie river which rises in a lake sixty-five miles northwest of Quebec city, and falls in great arcs through the high plateau country. We also see something of that wild Hell's river,—Rivière de l'Enfer,—which flows through great gashes in the rocks. Since out of all the rough and dangerous rivers in this Park the natives reserved for this one the most graphic of their place names, it is not difficult to imagine how terrible the travel along its route can be. Yet every corner of this reservation was known to Thomas Fortin. It was he who had traced its boundaries and penetrated into its unexplored and unsurveyed interior. His passionate and undeviating love of the land and its wild life marked him apart from all his neighbours and made of him a most unforgettable character of whom so many still speak with affection and admiration and respect.

Thomas was born on June 18, 1858, and was the oldest of ten children. His father was in his mid-forties before he married and had probably been a voyageur or a lumberjack before he settled down on a farm in St. Urbain, for his wife was Monique Tremblay whose brothers were all hunters and trappers and woodsmen. It was a small farm and it was difficult to maintain the large family in comfort. The little house still stands on the hillside on the road east of the village of St. Urbain.

Thomas had practically no schooling, only a few winter months in the tiny parish school before he was ten years old. He once told how he learned to read and write. As a young lad he was hired to accompany a party of surveyors who were laying out new farmlands. One of the staff carried with him a copy of "Round the World in Eighty Days", by Jules Verne, in the French version. Thomas listened avidly each night as the man read aloud by the camp fire. Then to his dismay, the owner of the book was recalled to Quebec. Thomas taught himself to read in order that he might finish the book. That, he said, was all the education he had.

After he was sixteen he became a trapper and hunter and he came to know the Montagnais Indians very well. From them he learned his skills in the woods and much of his knowledge of fish and animals and nature. When he was twenty-three, his father died. He had no choice but to return to his family to support his mother and the younger children. It was nine years later before Thomas was free to marry and make a home of his own. In spite of his love of the wilderness and of the trail and the camp site, Thomas was a family man. He loved his home and welcomed the children as they came. He was a benevolent and helpful man, hospitable, generous and gay. He was also a religious man but without ostentation and without false modesty. In the home the traditional courtesy was inculcated into all the family as a natural ingredient of normal family life. If the forests and its inhabitants, its trails and its mysterious sounds were an open book to him, so also were the village and the life of his neighbours, their cares and their joys. The man of the forest was also a good neighbour in the village. Every Sunday all the family came home to visit with him, sisters and brothers, sons and daughters, and in good time, the grandchildren. Emanating vigour and happiness, he greeted his guests and gave them all the same welcome, the relatives, the neighbours, the famous men of the world who all alike shared his hospitality.

Although Thomas was a habitant, unschooled and with little of the world's goods in his possession, he had the humble pride which comes from a sense of belonging to his community and of an ancestry as long as the history of the country. When I asked Rodolpe Fortin, a cousin, who is today the inspector of the St. Urbain section of the Park, if he could tell me something about the Fortins before they came to the Valley of the Gouffre, he promised to send me some notes. Twenty-four hours later a messenger arrived at Camp Lac Ste. Anne with a thick envelope. It contained six long sheets on which was written by hand, the entire family tree of the Fortins. This was characteristic of the Canadien, for in the province of Quebec the keeping of one's family tree is common practice and the government supplies any one who wants it was a large printed form, which can be framed, and on which is the necessary "tree" which can be filled in with one's ancestors all the way back to the beginning of the history of New France. Perhaps this sense of ancestry has something to do with the poise and gentle assurance of the average well-mannered and kindly habitant. The wealthy fishermen who sometimes go into the Park may be apt to use their wealth as a means of impressing their importance on these guides and woodsmen, but they soon find it a very weak weapon indeed. One of them, so the story goes, said to Thomas: "Fortin, I am a millionaire." Thomas smiled genially and responded, "Me, I am a habitant."

The Canadien is anxious to trace his family descent back to "the first ancestor" and there he is content to stop. For the first ancestor is the man who came to New France and helped to found the new nation. Thomas' first ancestor was Julien Fortin who was born in 1630 near Mans. He may have been a child of one of the families who came with Maisonneuve to found Montreal. For he was married in the little settlement in 1652 to Genevieve Gamache who was born near Chartres in 1635. Perhaps she too crossed from France as a child to join the colonists in Montreal. Thomas could read the record of every birth and marriage and death and burial in his family from that day on.

Genevieve was the sister of the Seigneur de l'Islet. Apparently Julien and Genevieve moved to Quebec where their children were born. It was one of their sons, Jacques, born in Quebec in 1660, who moved on to Petite Rivière du St. Francois near Baie St. Paul, and there he was buried. Some of his sons and daughters appear to have settled in Baie St. Paul, and apparently he ended his life there among them. Thomas' family lived in that parish until his father moved up to St. Urbain. The pride of the habitant is in continuity, in loyalty to the soil which nourishes him and to the family of which he is a part.

There is only one way by which the fisherman can win the respect of his guide and that is to act like a man,—a democratic man. The woodsmen have their own measuring rods and they are not easily hoodwinked. They are reserved and they expect their reserve to be respected, and since the Canadiens are courteous by birth and upbringing, they assume that their employers have had the benefit of the same instruction. Some one has said that today the Canadien guide represents "the most virile element in North America" and if they do, it is because they are "men of the north." Thomas was such a man, a Canadien and a guide whose story should be told comprehensively and sympathetically, for he was one of those great individuals who, although he was known to generations of visitors to the Park simply as Thomas, was a man of dignity and intelligence and integrity. If the fragments of his story are not gathered up very soon, while many yet live who knew him well, then we shall be much the poorer for allowing the significance of a fine life to be lost to us.

A few stories have been written and merely serve to whet the curiosity about what more might be told. One story relates how Thomas was once travelling towards a winter hunting ground with six Montagnais Indians. He was alone in his own canoe with his supplies when they came to a camping place at the foot of a portage. When they were ready to push on up the river they made the portage past a waterfall that plunged a sheer twenty-two feet over a ledge of rock and fell into a cauldron below. The hunters launched their canoes above the falls and prepared to paddle upstream. The launching place was a tricky spot where the paddler had to make a quick start to gain any headway against the strong current. Thomas was the last to embark. He pushed his canoe away from the rocks with the blade of his paddle. Then to his horror he discovered that the paddle was caught between rocks and was wrenched out of his hands. The canoe was moving swiftly out into the stream, was caught by the current and started down stream for the edge of the falls, stern first. Thomas acted in a flash of forest wisdom. He had to crawl over his baggage to get the second paddle and by the time he got it, he was near the crest of the falls. He paddled straight for the centre of the crest where the water curved outwards for its plunge. He shot out with all the force of the river and his powerful muscles, and, miraculously, landed on an even keel on the river twenty-two feet below and far enough from the cataract to miss the suction of the cauldron at its foot. His canoe broke in two but it carried him towards the bank and he grasped an overhanging tree. There the Indians found him and he lived to tell the tale for fifty years afterwards.

He had many narrow escapes from death and he saw many strange things in the Laurentian wilderness. He rarely spoke about the magic of the Indians except in confidence with such a friend as Blake, for he did not know what to make of it or how to appraise it. He lived like an Indian and knew the

239

tongue and the customs of his Montagnais friends and he had
to believe what he saw with his own eyes. He had to admit
that their magic worked. Explorers since the seventeenth
century had recorded some of the strange things done by the
medicine men who could, apparently transport such an object
as an axe-head from the trader's store, hundreds of miles
away, to the encampment, when an emergency arose. The
Indians merely claimed that their magic could *transport* the
object, not that it could *create* it. When an Indian asked the
medicine man to bring him an axe, or a pipe or tobacco to
replace something lost along the trail, both magician and
recipient were bound by oath and custom to compensate the
storekeeper for whatever they got, on their return to the
trading post: about this they were clear, there must be an
emergency and there must be an obligation. Brebeuf, Le-
Jeune, Henry, Thomson, all wrote about the same kind of
thing. Thomas saw this magic in action many times, watched
the performance with scepticism and sharp eyes and, good
Catholic that he was, perhaps with a little horror. But he
could not say that Indian magic did not work. He was content to say that he did not understand and that the matter
was incomprehensible.

When Thomas was a young man hunting with the Indians,
he came one day upon twin lakes that he never forgot. A
Montagnais family camped by one lake and the children
were taking many light coloured trout, averaging three or
four pounds apiece and which Thomas remembered as *bleues*.
They were very beautiful and game fish. He always spoke of
the place as The Lake of the Long Blue Ones. But the other
lake haunted him for twenty-five years before he told the
story to Blake. Thomas had wandered off to the second
lake to fish and was lazily floating in his canoe at the mouth
of a cool little stream that fed the lake when a pair of
fabulous trout swam along with their back fins out of water.
Thomas was astonished at the breadth of their backs and the

depth of their bodies. Whenever he told the story he would hold his hands together to demonstrate. Ribbed by his hearers who suggested that he should at least remove his thumbs, Thomas would solemnly refuse to do so. How heavy? he would be asked, nine pounds? ten pounds? "Maybe less, maybe more."

For years Thomas and Blake turned this story over in their minds, and mulled over its significance around the camp fires. Finally they decided to return to the two lakes. It was a difficult journey. First of all they would have to cut a trail for the canoe to be carried through many miles of forest. Also, only twice in the year would large trout concern themselves with surface food, during may-fly time and when they were spawning in shallow water. Eventually, however, a lumbering road was cut in the vicinity of the storied lakes. This was merely a cleared path for the transportation of cordwood or pulpwood in the winter time. In summer it might be boggy or rocky or crossed by creeks. However, an old horse wise to the ways of the woods was recruited and the canoe and supplies assembled and the proper time selected. Sometimes the wagon sank to its hubs in mud, sometimes they had to cut spruce trees and make little bridges. The route was along the valley of the La Cruche river near the northern Barrier, in the mountainous country we see from the highway as we drive to Lake St. John. This is high altitude, for the road rises to three thousand feet, and the flora is comparable with that of Labrador. There was no bridge across the river then, for in those days the road to Chicoutimi was not built. Beyond La Cruche they launced their canoe and crossed a lake to a portage which led them into Rivière Porc Epic,— The River of the Porcupine, for it was near the headwaters of this little tributary of the Malbaie river that Thomas' haunting lakes were to be found.

They came at last to the Lake of the Long Blue Ones and even found traces of the old Montagnais encampment and the spring bubbling up from the moss and bracken near the spot where the children fished. There had been no fishing in the lake for many years and the trout, left to themselves, had multiplied so greatly and had had to divide the food in the lake so many times that they had become *une race dégénérée.* For it is one of the strange things about *Les Belles Truites* that they need the fishermen to keep them from overcrowding their lakes. Where there are too many trout they get no chance to attain their normal and natural size. When a lake is intelligently fished, the trout grow big.

Fishermen can tell where there are big trout to be found by watching for the timid little ones hiding in the shallow waters by the shore. If the little trout are bold when the fishermen intrudes then he knows there are no big fish in the lake.

So the Lake of the Long Blue Ones had been too long secluded from men. Blake describes the lake as "a lovely sheet of glass-green water lapping clean sandy shores from which the unbroken woods stand back to give wide breathing space. A bold peak guards the upper end; the rounded summit, planed smooth aforetime beneath a mile of flowing ice, is now crossed by slow-moving clouds".

Blake explains that the colour of the trout depends upon his environment and changes with it. It has been proved scientifically that a blind trout does not change his colour with his environment. "The process," writes Blake, "is not automatic and unconscious, (as one might suppose it to be) but the trout has a chameleon power of harmonizing himself with his surroundings *as he sees them.*" The fish in this lake were "bright as herrings" and perhaps for that reason had seemed to Thomas, to reflect the cadmium blue of a Laurentian sky and so looked like "the long blue ones" of his memory.

Memory, too, of the trail between the lakes had made it seem a hundred yards or so but in middle age it took the two men a good half hour to cross the portage. At last, Thomas, with the canoe over his head, reached the shore of the Lake of The Big Red Ones. The shores of this lake were a mass of blossoms, not least among them the *fleur des savanes*, then lovely with coral blossoms, later to be quite as beautiful when the forest turned its leaves to red gold against the grey green of the mosses on the forest floor. The upper lake, shaded with the density of the forest seemed dark, mysterious and profound, just the kind of lake to linger in the memory of a man for a lifetime. They had come in over a moose trail to the little creek that fed the lake. But there were no myth-making trout there this time.

That is not to say they had not been there. Perhaps what Thomas saw was a mighty pair of trout that had seen the *fleur des savanes* with their scarlet leaves through a long lifetime, they may have been trout who lived in the lake for centuries. Thomas and Blake were welcomed at the lake by frightened little trout who made "curiously timid feints at the fly". So apparently there were big trout lurking in the cool depths of the lake. They caught only one two-pounder and another came to the surface and regarded them with an aloof fishy scorn and would not try the best flies they offered him. Nor did they live up to any of the traditions,—they did not rise in the evenings, they did not rise when it was warm and overcast, when it was sunny or when it was raining. The men decided that the undisturbed waters had plenty of food in it and the fish were probably few and large.

They left the Lake of the Big Red Ones without catching any trout to prove the story true, but, as Blake says, "the chill failure is not in missing the quarry but in losing the delight of the chase". "What perishes not in realization has its place forever among the treasures incorruptible by moth and rust." Perhaps the Big Red Ones are still awaiting a fisherman still unborn.

Thomas survived his old friend until 1941. Through many of the pages of Blake shines the spirit of the man from St. Urbain. And every visitor to the Laurentides Park, if he stays long enough to achieve a nodding acquaintance with the wilderness, will hear some of the legends of Thomas, the last of the coureurs de bois, and he may come away to seek the books that Blake wrote about the country that both men loved so well.

When we leave the Park we turn back to the St. Urbain Road and drive northwards through very beautiful mountain country and come out into the Lake Ha! Ha! district. Beyond these lakes and rivers the new frontier begins where colonists of today are making new farms and bringing to them the old traditions of the St. Lawrence. On as far as Grand Baie there is nothing but this new farming territory, some of it in lovely settings. The unit of colonization in Quebec is still the parish, not the township, and when colonists move into a frontier area the church and the curé go with them to teach them that "living is more important than achievement" and to establish a community with all its human relationships intact.

23

The Miracle of Shipshaw

THE Lake St. John country is a new Quebec, and in spite of it being a colonization area of comparatively recent times, it played a large part in the winning of the Second World War. It seems a long time now since the only way into the Lake St. John country was either by Jesuits' Road across the Laurentians from Quebec or by canoe up the Saguenay. A great industrial world has replaced the world of the missionaries and the fur traders.

Legend says that when the first explorers went up the Saguenay they turned into the wide deep waters of a bay which they thought was the continuation of the river. When they discovered their mistake they called it Ha! Ha! Bay. Later on they found a portage through to Lake Kenogami, which is as deep as the Saguenay itself, and so went on to Lake St. John.

It was to the rich alluvial soils around Ha! Ha! Bay that the first settlers to the new territory migrated, when the lumbermen had cut the forests and opened up the land to the sun.

When Napoleon shut the British out of the Baltic ports in the long war between Britain and France, Britain sent out William Price to survey possible new sources of tall straight pine trees. Price went into the Saguenay country and found great forests that beggared those of the Baltic countries. So when after the war Price began operating in this country as a lumber merchant he not only contributed enormously to the overseas trade of Canada, but he found work in the woods and lumber mills for the young men of Quebec and cleared

245

the land for new parishes. Colonists who could work on their farms in the summer and count on work in the lumber camps in the winter were assured of success in their settlement.

In the village of Grand Baie there is a memorial erected to the first comers who moved up from La Malbaie and settled here in 1838. The new settlement began as a co-operative venture. In 1837 The Society of Twenty-One was organized. Each one who joined contributed four hundred dollars to the treasury, from which all expenses were met. In the spring of 1838 the party set out and claimed their rich new land around Ha! Ha! Bay. But though the colony was well organized, disaster haunted it. For the first two years, in succession, the booms that held the wood the colonists had cut in the winter time broke, and the unhappy people saw all their work float away down the Saguenay, gone beyond retrieving. On top of that a forest fire swept around their colony not only threatening their new homes, but burning out the very forests which they hoped to cut.

After that, colonization in this area was forbidden for several years. Price and his company did not want settlers in the woods. However, some settlement went on secretly until in 1842 the ban was lifted and the habitants from the St. Lawrence were again permitted to move into the Lake St. John territory.

This time much of the settlement was due to the establishment of sawmills in the coves along the rivers where Canadiens were employed. When the timber was exhausted the mill was dismantled and moved on to a new area. Usually by this time so many of the habitants had become attached to the cove that they remained when the mill was removed and settled down to farming. It was in 1848 that colonization began to expand rapidly when Abbé Hébert became the agent of an association to settle Canadiens in the Saguenay and Lake St. John country. He was more successful and perhaps more astute than the leaders of earlier ventures and so colonists flowed in under his direction to become *Les Sagu-enéens*. For a long time he was the only missionary in the area and like the Jesuits of two centuries before he was constantly on the move among his parishioners.

As the forests were cut and the settlements spread, the unknown wilderness was explored and some astonishing discoveries were made. All the travellers had to avoid the upper Saguenay because of its frightening and fantastic turbulence. At Chicoutimi,—which means *Here the Water is Deep*,—the Saguenay narrowed and from there to Lake St. John, the Saguenay river was completely impassable and merely a place of legends of terror. But now the engineers began to be curious about the upper Saguenay. They discovered that in seventeen miles between Lake St. John and Chicoutimi, the river drops five hundred feet over broken, rocky terrain. Lake St. John is saucer shaped, round and shallow, and into it pours the water of five great rivers and many, many small ones, all flowing out of a basin of thirty thousand square miles. All this water finds only one outlet, where the Saguenay begins in a twin channel around Ile d'Alma, a large island in the throat of the river. The south channel is called La Petite Décharge and the northern channel is La Grande Décharge. The "little" channel is almost peaceful compared with the crested fury and the terrifying force of the water that flows through the larger channel.

Today these waters yield up two million horse power of electricity. The area served by this power is not only a great paper-making territory, but was one of the most "hush hush" places in Canada during the war when one of the most essential of war materials, aluminum, was produced here in colossal amounts, so great in fact that aluminum was the only industrial product to drop in price during the war years. This was the aluminum capital of the world and the war fought in the air depended upon aluminum planes for victory. This part of the country was guarded by the Royal Canadian

Air Force as atomic research plants are guarded today, for an enemy action to put out of service the power stations or the smelting plants might have meant victory for the Nazis and Fascists. Here at Arvida stands the largest aluminum plant in the world with a capacity of seven hundred million pounds of aluminum a year and for victory it worked to capacity.

There is something rather fantastic about the aluminum industry at the headwaters of the Saguenay. The one thing that this country had to offer to this industry, in which it excelled all other places, was power,—the power that since the glacial age has been wasting itself in foam and fury over the bare rocks of the valley. The present valley dates from the Great Ice Age when the continental glaciers, six or seven or eight miles thick, rubbed all the soil and loose rocks from this part of Canada, polishing, striating and engraving the rocky roots of ancient hills and ploughing up valleys where the ice fields rolled irresistibly southward to disintegration. A century ago the country was almost uninhabited. Today, suddenly, as a result of scientific experiments and the development of electrical and chemical engineering, and a re-orientation of world affairs, we find a community of one hundred and fifty thousand people in the area around the power plants that have replaced the portages. No longer does the white water of the Saguenay roar in undisciplined abandon through the chasms of the river, purposeless but beautiful. Within the last thirty years, within one generation, the waters have been taken into captivity and have been put to work to save the strength and labour of men. This power is the great alchemical energy of the twentieth century, and this is the greatest concentration of power in the world.

Today bauxite comes from New Guinea, cryolite from Greenland and coke from Texas to be transmuted by the power of the Saguenay into the silvery metal that is one of the wonders of our age. It requires as much power as would serve the average home for fifteen years to turn these raw materials into one ton of aluminum. Perhaps that gives us some idea of how many "white horses" are harnessed at the power plants of the Saguenay.

It was in 1886, in Oberlin, Ohio, that a young man of twenty-two, Charles Martin Hall, discovered a way to make aluminum cheaply. He did his work in a laboratory he built for himself in his father's woodshed. There was little aluminum in the world in those days and it was as costly as gold.

Before the end of the century there was an aluminum plant operating at Shawinigan Falls. The demand for it was so great that its manufacturers had to find some tremendous source of power which would lend itself to modern engineering methods. There was the Saguenay,—The Kingdom of the Saguenay that had lured men ever since the days of Champlain, the kingdom that legend said was richer than Cathay. And so presently the lonely and majestic Saguenay moved into the forefront of the world's economic stage.

The first power plant was at Ile Maligne where, so engineers said, the waters could be turned into tunnels and forced through generators. This was a place to challenge the imagination of the greatest engineers of the day. It was in 1926 that the first power plant came into operation. There was a piece of work to be done here that will go down into the history of engineering. The river was too wild to dam by conventional methods and the builders contrived an ingenious experiment. Abutments were built from the shores and the river bed carefully explored so that a model of it could be built. From that model they built the dam on its side, the jagged edge made to fit the bottom of the river, rearing far overhead. When it was complete, and an enormous structure it was, the engineers removed the props which had held it and in one of the most breathless moments in Saguenay history, the enormous wall was allowed to fall into the river. Would it fall into its proper place? would it reach the bottom intact? So finely calculated had been the engineering

work that in the few moments of almost intolerable anxiety
that ensued, the tens of thousands of tons of concrete slid into
place like a card in a file. Even the beavers could do no
better.

The dam held and for the first time in their history, the
waters of the Saguenay were stopped. They were driven by
natural law into the turbines and trapped for human service.

No sooner was this half million horse-power project completed than engineers began work on another project three
times as great as that of the damming of La Petite Décharge,—the damming of La Grande Décharge. The plans
were drawn to the minutest detail and stowed away as something that belonged to the dreams of the future.

One of the things that Herr Hitler did not count upon
when he started his bleitzkrieg into the lands of his European
neighbours, was the power of the Saguenay and the skills
and ingenuity of *Les Saguenéens*. The plans for La Grande
Décharge were brought out of hiding and with the co-operation of all concerned with war and industry, Canada began
the colossal task of building the power plants and factories
to win the war for democracy.

The power plant at La Grande Décharge was a job that
required five years work. But we couldn't wait for five years
for the power and aluminum to win the war. So the job was
done in half the time,—two and a half years. It cost forty
million dollars more to do the work so quickly but that was
only the price of a battleship. Nearly fifty thousand men
worked on the project and when it was finished the Saguenay
was contributing two million horse power of electricity to
the war effort. Shipshaw was the magic Indian word that
defined the project. the name of a great place spirit out of far
antiquity.

What we see hereabouts is only part of the whole power
project. Far away to the northwest are the great man-made
lakes at Manouan, one of the sources of the Peribonka river,
and another at Passe Dangereuse, a great arm of the river that

flows from the height of land to the north. Everything for the construction of these great dams,—one of which creates a lake eighty miles long,—had to be flown in by air. The combined storage behind these dams, intended to regulate the flow to the power plants, is four hundred billion cubic feet of water.

Little wonder, then, that a new world was born behind the power plants and that around them has grown up a community far more modern in every way than most of the rest of Quebec province. The power plant at Shipshaw is beautiful with that beauty of functionalism that must impress itself upon the consciousness of the community around it. Like an iceberg, Shipshaw is mostly unseen, but the one-eighth of the plant that rears itself above the rocks is as symbolic of our age and our civilization as is the Sphinx of its age and civilization.

The way back to Quebec lies through Hébertville,—named for the wise and priestly colonizer,—and into the country of La Belle Rivière. This was part of the canoe route from Quebec to Lake St. John in the pioneer days. The road runs for ninety miles across the Laurentides Park. This was the fishing country to which Winston Churchill and Franklin D. Roosevelt travelled in an interlude in the Quebec Conference at which the fate of Europe and of the world was fixed during the Second Great War. To one of the famous fishing lodges in this part of the Park they came for rest and relaxation,—and *la belle truite.*

Not least of the lovely things to be seen along this way as we return to Quebec are the beautiful transmission towers, appearing to be so fragile and yet so functional as they leap through the Laurentian wilderness, on hill tops and down into the valleys, bearing aloft the lines through which the power of the Saguenay goes down to old Quebec to serve the life of a people who are interweaving so much that is new with so much that is old.

Index

Index

Index

Terrace, Quebec, 9, 12, 41
Tetes de Boule, 82
Tesserie, Jacques de la, 56
Thierry, Catherine, 118
Three Rivers, 1, 70, 74, 75, 76, 77-89
Timber Trade, 44
Timmins, Noah, 186
Tracy, Marquis de, 8, 118
Trappists, 132

University City, 40
Ursulines, 104, 111

Varennes, 140
Vaudreuil, Marquis de, 36, 67, 156
Vaudreuil, 133
Vercheres, Madeleine de, 66-68, 141-149
Vercheres, Francois Jarret de, 77
Versailles, 155, 215
Vezin, Olivier de, 85, 86

Vicier, Adrienne de, 176
Vikings, 210, 213
Ville Marie de Montreal, 90, 94, 115
Victoria Bridge, 92, 137
Victoria, Queen, 185

Walker, Sir Hovedon, 16
War of 1812, 35, 122, 127, 156
Weavers, New England, 192
Wellington, Duke of, 127
Wentworth, Sir John, 167
Williams, Rev. John, 156-159
William of Orange, 190
Wolfe, General James, 14, 23, 24, 29, 49, 51, 63
Wolfe's Cove, 48
Wright, Philomen, 45
Wrong, Professor George, 122, 190

Yamachiche, 84
Yamaska River, 172

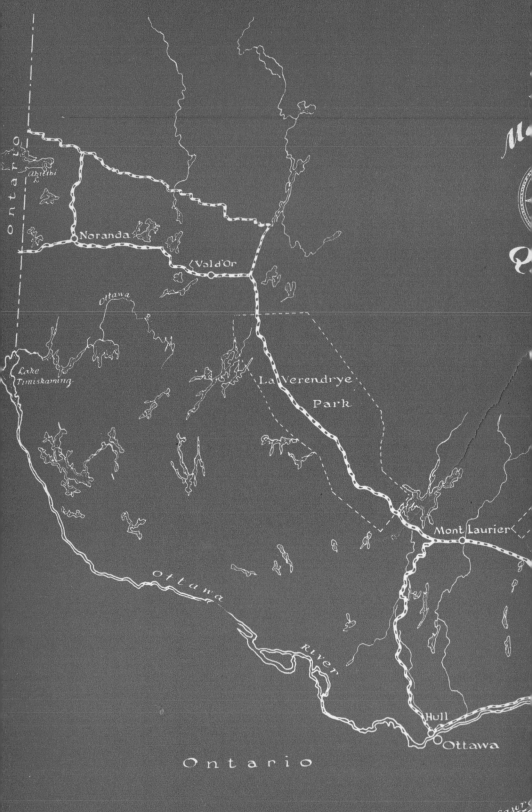